ANTIPHON THE ATHENIAN

ANTIPHON
THE ATHENIAN
*Oratory, Law, and Justice
in the Age of the Sophists*

Michael Gagarin

 UNIVERSITY OF TEXAS PRESS, AUSTIN

This book has been supported by an endowment
dedicated to classics and the ancient world and
funded by the Areté Foundation; the Gladys Krieble
Delmas Foundation; the Dougherty Foundation;
the James R. Dougherty, Jr. Foundation; the
Rachael and Ben Vaughan Foundation; and the
National Endowment for the Humanities. The
endowment has also benefited from gifts by Mark
and Jo Ann Finley, Lucy Shoe Meritt, the late Anne
Byrd Nalle, and other individual donors.

First edition, 2002

Requests for permission to reproduce material from
this work should be sent to Permissions, University
of Texas Press, Box 7819, Austin, TX 78713-7819.

⊛ The paper used in this book meets the minimum
requirements of ANSI/NISO Z39.48-1992 (R1997)
(Permanence of Paper).

Library of Congress Cataloging-in-Publication Data

Gagarin, Michael.
    Antiphon the Athenian : oratory, law, and justice
in the age of the Sophists / Michael Gagarin.
        p.   cm.
    Includes bibliographical references and index.
    ISBN 0-292-72841-7 (alk. paper)
    1. Antiphon, ca. 480–411 B.C.—Criticism
and interpretation.   2. Speeches, addresses, etc.,
Greek—History and criticism.   3. Justice,
Administration of—Greece—Athens—History.
4. Forensic orations—Greece—Athens—History.
5. Antiphon, ca. 480–411 B.C.—Authorship.
6. Athens (Greece)—Civilization.   7. Oratory,
Ancient.   8. Law, Greek.   9. Sophists.   I. Title.

PA3869 .G34   2002
885′.01—dc21   2001046483

For Tom Cole

CONTENTS

PREFACE

My interest in Antiphon was first awakened in a course taught by Tom Cole some forty years ago, when I was an undergraduate at Stanford. At the time I put Antiphon aside to write a dissertation on Protagoras, and then went on to write on Aeschylus, justice, law, and rhetoric, which has now brought me back at last to this book on Antiphon. Another important stimulus came in 1977, when, while working on Athenian homicide law—and thus, naturally, encountering Antiphon again frequently—I had an opportunity to teach the Attic orators at Berkeley. I included a good bit of Antiphon in the course, and the students (a mixture of undergraduates and graduates) responded enthusiastically. I became convinced that Antiphon should be included in every Classics student's reading, as he rarely was at that time. In the last two decades, as I have worked on other subjects, I have never strayed far from Antiphon, and the conviction has strengthened that his work is important for understanding the intellectual movement of the last half of the fifth century, and especially the origin and nature of forensic oratory. Antiphon's various identities—logographer, Sophist, political adviser, political leader, even dream-interpreter—suggest not so much a multiplicity of persons with the same name living and working in roughly the same time and place, but rather a single individual with a wide-ranging mind, ready to tackle most of the diverse intellectual interests of his day. In this book I try to do what no one else has yet attempted: to bring together into a single, complete picture the many parts of this multidimensional fifth-century intellectual, Antiphon the Athenian.

Not that scholars have not written about Antiphon before now. The first edition of his speeches, the Aldine, appeared in 1513. The first modern edition and commentary was produced by Maetzner in 1838, but a century and a half would pass before there was another commentary on all the speeches (Gagarin 1997). Other notable texts of all the speeches are the editions by Blass (later revised by Thalheim), Gernet, and Maidment. In addition, several books have been devoted to Antiphon's three court speeches, beginning with the influential work of Solmsen (Solmsen 1931, Vollmer 1958, Due 1980, Heitsch 1984). Fewer scholars have interested themselves in the Tetralogies, where the question of authorship has dominated discussion, though Decleva Caizzi (1969) produced a good commentary on them. And the publication of the papyrus fragments in the early twentieth century stimulated many papers on "Antiphon the Sophist."

All these studies have isolated pieces of the work of Antiphon, and so have continued to foster the view that these were the products of more than one individual. In recent years, however, more and more scholars have been inclined to see Antiphon as a single person. Thus, the time seems ripe for a study that takes this unitarian premise as its starting point, and reassembles these pieces as the work of one man. To the extent that the resulting picture is coherent and interesting, it will help justify the premise from which this work begins.

ACKNOWLEDGMENTS

Work on this book was greatly aided by a fellowship from the National Endowment for the Humanities in 1997–98, supplemented by a research grant from the University of Texas. In addition, the digital database supplied by the Thesaurus Linguae Graecae was indispensable to my work, as it now is for the work of most Hellenists. As I was writing, I showed drafts of all the chapters to my friend and colleague Paul Woodruff and benefited greatly from his feedback. He and I have discussed these and related ideas regularly for many years, and I could not have written this book without his advice and support. The full manuscript was also read by Alan Boegehold and Michael Edwards, who made many helpful suggestions.

Finally, I thank the staff at the University of Texas Press. As always, it has been a pleasure to work with all of them, in particular Director Joanna Hitchcock, Humanities Editor Jim Burr, Managing Editor Carolyn Wylie, Assistant Managing Editor Leslie Tingle, and Copyeditor Sherry Wert.

ANTIPHON THE ATHENIAN

INTRODUCTION

The second half of the fifth century[1] was a period of intellectual innovation and excitement throughout the Greek world, nowhere more so than in Athens. Poets, philosophers, medical writers and practitioners, religious reformers, historians, and others introduced new ways of thinking. They discussed and debated ideas, experimented with new methods of communicating orally, often in public forums, and explored the possibilities offered by the relatively new medium of communication, writing. At the time, some regarded it as a period of intellectual chaos and moral degeneration; Aristophanes took much of his comic material from these new trends, and Plato often attacks them in his dialogues, determined to separate his teacher Socrates from the entire period. Much of Plato's attack was directed at a group of intellectuals he labeled Sophists—a name that has retained much of its Platonic coloring ever since.

During most of this period, the Peloponnesian War was creating bitter divisions among the different Greek cities and within the cities themselves, and Athens experienced the most serious internal challenges it had known since the foundation of the democratic order at the end of the sixth century. Yet with the end of the war and the eviction of the Thirty, Athens and the other Greek cities settled into a period of relative stability lasting until they were all overtaken by the military might of Macedon more than half a century later. Some cultural institutions, such as tragedy, declined during this period, but philosophy[2] and oratory in particular thrived, as Athens solidified its position as the intellectual and cultural capital of Greece.

---

[1] All dates in this book are B.C.E. unless the contrary is either indicated or obvious.

[2] I am using "philosophy" in the modern Western (Platonic) sense, aware that this begs many questions (e.g., Isocrates' *philosophia*); but this is not the place to explore the complex history of the term or the fourth-century struggle among rival claims to the discipline.

Each of these two fourth-century cultural products, philosophy and oratory, owed its success to a pivotal later fifth-century figure who steered the
intellectual currents of the sophistic period toward their fourth-century
course. For philosophy, this figure was Socrates, whose contribution is well
known; for oratory, the pivotal figure was another Athenian, Antiphon,
whose career bears some interesting resemblances to Socrates': both were
intellectuals, friends of important public figures (though for the most part
not politically active themselves), who were tried, convicted, and executed
by a recently restored democratic government. Antiphon's work is not so well
known today, both because of the relative scarcity of ancient information
that survives about him and because for the last century or so, his accomplishments have been divided up and treated separately. The aim of this study
is to reunite the person Antiphon and all his surviving works into one coherent figure, so that we may begin to assess his career and the important
role he played in the creation and development of the genre we now call Attic Oratory.

Antiphon (ca. 480–411) was the first "logographer" (speechwriter); he
began writing speeches for use in the lawcourts about 430–425. Greeks had
been giving speeches, of course, in many different settings from the time of
Homer and undoubtedly earlier, but Antiphon was the first to write down
a speech for delivery in court.[3] We can plausibly connect this innovation
with the earliest report of his career (Thucydides 8.68) that, although he
had great skill with words, he did not like to appear in public but confined
himself to giving advice to others who were involved in legal or political disputes. It is not hard to imagine that giving advice for a legal dispute could
soon include providing an outline of the speech that would be delivered in
court, and eventually the full text of the speech. It might have been difficult
to prepare beforehand the text of a speech to the Assembly, where a person
could not easily predict just how the debate would go before his turn came
to speak,[4] but speeches in court went in a fixed order—plaintiff followed
by defendant, and in some cases second speeches by each—and a litigant
would have had a fairly good idea from preliminary hearings what lines of ar-

---

[3] I exclude sophistic display speeches, such as the speech Gorgias reportedly gave to
the Athenians in 427 (Diodorus Siculus 12.53.3–5 = 82A4 DK), which may have been
written beforehand. Pausanias reports (6.17.8) that Tisias of Syracuse (active around
450) composed a speech for a Syracusan woman in connection with a property dispute;
if the report is true, it may also refer to a model argument for display, perhaps involving
probability; see Cole 1991b: 82.

[4] As a result, fewer Assembly speeches survive; see Trevett 1996.

gument his opponent would probably take. Thus, a logographer could provide not just advice on how to present the case, but a complete text, generally for a handsome fee. And since the litigant was expected to present his case himself, Antiphon would have had to write the speech down so his client could learn it by heart, maintaining the fiction that he was speaking extemporaneously.

The art of logography grew rapidly after Antiphon's death and was practiced by many others besides those whose speeches survive. Survival of these speeches depended in the first place on the interest of friends and families (and perhaps of booksellers and others),[5] and then on the inclusion of one's works in the great collection of the library at Alexandria, which began to acquire material early in the third century. At some point the number of Athenian "orators"[6] selected for preservation was fixed at ten, from whom some 150 speeches survive more or less complete today;[7] they address a range of topics, from important public issues to private disputes between individuals arising out of lovers' quarrels, business dealings, inheritance disputes, and other matters. Some of the speeches were delivered by their authors, but most were written for others. Antiphon delivered only one speech himself—at his trial for treason in 411; though much admired, this speech failed to win his acquittal, and he was executed shortly thereafter. His other surviving speeches all concern homicide cases, although this is an accident of preservation; fragments and titles of speeches that do not survive indicate that they dealt with many other kinds of cases as well.

From the perspective of the fourth century, Antiphon stands as the founder of logography, but in his own day he also made notable contribu-

---

[5] See Dover 1968a.

[6] "Orator" is a misleading label, since several of the canonical ten seldom or never delivered a speech themselves. It is a translation of the Greek *rhētōr*, which in the classical period means "speaker" and is especially used of a speaker in the Assembly, or, in other words, a "politician." Antiphon would not have been called a *rhētōr* in his own day (see further below, chapter 2, notes 23 and 24). The word *rhētōr* was probably not applied to him and others who composed speeches but did not themselves speak in court until their works were catalogued in Alexandria together with those of others, like Demosthenes, who were orators in the strict sense. I shall sometimes use the term "orator" in this later sense (i.e., as equivalent to "logographer") for one or more of the Attic orators, but in discussing Antiphon, I will generally use "logographer," which more accurately describes his career as a speechwriter who did not normally speak himself.

[7] It is now generally agreed that several of the speeches preserved among those of Demosthenes were actually written by Apollodorus, son of Pasion, who is thus sometimes called "the eleventh Attic orator"; see Trevett 1992.

tions to the intellectual discourse of the sophistic period. He wrote on many of the prominent and controversial topics of the time, from mathematics, physics, and metaphysics to social and political issues. His behind-the-scenes involvement in public life gave him a thorough knowledge of Athenian politics and law and a deep concern with legal, moral, and philosophical aspects of justice. This is reflected in *Truth,* where the debate between the claims of *physis* ("nature") and the demands of *nomos* ("law, custom") is directed primarily at the theory and practice of justice. Some scholars have understood Antiphon as proposing to dispense with law altogether; but more likely he, like his younger Athenian contemporary Socrates (469–399), sought insight by drawing out the logical consequences of various positions and exploring the contradictions and paradoxes posed by traditional institutions and beliefs, without necessarily rejecting all aspects of traditional thinking. In this sense, Antiphon was a true Sophist, and he shared with Protagoras and others the major shortcoming, in Plato's view, of not presenting a coherent positive doctrine.[8] For Plato, this disqualified the Sophists as "philosophers," and they still have a rather tenuous position in the modern history of philosophy.

One obstacle to appreciating the work of the Sophists is, of course, that much of our evidence comes directly or indirectly from this hostile source, Plato. In the fourth century, Plato won the struggle against Isocrates and perhaps others to control the content of the emerging discipline, philosophy. By this victory, Plato succeeded in controlling our view of the Sophists not just as bad philosophers, but as not really philosophers at all. Plato's attack on Homer and other poets has not caused later ages to view them as bad poets, since poetry, which continued to thrive in Greek and later cultures, has simply been considered a separate enterprise from philosophy. But Plato's attack on the Sophists has influenced us to treat them (in contrast to the Presocratics) essentially as nonphilosophers, as Plato defined the discipline, and this has diverted our attention away from their important influence in other areas, such as history, poetry, and medicine. Thucydides' *History,* for example, is inconceivable without the work of the Sophists.

The other main area of sophistic success was oratory and rhetoric. Although rhetoric is becoming better appreciated today as a positive cultural force than it has been in the recent past, it is still far from regaining the high position it held for so many centuries in antiquity and later. Classical oratory and rhetoric remain less highly valued in our culture than philosophy

---

[8] See Striker 1996.

or history. We may be aware of Isocrates' success, both in his own time and in subsequent ages, but a search of any bookstore or library catalogue for translations of, or scholarly works about, Plato and Isocrates will show immediately the dominance of philosophy over rhetoric in our own culture. Indeed, we could include all ten Attic orators in the balance and Plato would still outweigh them considerably. But Plato's influence on fourth-century Athenian culture was relatively slight, whereas oratory was central to the lives of most Athenian citizens, who regularly attended meetings of the courts or the Assembly in some capacity, even if they did not actively engage in legal or political affairs. It is no exaggeration to say that oratory in the fourth century took the place of drama as the most vital medium of cultural activity in Athens, and this, I would argue, is in part the legacy of Antiphon.

As a Sophist, Antiphon was unusual in being Athenian.[9] The other major Sophists, Protagoras, Gorgias, Thrasymachus, Hippias, and Prodicus, came from widely different parts of the Greek world. They traveled frequently, and although they spent some time in Athens, they would not have had the same impact on Athenian life as a native Athenian like Antiphon or Socrates.[10] Antiphon probably also traveled, but Athens was always the center of his activity. Unlike his contemporary Socrates, however, he remained out of the public light until the coup in 411, and instead worked behind the scenes to advise and influence others. Xenophon presents the two as rival teachers (*Memorabilia* 1.6), and although we cannot put much trust in the historicity of the conversations he reports, it is hard to imagine that the two did not encounter each other often. The main difference between the lives of the two intellectuals is that Antiphon came from an aristocratic family, and thus was probably more involved than Socrates in the political life of Athens, albeit behind the scenes. Socrates, on the other hand, came from a working family; however, he enjoyed the company of the aristocratic youth of Athens, many of whom were or would soon be politically prominent, and he led a generally public life, though he avoided political engagement of any sort himself.

Despite his concern for self-understanding, Socrates' teachings generally remained abstract and theoretical. In Plato's accounts, at least, he does not offer political advice, and his pretrial discussion with Euthyphro, far from

---

[9] The Athenian Critias is also generally classed as a Sophist; but as far as we can tell, although important in Athenian politics, he was a rather minor intellectual figure, especially if the famous fragment from *Sisyphus* is not his (*Tragicorum Graecorum Fragmenta* I 43 F19; see Davies 1989).

[10] This is probably the main reason why Aristophanes chose Socrates, a well-known local figure, to represent the Sophists in his play, the *Clouds*, rather than, say, Protagoras.

providing assistance with arguments Euthyphro might use in court, quickly moves away from Euthyphro's legal case to the more abstract subject of the nature of piety. By contrast, Antiphon, though concerned about theoretical issues in areas such as geometry and psychology, seems to have devoted most of his attention to law and justice, areas important for his role as adviser to those engaged in litigation. The second half of the fifth century was a period of rapid growth for the courts in Athens, and new ideas about forensic discourse were clearly of great interest to many thinkers at this time, whether or not we accept the story of the birth of rhetoric in Syracuse in 467.[11] Many non-Athenian Sophists, particularly Protagoras, Gorgias, and Thrasymachus, made important contributions to the study of discourse (*logos*); but Athens provided so many more opportunities for speaking than did other Greek cities that Athens became the focus of interest in rhetoric and oratory, and more specifically in law, justice, and forensic discourse. Living in the center of this activity, Antiphon not surprisingly devoted some important work, including the Tetralogies and part of *Truth,* to these subjects.[12]

Despite his lack of direct involvement in politics, Socrates was tried and executed in 399 under the influence of democratic politicians who had regained control of Athens after a short-lived aristocratic coup, just as Antiphon was a decade earlier (in 411). Both men remained in the city to face trial when they could easily have left and lived the rest of their lives elsewhere (Socrates was 70 at the time, and Antiphon probably about the same age); and there is some evidence that Socrates' speech at his trial, at least in the version Plato gives in the *Apology,* was influenced by Antiphon's famous speech in his own defense.[13] The trial of Antiphon is usually viewed as a purely political event, but there seems to have been an intellectual (or rather, anti-intellectual) aspect to it as well, just as political and intellectual factors apparently came together in Socrates' trial. In any case, it remains a blot on

---

[11] We may wish to call the Sophists' teaching in this area "rhetoric," though I am persuaded that rhetoric was not recognized as a formal discipline until the fourth century and that the major force in identifying it as such was Plato, whose motive was certainly hostile (Cole 1991b; also Schiappa 1999). On the other hand, fifth-century figures like Gorgias and Thrasymachus talked, and probably wrote, about methods or techniques of speaking and arguing, and I may sometimes use "rhetoric" to designate this area of intellectual activity.

[12] Also attested are an *Art of Speaking* and an obscure work titled *Politicus* (*Public Citizen*).

[13] See Gagarin 1997: 1–3; Gagarin forthcoming.

the otherwise positive record of Athenian democracy that it executed its two most important fifth-century thinkers.

Although he was a leading Athenian intellectual, an important contributor to the debates of the Sophists, and a pioneer in forensic rhetoric who laid the groundwork for this flourishing genre of oratory, especially forensic oratory, in the next century, Antiphon remains largely unread and unstudied. To some extent, he shares the fate of the orators as a group, whose works, until the last third of the twentieth century, were used as sources for legal and historical data but otherwise were read largely as examples of Greek prose style.[14] But Antiphon has suffered the special fate of having been divided into (at least) three parts:[15] the orator (i.e., logographer), who wrote speeches for the courts and was a political conservative; the author of the Tetralogies, who may have been an Ionian or lived later than the fifth century; and the Sophist, whose main contribution was a radical, even anarchical, view of human society. Sometimes a separate dream-interpreter was added to the group. Only recently has a "unitarian" view of Antiphon begun to prevail, enabling us to appreciate the full range of his activities and accomplishments. I shall present the arguments for this unitarian view in chapter 2, but in a sense this whole book is the most important argument for unity: to the extent that putting the pieces of Antiphon back together again produces a coherent, interesting, and plausible picture of this fifth-century Athenian intellectual, it will support the case for a single Antiphon.

Chapter 1 presents a brief survey of sophistic activity in the second half of the fifth century as background for the life and work of Antiphon. Chapter 2 treats the two main controversies concerning the unity of Antiphon, whether there were two separate Antiphons, a "Sophist" and an "orator," and whether Antiphon wrote the Tetralogies. Chapters 3 through 6 take up Antiphon's works, first *Truth,* then *Concord* and his views on dream-interpretation, then the Tetralogies, and finally the six court speeches and

---

[14] Jebb, for instance, refers to his hugely influential work on the Attic orators as an "attempt to aid in giving Attic Oratory its due place in the history of Attic Prose" (1875, 1:xiii). The first scholar to perceive the broader importance of the orators was Kenneth Dover (e.g., Dover 1974, 1978); as he later noted (Dover 1994: 157), "When I began to mine the riches of Attic forensic oratory I was astonished to discover that the mine had never been exploited."

[15] A number of other Antiphons can with certainty be excluded as separate figures; these include the fourth-century tragedian from Syracuse and the politician executed by the Thirty; see further below, 2.1.

the fragmentary speeches. Chapter 7 brings all this material together in order to assess Antiphon's full accomplishment. As noted above, the ultimate argument for a unified Antiphon is the coherence of the picture that results. Not that all his works are similar or treat the same issues—far from it. But if, when due account is taken of differences in the purpose of each work and its intended audience, the issues treated and the attitudes underlying them are seen to have an overall coherence, then our attempt to reassemble the complete Antiphon will be justified.

I. THE SOPHISTIC PERIOD

Antiphon was active in the second half of the fifth century, a period of great intellectual activity generally associated with the group of thinkers we call Sophists. In using this term and expressions like "the sophistic movement," I do not mean to imply any strict unity of belief or coordination of activity; indeed, the sophistic period is more notable for rivalry than for agreement or cooperation, as the vivid picture Plato draws of three Sophists (Protagoras, Hippias, and Prodicus) in *Protagoras* indicates. But the Sophists do share certain common interests, attitudes, and methodologies, and a review of these will provide the background for Antiphon's work. The following sketch is not intended to be either comprehensive or balanced, but rather to highlight especially areas and aspects of the Sophists' activity that are significant for Antiphon's work.[1]

1. WHO WERE THE SOPHISTS?

Since Plato, the word "Sophist" has come to designate in the first instance a member of a specific group of fifth-century intellectuals, but in the fifth and fourth centuries the name was widely applied to poets and other sources of wisdom, including Socrates, whom Plato sharply separates from the Sophists, and to orators and logographers such as Demosthenes and Lysias.[2] One characteristic often singled out is that the Sophists were teachers who took pay. Both features must be understood in context: before the Sophists, the only professional teachers in Greece were elementary-school masters (*grammatistai*), who taught reading, writing, and other subjects.[3] There were no

---

[1] For a fuller survey of the Sophists' accomplishments, Guthrie (1971) and Kerferd (1981) have not been superseded. For a different approach, see Cassin's recent book (Cassin 1995) and her brief article on "Sophistique" (Cassin 1996).

[2] Kerferd 1950; Guthrie 1971: 27–54.

[3] Beck 1964.

established institutions for postelementary education. Young men attracted to intellectual pursuits might arrange privately for a tutor, or might join the circle of an established thinker like Pythagoras, but teaching at this level was in general ad hoc and loosely structured.[4] In this context, some of the Sophists (but not necessarily all) offered formal courses of study for a fee. We have good evidence for this sort of teaching by the four most prominent Sophists, Protagoras, Gorgias, Prodicus, and Hippias, but Thrasymachus and Critias are never referred to as teachers, and reports about Antiphon have been disputed. It may be, then, that only some Sophists offered formal lectures or courses of study for a fee; but all Sophists were probably teachers in the broader sense of influencing younger men who associated with them. Teaching was thus an important activity of many Sophists; but Plato's real objection to the Sophists was not that they taught per se but the content of their teaching.

Plato objects to the Sophists' taking pay for two reasons: because they cannot say exactly what it is they are selling or show its value; and because anyone who accepts pay is obligated, like a merchant, to sell his wares to anyone who can pay for them, whereas higher education should be reserved for those with superior intelligence who have already advanced to a certain point in their studies. The first objection is characteristic of Plato's insistence on a rigorously intellectual and theoretical approach; no one before him was able (in his view) to give an adequate account of his profession. The second objection is more political. As Kerferd notes, Plato's implied criticism that Sophists display their wisdom to "all sorts of people" ($\dot{\epsilon}\nu$ $\pi\alpha\nu\tau o\delta\alpha\pi o\hat{\iota}s$ $\dot{\alpha}\nu\theta\rho\dot{\omega}\pi o\iota s$, *Hippias Maior* 282c) is contemptuous, and aristocratic prejudice is also evident in Xenophon's analogy of a prostitute who sells his beauty to all comers (*Memorabilia* 1.6.13).[5] Such remarks suggest that although those who studied with the Sophists must have been fairly wealthy and (even more important) must have had leisure time, the Sophists were intellectually more egalitarian, and probably politically, too,[6] than outspoken elitists like Plato, Xenophon, and perhaps also Socrates.

---

[4] Cf. Anytus's assertion that "any Athenian gentleman he happens to meet" can teach a young man virtue (*aretē*) better than the Sophists (*Meno* 92e; the entire conversation 89e–94e is revealing on the matter of postelementary teaching).

[5] Kerferd 1981: 25–26.

[6] On possible political leanings of individual Sophists, we are very poorly informed and can only speculate; see Gagarin and Woodruff 1995: xxiii, to which we should add that Hippias often served as an ambassador for Elis, which seems to have been governed by an oligarchy in the fifth century.

Another contrast with Socrates is that the other Sophists were mostly non-Athenian and itinerant. We have direct reports of travel for most of them, as well as the indirect evidence of, for example, Critias's writings on Sparta. It appears, moreover, that most Sophists were from aristocratic backgrounds, and had the wealth and leisure to travel and pursue their careers. Despite their travels, however, Athens remained a center of sophistic activity,[7] and its importance is confirmed by the fact that all the major Sophists (to judge from the surviving works) wrote in Attic Greek rather than in local dialects or in Ionic, which was the language of most intellectual communication until after the middle of the fifth century.[8] Perhaps related to their traveling is the wide range of interests pursued by most Sophists. Hippias was a famous polymath, and Protagoras, Prodicus, Antiphon, and Critias all had wide interests. Even Gorgias and Thrasymachus, who are best known for their contributions to rhetoric, had other interests, especially Gorgias.

More significant is the fact, first emphasized by Grote, that the Sophists' interests (as opposed to Plato's) were practical, not theoretical.[9] Plato regularly moves from practical concerns to ever more theoretical levels, as for example in the progression of questions in the *Protagoras:* Should the young Hippocrates study with Protagoras? What does Protagoras teach? Can *aretē* be taught? What is *aretē?* By contrast, the Sophists were more oriented toward practical knowledge, which was in part responsible for their success, as young men with expectations of later careers in public life came to study with them. The Sophists' teaching was not narrowly vocational, however, and indeed must have often appeared unrelated to any practical concerns. Protagoras's pronouncements on the proper genders of words, Gorgias's speeches for mythological characters, or Antiphon's (and others') attempts

---

[7] On the Sophists and Athens, see Wallace 1998. He rightly stresses their activity outside Athens, then argues that before 430 they contributed positively to the Athenian democracy, but after that date "sophistic philosophy had become more extreme" and "less sympathetic to the interests of the democracy," which simultaneously became less sympathetic to the Sophists (ibid.: 221). Wallace makes some good points, but with respect to Athenian democracy he disregards his own strictures against treating sophistic thought as a unity. He also considers only the work of those specifically considered Sophists; if we consider sophistic ideas more broadly, the role of Athens becomes more prominent (see below, 1.2).

[8] The main exceptions are the early medical treatises, written in Ionic, and the *Dissoi Logoi,* written in Doric, though most consider this a minor work. Most Presocratics wrote in Ionic, though Anaxagoras (mid-fifth century) wrote in Attic.

[9] Grote 1869, 8: ch. 67, p. 158.

to square the circle could hardly have been of direct use in real life—a point Aristophanes ruthlessly parodies in the *Clouds* (as Strepsiades learns to measure the distance a flea jumps when he had hoped to learn how to escape from paying his debts). But this play also reveals the strong popular conviction that the Sophists' teaching is fundamentally of practical value. In the dialogue named after him, Plato has Protagoras say that he teaches what a student wants to learn, namely "good judgment (*euboulia*) about domestic matters, so that he may best manage his own household, and about political affairs, so that in affairs of the polis he may be most able both in action and in speech" (Plato *Protagoras* 319a). *Euboulia* nicely captures the tenuous conjunction of theoretical reasoning and practical management that teachers of liberal arts in the modern university know well—the belief that general, nonprofessional intellectual training has ultimate practical value, a greater value, in fact, than the more directly practical but narrower training in, say, accounting.

This ambivalence about the value of a Sophist's teaching reflects ambivalence about the name "Sophist" itself and the activities associated with members of this group. The Sophists' critics, Plato, Xenophon, and Aristophanes, give the impression that the negative connotations of the term dominated public thinking by the last quarter of the fifth century, and, to some extent, their continual use of the term in a derogatory sense undoubtedly fostered this view of the Sophists among the general public. We have seen how in the United States at the end of the twentieth century, constant denunciation of political "liberals" rendered this word almost unusable in any positive sense, so that almost all politicians who might once have welcomed the label learned to substitute other designations, such as "progressive." Similarly, it is impossible to find in the fourth century an unequivocally neutral, let alone a positive, use of *sophistēs*.[10] And yet scenes like the opening of Plato's *Protagoras* reveal a more complex picture. Although the young Hippocrates vehemently denies that he wants to become a Sophist himself, he (and apparently others, too) is excited to have a chance to hear Protagoras and to learn what he is teaching. In short, it should not surprise us if the kind of teaching we associate with the Sophists stirred considerable interest among many Greeks in the last half of the fifth century, especially among the young, while at the same time arousing considerable hostility among the more traditionally minded members of the commu-

---

[10] The latest example of a neutral (perhaps even positive) use may be in the fifth-century treatise *On Ancient Medicine* (20): "certain doctors and Sophists."

nity. Thus, although the word *sophistēs* appears to have acquired negative connotations soon after it began to be used of this particular group of intellectuals, public perceptions of the Sophists themselves remained ambivalent. Thucydides testifies explicitly to this ambivalence in the public perception of Antiphon.

2. INQUIRY AND EXPERIMENT

Perhaps the most fundamental characteristic of the Sophists' activity is a spirit of inquiry (*historia*), which manifests itself as both curiosity and skepticism. These are exemplified in the great work of Herodotus, who compiled an account (*logos*) of his inquiry and made a public display (*apodeixis*) of this account, at times orally.[11] Herodotus's inquiries took him all over Greece and much of the non-Greek world in search of information. He asked questions of local authorities such as priests, and often his *logos* simply reports their answers, but he also reveals his own conclusion on some issues, and sometimes his reasoning as well. Sometimes he repeats a tradition without comment, but he is not averse to challenging tradition, as in his conclusion that Homer was wrong about the Trojan War (2.120). These attitudes are widespread among the Sophists and in the work of Antiphon.[12]

Herodotus undertook his inquiries in the direct aftermath of the Persian War, which ended in 479. The victory infused the Greeks with confidence in their ability to overcome obstacles and the desire to learn more about the world they had conquered and to draw lessons for understanding their own world. Herodotus was born a little before the war, in Halicarnassus, which was under Persian control at the time. Protagoras was born about the same time in Abdera in Thrace, and would have witnessed the might of Persia in his youth. Gorgias (also born ca. 490) came from the other end of the Greek world, Leontini in Sicily, but he, too, may have had contact with non-Greek cultures on that island. All three would have begun their careers

---

[11] On *apodeixis,* see Nagy 1987. Johnson's arguments against oral performance by Herodotus (Johnson 1994) apply only to the work as a whole, but Herodotus may have presented many parts of his work orally before committing the whole to writing; see further Thomas 1993.

[12] Lloyd 1979 argues that this fondness for controversy is uniquely Greek, inspired in part, at least, by the absence in Greek culture of powerful central authorities, whether political or religious. The poetry of Homer did not have the same degree of authority as the Hebrew bible, and a Homeric "king" (*basileus*) had none of the authority of a Near Eastern king, Chinese emperor, or Egyptian pharaoh.

in the aftermath of the Greek victory and would share in the confidence it engendered and the spirit of inquiry stimulated by contact with other cultures. Even someone as homebound as Socrates (born 469) could hardly have escaped the inspiration provided by the epic victory a few years before his birth.

In this spirit of inquiry, the Sophists questioned in particular the authority of the poets. Protagoras claims that "the greatest part of a man's education is to be clever (*deinos*) about poetry" (Plato *Protagoras* 338e—339a) and adds that this means distinguishing poetry that is "correct" (*orthos*) from poetry that is not. The example Protagoras chooses of incorrect poetry, which appears to present contradictory views on human virtue, is from Simonides. We know that he also challenged Homer on questions of gender and the mood of a verb, but for the most part the Sophists challenged ethical or religious aspects of traditional thought, particularly on points such as the existence and nature of the gods and of justice. They reached no consensus on the correct alternatives to traditional views, or even on the right questions to ask; rather, their main concern seems often to be simply to find questions or answers that would be new and different from those of others. This search for novelty owed something to the Greek spirit of competition, which I shall discuss below, and it often took the form of what Solmsen calls "intellectual experiments," [13] in which the Sophists explored arguments or methods of argument without being certain where they might lead. Solmsen takes much of his material from authors not traditionally considered Sophists, especially Euripides and Thucydides, and demonstrates that these authors are fully in tune with the spirit of the sophistic period. Indeed, their work is unimaginable without the work of the Sophists, as is the work of others Solmsen could have added—Herodotus, other tragedians, comic poets, medical writers, and others, such as the "Old Oligarch."

The expansion of the group in this way points again to the Athens-centered nature of sophistic activity.[14] Although most Sophists were not Athenian, by around 430 the kind of intellectual activity associated with the Sophists dominated the intellectual life of Athens. Take the Corinthians'

---

[13] Solmsen 1975: 6. These are not to be confused with scientific experiments, in which one creates a method for testing a hypothesis; this is a later development.

[14] Herodotus certainly spent time in Athens, perhaps a great deal of time, and probably gave oral performances in the city. Thucydides left Athens in 424 and wrote his work outside the city, but intellectually he was as much a product of Athens as any of the dramatists. And the "Old Oligarch" has a thorough knowledge of Athenian life and customs, even if we cannot be certain of his nationality.

description of the Athenian character during the debate at Sparta just before the Peloponnesian War (Thucydides 1.170):[15]

> They love innovation, and are quick to invent a plan and then to carry it out in action . . . they are bold beyond their power, take thoughtless risks, and still hope for the best in danger . . . above all, they never hesitate . . . they are never at home . . . they count on getting something by going abroad . . . they alone get what they hope for as soon as they think of it, through the speed with which they execute their plans . . . what they have, they have no leisure to enjoy, because they are continually getting more . . . they think that an idle rest is as much trouble as hard work . . . in a word, it is true to say that they are born never to allow themselves or anyone else a rest.

This spirit of restless and relentless adventure and search that Thucydides identifies as characteristically Athenian also characterized the Sophists who gathered in Athens.[16] However much they may have traveled throughout the Greek world, they must have found a congenial and stimulating atmosphere in Athens. Not only did most of them write in Attic, but their works reflect their Athenian audience in other ways, too. Gorgias, for example, wrote a funeral oration for an apparently Athenian setting, and his Palamedes refers to the characteristically Athenian institution of *euthynai* (the public accounting all officials underwent after their term in office).[17]

Finally, Athens seems remarkably tolerant of the presence of these Sophists, despite occasional reactions in times of political stress.[18] Socrates claims that the production of Aristophanes' *Clouds* in 423 generated considerable hostility against him, but he continued his probing inquiries for almost a quarter century without trouble, until (apparently) his political associations with the failed tyranny of the Thirty provoked his enemies in 399. Antiphon, too, was put to death in 411 after participating in the short-lived

---

[15] The translation is from Gagarin and Woodruff 1995: 89–90; the parts I omit describe the Spartan character, which is in every way the opposite. Whether these views were really expressed by a Corinthian at the time or are Thucydides' own (or some combination of the two), this is still a contemporary account of the special nature of Athens.

[16] Note also the Athenians' great interest in *logoi* (see below, 1.5), which is defended by Pericles (Thucydides 2.40) and condemned by Cleon (Thucydides 3.37–38).

[17] *Palamedes* 28. Note that the constitutional debate in Herodotus (3.80–82) also assumes a form of democracy that is clearly identifiable as Athenian (election by lot, *euthynai*, etc.).

[18] Dover 1988; Wallace 1994.

regime of the 400, but as far as we know, neither his politics nor his intellectual activities, which had raised suspicion among the people (Thucydides 8.68), were threatened before this time. And the reported trials of Protagoras and others, even if they are not later fictions, as seems likely in most cases, were in part intended as attacks on Pericles, whose own popularity prevented his opponents from challenging him directly. It is possible that the Sophists were just as welcome in certain other cities (though it is hard to imagine their being well received in Sparta), but Athens was surely a most congenial center for their activities.

3. PARADOX AND PLAY

The innovative, experimental nature of sophistic activity commonly found expression in challenges to traditional ways of thinking. Sophists favored challenges that were provocative, often to the point of shocking, and paradoxical. Such practices are, of course, much older than the Sophists. Thales may not have said literally "Everything is water," but whatever he did say on the subject—perhaps "Everything comes from water"—is likely to have appeared nonsensical to many of his contemporaries, accustomed to traditional pictures of the cosmos presented by Homer and Hesiod. Thales' successors continued this tradition of seeking an ever more extreme and surprising unity for the world, from Anaximenes, whose "Everything is air (ἀήρ)" would have been even more shocking than Thales' dictum—implying, as it does, that not only is the world not what it seems, it is hardly anything at all—to Parmenides' insistence that only "is" is and nothing else can even be thought, and Zeno's paradoxes (how could Achilles possibly fail to catch the tortoise?), and finally to Gorgias, who arrived at the most extreme possible position, that nothing at all exists.

Poets shared these attitudes. All three tragedians presented new versions of traditional myths that must have surprised and sometimes shocked the audience. Euripides is the most obvious example: not only did he radically change traditional plots, but some of his characters, particularly his women, departed shockingly from traditionally appropriate behavior. But Euripides' (supposedly) more conservative predecessors, Sophocles and Aeschylus, also presented highly innovative versions of the myths, and earlier poets from Archilochus to Pindar also made their mark in part by challenging or altering the tradition.

Heraclitus introduces a new element with aphorisms that are as paradoxical in form as in substance. For example, "road up down one and the same" (ὁδὸς ἄνω κάτω μία καὶ ὠυτή, 60 DK) could be simply a statement of the obvious, that the road going up (a hill) is the same as the one that comes down. But its form, especially the elliptical juxtaposition "up down," suggests a more paradoxical claim, the identity of up and down. Heraclitus is clearly experimenting with unusual stylistic effects at the same time as he seeks a better understanding of the world. Some Sophists have a similar interest in style, notably Gorgias. The stylistic effects that amazed his Athenian listeners on a visit in 427 have not lost their impact today. And Gorgias's innovations are not just stylistic. Earlier defenses of Helen relied on a version of events different from Homer's, one in which Helen never went to Troy. Gorgias defended Helen while retaining the traditional version that she went to Troy with Paris. His encomium is thus a tour de force, demonstrating that even on the traditional facts, a defense is possible, no matter how improbable it might seem at first glance.[19]

Gorgias's most extreme work is *On Not-Being,* where he argues that (a) nothing exists, (b) if anything exists it cannot be known, and (c) if anything exists and can be known, it cannot be communicated to others. To many this argument appears absurd, and scholars have often wondered whether Gorgias is really serious or just playing—seeing how far he can support an obviously wrong conclusion with apparently sound reasoning.[20] The accusation of playfulness is supported, of course, by the last words of *Helen,* where Gorgias remarks almost boastingly that he wanted to write his speech as "an encomium for Helen and for myself an amusement (*paignion*)." Obviously *paignion* is intended to shock: until the end, *Helen* appears to be a serious defense of Helen, with important observations along the way on other topics, such as language, perception, and the emotions. Some of the more extreme stylistic effects may raise doubts, but the final word still leaves many readers perplexed and uncertain whether to dismiss the earlier arguments entirely or disregard the end as irrelevant to the substance of what precedes. Neither course is warranted unless we insist that playful and serious cannot coexist. For Gorgias, they can, and his final words, "an encomium for Helen and for myself an amusement," in fact affirm both qualities simultaneously.

This same combination of seriousness and playfulness is found in the work of Gorgias's contemporary, Zeno of Elea (born ca. 490–485), whose paradoxes are still taken seriously by mathematicians and philosophers. We

---

[19] A defense along the same lines as Gorgias's is found in Euripides' *Trojan Women,* produced in 415, when Gorgias would have been about 75 years old. We cannot date Gorgias's *Helen,* but it seems likely that it was an early work.

[20] Scholars rarely ask whether Parmenides is serious, though some of his claims are nearly as paradoxical as Gorgias's. Perhaps the fact that we have his exact words, whereas we only have summaries of Gorgias's makes a difference.

have no evidence that Zeno called his paradoxes amusements, but it is hard to imagine he was not amused by the effect these would have had on others. Gorgias's *On Not-Being* may have had much the same purpose as Zeno's paradoxes,[21] but perhaps because he is classed as a Sophist, scholars often discount the possibility of a serious purpose. A combination of serious and playful also appears in other Sophists. Antiphon in the Second Tetralogy (3.4.4) proposes that a boy who was struck dead by the throw of another youth's javelin had in fact killed himself. Protagoras says in the first line of the *Iliad*, Homer should not have addressed the Muse with an imperative verb, "sing" (because a mortal should not give a command to a divinity). The author of the *Dissoi Logoi* presents an argument that good and bad are one and the same thing. Underlying such arguments may be the attitude that a paradoxical, shocking, or outrageous statement can draw the audience's attention to a serious argument. Defense of the "weaker" argument (see below) was another manifestation of this attitude. One of the best practitioners of paradox, in fact, was Socrates, who clearly has a serious purpose in proposing paradoxes like "The only thing I know is that I know nothing." The dual effect such a paradox could have on others—leading them to explore its further implications while at the same time irritating them so that they are put off from such inquiry forever—is well illustrated in Plato's works, perhaps most brilliantly in the character of Alcibiades in the *Symposium*.

The Sophists provoked the same contradictory reactions of hostility and attraction, not just by the content of their arguments but also by their stylistic novelties. Gorgias may have the most extreme style, though most of the features he takes to an extreme (parallelism, balance, assonance) are found in earlier poetry. A different stylistic direction was tried by Antiphon, especially in the Tetralogies, and further developed by Thucydides. These two writers favored unusual forms of syntax (particularly involving participial and infinitival constructions) that may seem needlessly complex. But such conscious divergences from traditional prose style went hand in hand with the rejection of traditional beliefs. New ideas and new styles of writing are related features of the Sophists' achievement.

4. PUBLIC COMPETITION

In addition to new thoughts and new styles, the Sophists developed new methods and forms of intellectual activity. These centered on the oral pro-

---

[21] The form of Gorgias's argument, as best we can tell, strongly resembles the form of Melissus 1 DK.

cesses of question and answer and debate, which were recreated in writing by means of paired speeches and (later) dialogues. Both forms grew out of the Greek culture of competition.[22] Most poetry and prose from at least as early as Homer through the classical period was created for or performed in a competitive environment, often in a formal contest. The Sophists entered fully into this competitive spirit, challenging earlier authors and striving to outdo their contemporary rivals. In earlier writers, competition took the form of explicit criticism and rejection of one's predecessors and contemporaries. Xenophanes criticizes Homer and Hesiod; Heraclitus criticizes Hesiod, Pythagoras, Xenophanes, and Hecataeus; Hecataeus dismisses the Greeks in general for telling foolish stories; and Heraclitus complains that people do not understand his *logos*. The Sophists were just as critical, both of earlier writers, especially the poets, and of each other. They also criticize specific institutions, such as the legal system. But unlike Heraclitus and other Presocratics,[23] they do not criticize or belittle people in general for lacking intelligence or for having no comprehension. On the contrary, in the *Protagoras*, Protagoras defends the practice of allowing everyone a say on matters of public concern. Not all Sophists would go so far, but in contrast to the explicit elitism of the Presocratics, the Sophists tend to be more populist, criticizing primarily the views of traditional authorities, not those of ordinary people.

As we saw earlier, the Sophists presented their ideas to "all sorts of people." They presumably desired the approval of their fellow Sophists and their pupils, but they especially sought the acclaim of a larger audience, and they presented their work in public settings, often in competitions or debates. The author of the Hippocratic work *On the Nature of Humans* (section 1) notes that the deficiencies in other accounts of human nature can best be seen by "attending their debates" (*paragenomenos autoisin antilegousin*), for the same person never wins three times in a row, but sometimes this one wins, sometimes that one. If someone had correct knowledge, he should win every time, but "such men seem to me to overthrow (*kataballein*) themselves in their own words through ignorance."[24] The imagery is from a wrestling match, where three falls determined the winner, an image often used at the

---

[22] Griffith 1990; cf. Lloyd 1979.

[23] Xenophanes criticizes mortals for their ideas about the gods, and Parmenides (6 DK) pictures these same mortals wandering on the Way of Seeming, knowing nothing.

[24] ἐμοί γε δοκέουσιν οἱ τοιοῦτοι ἄνθρωποι αὐτοὶ ἑωυτοὺς καταβάλλειν ἐν τοῖσιν ὀνόμασι τῶν λόγων αὐτέων ὑπὸ ἀσυνεσίης. The passage is translated in Gagarin and Woodruff 1995: 166.

time to describe intellectual debate, and Protagoras apparently gave his work *Truth* the alternate title *Overthrowing (Arguments)* (*Kataballontes*).[25] Kerferd is skeptical about such public debates,[26] and argues that lectures and debates before small groups, such as we see in the *Protagoras,* were the rule. But Gorgias's reference to "contests of philosophical arguments" (*Helen* 13), Thucydides' characterization of the work of others as "a contest-piece for the audience of the moment" (1.22), and Cleon's expression of scorn for "the more intelligent . . . who wish to outdo whoever is currently speaking" and criticism of members of his audience, who are like "spectators of the Sophists" (Thucydides 3.37), strengthen the case for open public debate.[27]

Even if the Sophists did not often engage in direct competition, public performances such as the delivery of a funeral oration would indirectly involve competition with others. Both Hippias and Gorgias gave public presentations at Olympia and other panhellenic gatherings, and even if each had his separate occasion or set himself up in a separate place, they would have been competing indirectly. Thus all public performance could evoke a spirit of competition, whether it was Herodotus presenting his work orally to the Athenians or a Sophist giving a public lecture.[28] Many of the Sophists' surviving works take the form of a speech or debate and were probably performed orally in public. The effects of extreme assonance in a work like Gorgias's *Helen* cannot be fully appreciated if the speech is simply read to oneself (even if out loud), but it is easy to imagine Gorgias dazzling a public audience with this speech "by the strangeness of his style," as Diodorus Siculus reports (12.53).

Even if a speech like *Helen* was performed by itself, moreover, it competed with presentations on the same topic by poets, dramatists, and others. Thus opposing views would often be implicitly present in a single speech. The notable exception to the practice of public performance was Antiphon, who, Thucydides tells us, "did not come forward in public or willingly en-

---

[25] Cf. Thrasymachus's ὑποβάλλοντες (7 DK). Heitsch (1969: 299 n. 4) gives examples of καταβάλλω applied to arguments in other authors; for other wrestling imagery during this period, see Stanford's (1958) note on *Frogs* 775 and O'Sullivan 1992: 65 with notes.

[26] Kerferd 1981: 29–30; he allows the possibility of such debates, but suggests that the Hippocratic passage cited above may be describing a succession of individual presentations, not a single occasion.

[27] Slightly later is Lysias's reference (2.80) to contests of strength, wisdom, and wealth (ἀγῶνες . . . ῥώμης καὶ σοφίας καὶ πλούτου) held at the tombs of warriors.

[28] Kerferd 1981: 28–29 presents evidence for such lectures.

ter any other debate";[29] clearly this was unusual for someone of Antiphon's intellectual ability. Performances and debates would have been especially appealing to the young men who would soon be entering careers that would include performances and debates in the lawcourts and Assembly. These young men could get direct, specialized training simply by attending actual meetings of the courts and Assembly (particularly in the company of an older, experienced participant); but sophistic performances would demonstrate the more general intellectual discourse that would be useful in other, more private settings, such as symposia. Thus sophistic performances and competitions would have been good settings for the kind of broad general education offered by the Sophists for young men intending to enter public life.

In addition to oral performance and debate, it is clear that writing was also important to the Sophists' work. The evidence for writing and literacy in general at this time is scarce and difficult to interpret,[30] but it appears that during the second half of the fifth century, communication by means of writing was becoming more common, at least among the elite. The Sophists seem to have understood some of the possibilities offered by this medium, perhaps initially just in helping to preserve oral performances and transmit them to others. Although Gorgias undoubtedly gave public performances of *Helen,* he may have composed the work in writing, and he certainly produced a written text at some point, enabling others to read, study, or perform the text for themselves. Similarly, logographers would write a speech for later performance by a client, which could also be read later by others.[31] And writing was probably used in the composition of large-scale works, even though parts of these might retain their oral character. Herodotus's

---

[29] Thucydides 8.68: ἐς μὲν δῆμον οὐ παριὼν οὐδ' ἐς ἄλλον ἀγῶνα ἑκούσιος οὐδένα. This may be another reference to sophistic debates, though it may just refer to court "contests." Thucydides himself probably also avoided public performance.

[30] Harris 1989; Thomas 1989.

[31] It is uncertain whether (or how closely) the texts we have correspond to the texts actually spoken in court or in the Assembly. In my view, the arguments on both sides of the question are largely subjective, and many cut both ways. However, it is hard to envision a logographer seeking to improve a forensic speech after the performance, unless the speech had political interest and was intended to circulate as a political pamphlet after the fact. It would not help a forensic logographer's business to produce a better speech for publication than the one he wrote for delivery in court, especially if the actual court speech failed. Thus it seems more likely that speeches on important public issues may have later been revised than those written for private cases. See Trevett 1996, with references to previous work.

History is almost certainly not an exact record of an oral performance but was most likely composed out of smaller *logoi,* many of which had previously been presented orally.

The writing down of oral performances led to a new form of sophistic discourse, *Antilogiae,* or opposing arguments. Protagoras reportedly was the first to say that "on every subject (*pragma*) there are two *logoi* opposed to one another" (6a DK, 24 GW),[32] and though nothing survives of his own *Antilogiae,*[33] we may infer that it contained pairs of opposed arguments on various topics. Others followed Protagoras's lead, and several works containing arguments on both sides do survive, most notably Antiphon's three Tetralogies, each of which (following the form of Athenian homicide procedure) contains two alternating speeches by the plaintiff and the defendant. A lesser work, the *Dissoi Logoi* ("Double Arguments"), presents a series of theses (e.g., "Good and bad are the same thing"), each followed by arguments in support of and opposed to the thesis. Xenophon (*Memorabilia* 2.1.21–34) presents a version of a work of Prodicus in which two women, Virtue and Vice, give opposed speeches, each seeking to attract Heracles to her way of life. And many speeches in Thucydides are either directly paired, as in the Mytilenean debate, or indirectly paired to respond to one another, as in the characterizations of Athens by the Corinthians in 1.71 and by Pericles in 2.36–46.

It is unlikely, even in the case of Thucydides, that these *Antilogiae* are direct records of actual oral debates, though their authors may have drawn material from actual debates, and of course others may later have performed these *Antilogiae* orally. But they were written not for oral performance, but rather to practice and display skill in argument, and to explore new ways of thinking about ethical, legal, and political issues.[34] In sum, public performance, whether a single speech or a debate, not only was an important means of communicating one's views to others, but also provided the basis from which the Sophists created a new written form of intellectual communication.

---

[32] Cf. Cicero's report (*Brutus* 12.47 = DK 82A25) that Gorgias thought an orator should have the special ability "to amplify a subject with praise and to diminish it with criticism."

[33] Aristoxenus is reported to have said that it contained virtually all of Plato's *Republic* (Diogenes Laertius 3.37); this is obviously an exaggeration, at best.

[34] I argue below (5.1) that the Tetralogies were intended primarily for reading and studying.

5. *LOGOS*, ARGUMENT, RHETORIC

It is sometimes said that the primary interest of all Sophists was rhetoric.[35] This is misleading.[36] There is little evidence for Prodicus's interest in rhetoric besides his famous concern for using synonyms correctly, and the only aspect of rhetoric mentioned among the many subjects professed by Hippias is the art of memorization. Even Protagoras does not appear interested in methods or techniques of speaking, though his concern with methods of argument is evident. Rhetoric was important in varying degrees for Gorgias, Thrasymachus, and Antiphon, but Gorgias is the only one whose primary interest may have been the art of speaking. On the other hand, if we substitute the broader area of *logos* ("word," "argument," "speech," "reasoning") for "rhetoric," then we can say that most Sophists were intensely interested in this subject. Different Sophists explored everything from specialized linguistic areas, like semantics and etymology, to style and methods of argument, to such overriding issues as truth and falsehood, and the relation of words to reality. These interests were undoubtedly stimulated by the fact that the Sophists regularly performed their *logoi* in public and private settings, and that public speaking was a vital part of the lives of many Athenians, and probably of many Greeks outside Athens, too. Thus every Sophist would have reason to interest himself in *logos* in addition to whatever other interests he might have.

Certain aspects of the subject drew especially wide attention. One broad theme (discussed briefly above) was that of writing or speaking on both sides of a subject. This practice was probably inspired by Greek legal procedure, which everywhere insisted on the basic rule that both litigants should present their case orally before a judge or judges, normally in a public forum, as we see pictured as early as the trial scene on the shield of Achilles (*Iliad* 18.498–508).[37] Automatic means of deciding disputes, such as the ordeal, that are common in most other premodern legal systems are quite

---

[35] "One subject at least [the Sophists] all practised and taught in common: rhetoric or the art of the *logos*" (Guthrie 1971: 44). Protagoras "was the first to call himself a 'sophist,' a term which came to be applied in a more or less loose way also to other teachers of rhetoric who appeared in Athens from abroad during the next two or three decades" (Ostwald and Lynch 1994: 592; cf. Winton 2000: 91). Ostwald's earlier treatment (1992: 341–69) is more balanced.

[36] Cf. Introduction, note 11.

[37] Cf. the fragment attributed to Hesiod (338 MW): "Do not render a judgment until you have heard the story (*mythos*) of both sides."

rare in early Greek law and are generally limited to minor issues. Justice for the Greeks was generally a process of adjudicating conflicts between opposing claims, and a trial thus normally involved a pair (or sometimes two pairs) of *logoi*. A dramatic poet representing a trial (as in Aeschylus's *Eumenides*) or any less formal dispute would compose one or more pairs of *logoi* as part of his dramatization of significant issues. Then, in the second half of the fifth century, the technique of writing paired speeches began to be used as an intellectual tool. Of course, structuring thought in terms of opposition is common throughout Greek culture, and scenes of debate are plentiful in epic and tragedy, but before Protagoras, the reduction of a debate to a single pair of opposed speeches generally occurs only in a legal or quasi-legal setting. An early example of nonlegal paired speeches is the debate between Mardonius and Aristobanus in Herodotus (7.9–10), and this may already show the influence of Protagoras's theory of opposed *logoi*.

The practice of speaking or writing speeches on both sides requires that one learn to support positions that may at first seem unlikely or even impossible. The ability to compose the best possible argument for such positions was referred to by the expression attributed to Protagoras, "to make the weaker *logos* stronger."[38] The notoriety this practice gained in the public perception of the Sophists is evident in *Clouds*, where the *agōn* (889–1112) presents a debate between characters named "Weaker *Logos*" and "Stronger *Logos*."[39] It is probably no accident that the expression, particularly the two adjectives *hēttōn* and *kreittōn*, is essentially ambiguous.[40] For some, "weaker" meant "less just" or simply "wrong." Strepsiades reports (*Clouds* 113–18) that people say there are two *logoi* in Socrates' school, the stronger and the weaker, and "they say the weaker can present the less just case (*ta adikōtera*) and win." This probably represents the popular view of the Sophists' teaching, and it is reinforced when the weaker *logos* wins the debate.[41] But there is no evidence that Protagoras or the other Sophists intended "weaker" to mean

---

[38] τὸν ἥττω λόγον κρείττω ποιεῖν, Aristotle *Rhetoric* 2.24.11, 1402a23 = 6b DK, 27 GW.

[39] For the names, see Dover 1968b: lvii–lviii; cf. Plato *Apology* 19b, where Socrates complains about the false allegation that he makes the weaker *logos* stronger.

[40] *Logos* has (as we have noted) a broad range of meanings, but this causes relatively little difficulty in interpreting this expression, since on any view the meanings "argument" and "speech" are probably both present.

[41] Whether the weaker *logos* speaks more unjustly than the stronger *logos* in the actual debate is questionable; Aristophanes gives a cleverly mixed picture of both.

only "morally inferior." Nor did they necessarily wish to make the weaker *logos* prevail. Only Aristophanes speaks of the weaker *logos* winning, and this outcome is clearly motivated by his plot. Other citations of the expression do not give an article to the second adjective: one should make the weaker *logos* "stronger," not "the stronger."[42] It can be a useful exercise to make the weaker *logos* as strong as possible, even though it may still be weaker no matter how much stronger one makes it.

What, then, do these two adjectives mean? "Stronger" and "weaker" refer in the first instance to physical strength or power. But in Greek, these terms also mean more generally "better" and "worse." Thus, for a *logos* these assessments could designate anything from technical skill to moral content, and it is hard to believe that Protagoras did not intend at least some ambiguity among this range of meanings. Certainly, if he had wished to be unequivocal, he could easily have chosen more definite terms.[43] But the broad range of these terms allows him to pursue his interests in every aspect of *logos,* from technical details of gender or mood to larger issues of truth and justice.

Another ambiguity in Protagoras's expression is that it is not always evident which *logos* is the weaker. Is it the case that loses? Or the novel argument? Or the minority view? What if one makes the weaker *logos* so strong that it prevails; is it then the stronger *logos?* Here, too, the Sophists probably exploited the ambivalence. Gorgias's two complete speeches illustrate the possibilities.[44] In defending Helen, he explicitly challenges the traditional view and also provides arguments that seem quite unpersuasive, at least to many; presumably his speech is the weaker *logos.* By contrast, in *Palamedes* he defends a person who, according to tradition, was tried and convicted despite being innocent.[45] Is this a case where Gorgias presents the stronger *logos* because it is the just case? Or is it the weaker *logos* because it loses? And

---

[42] In an otherwise good treatment of this fragment, Schiappa (1991: 103–16) translates it throughout with a second definite article—"make the weaker *logos* the stronger"—implying a victory.

[43] E.g., *agathos* and *kakos* or *ponēros* (cf. Dionysius of Halicarnassus *Isaeus* 4: λόγους ἐπὶ τὰ πονηρότερα).

[44] Cf. Long 1984: 238: "Gorgias could make the worse appear the better cause [in *Helen*], but he could also apply equally strong eloquence to an innocent man's defence."

[45] As Gantz (1993: 604–6) notes, the tradition is "remarkably consistent" on the main points of the story: that Palamedes was framed (by Odysseus) and subsequently convicted and executed. Alcidamas's *Odysseus,* which presents the prosecution's case, is a later response to Gorgias's work.

what if a writer presents a pair of *logoi,* as in Antiphon's Tetralogies, without rendering any verdict or indicating which side would prevail?[46] How can we tell which case is the stronger?

Such questions are unanswerable because Protagoras's claim is intentionally problematic. The terms "weaker/worse" and "stronger/better" were traditionally used of unambiguous contrasts, as we see in Herodotus's report of Themistocles' address to the ship captains before the battle of Salamis in 480: "His whole speech presented a contrast between the better and the worse features of human nature and the human condition; and he urged them to choose the better of these."[47] Herodotus implies that for Themistocles, better and worse were unambiguous judgments about human conduct. When Protagoras proposes to make the worse *logos* better, however, he is implicitly challenging the idea that these values are fixed. This course might lead to complete moral relativism, in which no position is in itself better or worse than any other, and this is part of Plato's criticism of the Sophist; but it is not clear that Protagoras drew this conclusion.[48] Although nothing survives of Protagoras's *Antilogiae,* works such as Antiphon's Second Tetralogy (as we shall see) show that making a strong case for the prima facie weaker *logos* (in this case, the defendant's) can have the serious and constructive result of deepening the reader's understanding of important issues concerning causation and responsibility. The weaker *logos* sometimes turns out to be the just *logos.*

Another term with a similarly ambiguous range of meaning that became important for Protagoras and others is *orthos* ("straight, correct, right"). In its simplest sense, it designates "correct" usage, as for example in Prodicus's insistence on "the correctness of words" (ὀνομάτων ὀρθότης),[49] which is illustrated and parodied by his repeated drawing of fine distinctions between near synonyms in Plato's memorable picture (*Protagoras* 337a–c). For Protagoras, *orthos* had a broader range of meanings.[50] He is reported to have

---

[46] Antiphon seems to indicate that the verdict in the Third Tetralogy goes against the defendant, who voluntarily goes into exile before his second speech—an apparent admission of the weakness of his case.

[47] Herodotus 8.83: τὰ δὲ ἔπεα ἦν πάντα ⟨τὰ⟩ κρέσσω τοῖσι ἥσσοσι ἀντιτιθέμενα, ὅσα δὴ ἐν ἀνθρώπου φύσι καὶ καταστάσι ἐγγίνεται· παραινέσας δὲ τούτων τὰ κρέσσω αἱρέεσθαι.

[48] Woodruff 1999.

[49] See Plato *Cratylus* 384b, *Euthydemus* 277e.

[50] O'Sullivan 1992: 17–18, 77.

taught "correctness"[51] and "correct speech" (ὀρθοέπεια, *Phaedrus* 267c), and although we know of no specific work of his on this subject, two reports may illustrate some of the matters included in it. First, Plato represents Protagoras as saying (*Protagoras* 338e–339a), "I think the greatest part of education for a man is to be clever (*deinos*) about verses; by that I mean to be able to grasp which of a poet's lines are composed correctly (*orthōs*) and which are not, to know how to distinguish them, and to give a reason (*logos*) when questioned." Correct composition for a poet could encompass certain technical skills that we know Protagoras investigated; but the example of incorrect poetic composition given in *Protagoras* involves an apparent contradiction between two ethical generalizations. This goes well beyond correct usage of words into the areas of correct reasoning and moral truth.

The other report suggests an even broader sense for *orthos*. Plutarch reports (*Pericles* 36) that "when an athlete unintentionally struck Epitimus the Pharsalian with a javelin and killed him, Pericles spent an entire day with Protagoras puzzling over whether one should believe that the javelin or the javelin-thrower or those who arranged the contest were more to blame according to the most correct account (*kata ton orthotaton logon*)." It appears that the two intellectuals discussed several different arguments regarding the responsibility for Epitimus's death, seeking to determine which of these is the "most correct." *Orthos* here clearly includes more than technical skills, such as diction, grammar, and syntax. Since, as in the Second Tetralogy, the facts are apparently undisputed, the dispute must concern the "most correct" interpretation of guilt or liability based on these facts. In other words, which *logos* contains the best reasoning and is the most consistent with law and morality? Correctness here includes almost every aspect of *logos*.

Another attribute of *logos* that became important for the Sophists was precision (*akribeia*), in particular the precise differentiation among terms or concepts. The pursuit of *akribeia* was sometimes seen as hairsplitting. Aristophanes parodies this in *Clouds* (740–42), when Socrates instructs his pupil to "slice your thought fine (*leptos*) and contemplate the matter in detail (*kata micron*), dividing and examining it correctly," and Plato parodies Prodicus for his overly fine distinctions between synonyms (see above). In recognition of this popular attitude, the defendant in the Second Tetral-

---

[51] Plato *Cratylus* 391c. We should resist the assumption of Diels-Kranz that for Protagoras, correctness meant only correctness of words (O'Sullivan 1992: 18 n. 83; Pfeiffer 1968: 280–81).

ogy begins by apologizing to the jurors if his speech seems "more precise" (ἀκριβέστερον) than they are accustomed to. He thereby acknowledges that his case will depend on a detailed and precise set of arguments that some may see as hairsplitting. Precision is also a goal of Thucydides, who writes (1.22) of the difficulty of remembering the precise wording (τὴν ἀκρίβειαν αὐτὴν) of speeches and of his efforts to report events (erga) with as much precision as possible (ὅσον δυνατὸν ἀκριβείᾳ . . . ἐπεξελθών).

It appears that precision came to be associated particularly with written communication. It is promoted in Antiphon's Tetralogies and Thucydides' History, which were intended to be read, and is downplayed by Gorgias in his funeral oration, which was clearly composed for oral performance.[52] And Alcidamas recommends in his treatise On Those Who Write Written Speeches or On the Sophists (13) that if one writes a speech for oral delivery, one should "avoid precision (akribeia) and imitate instead the style of extemporaneous speakers."[53]

Far more complex than their quest for correctness and precision is the Sophists' view of and attitude toward truth. Plato attacks them on this point, maintaining ironically that "Protagoras's Truth is true to nobody" (Theaetetus 171c), that rhetoric deals in falsehood (Gorgias 458e–459c, etc.), and that his predecessors honored probabilities more highly than truth (Phaedrus 267a, 272d–273c). Although both Protagoras and Antiphon wrote works entitled Truth, none of their preserved fragments explicitly discusses this subject. In their surviving works, however, the Sophists and orators consistently present truth as a positive value, even a primary goal, while recognizing that truth is often a matter of judgment rather than fact, and is often difficult if not impossible to determine.[54]

On one level, truth lies in the facts of the real world.[55] In this sense, Thucydides and the orators strive to present to their audiences "the truth of things" (ἡ ἀλήθεια τῶν πραγμάτων). But truth must be constructed and conveyed by logoi, and the same set of facts may give rise to different logoi.

---

[52] "These men [i.e., the dead] often preferred gentle fairness to obstinate justice and correctness of speech to precision of law (προκρίνοντες . . . νόμου ἀκριβείας λόγων ὀρθότητα)" (Gorgias 6 DK, 3 GW).

[53] In this work, Alcidamas frequently and consistently uses akribeia of written prose (13, 14, 16, 18, 20, 23, 25, 33, 34; cf. 12). On akribeia, see further Gagarin 1999.

[54] See further Gagarin 2001a.

[55] I cannot deal here with the many complex issues surrounding the notion of "reality," but in my view, even if reality is a social construction, the term usefully conveys a meaningful notion. See further Searle 1995: 149–97.

The defendant in the Second Tetralogy warns the jurors that they must decide the truth of this case from the two competing *logoi;* each *logos* corresponds to the same set of facts, but each understands those facts from a one-sided perspective (3.4.1–2; see below, chapter 3). Truth is thus not simply a matter of knowing the facts; it is also dependent on its expression by means of *logoi,* and the relationship between *logoi* and facts (*erga* or *pragmata*) is problematic.[56] To our knowledge, the Sophists never posited a single, knowable truth grounded in a higher reality like Plato's Forms; rather, their problematic view of truth led them to focus their interest on other matters, such as probability, that had immediate practical importance.

The argument from probability (*eikos*)[57]—the demonstration that something is likely, though not certain—was, according to tradition, the main interest of the earliest rhetorical theorists. Probability arguments, of course, existed from the earliest times (e.g., Homer *Odyssey* 22.321–25), but in the middle of the fifth century, two Syracusans, Tisias and Corax, apparently took special interest in this subject and may have invented the "reverse probability" argument—that the most obvious suspect is least likely to be guilty, since, knowing that he would be the main suspect, he would have avoided committing the crime.[58] The argument from probability was primarily of interest to those Sophists who wrote hypothetical forensic speeches, Gorgias and Antiphon.[59] Antiphon's First Tetralogy is an exercise in probability arguments (and contains the only example in oratory of the reverse probability argument), and Gorgias's *Palamedes* is a similar exercise, employing a succession of rhetorical questions that have the effect of probability arguments without using the word *eikos.*[60] Neither of these works supports

---

[56] Nowhere more so than in Thucydides' work; see Parry 1957.

[57] On the ideas in this paragraph, see further Gagarin 1994. "Probability" may be a misleading translation of *eikos* if it suggests mathematical calculations. But in saying "He will probably come," we do not think of a mathematical probability; rather, we mean, "It is a reasonable expectation that he will come." This is how I use the term.

[58] The classic example is the question, Who started the fight between a weak and a strong man? The strong man is the likely suspect, and so he argues that for that very reason he is unlikely to have been the assailant (Aristotle *Rhetoric* 2.24.11, 1402a17–21).

[59] It is unclear whether Protagoras was interested in probability arguments. Aristotle asserts that making the weaker argument stronger promotes a false, not a true, probability (*Rhetoric* 2.24.11, 1402a23–28), but this does not mean that Protagoras took this step. Kennedy (1991: 210 n. 254) suggests that Protagoras's declaration of agnosticism was followed by probability arguments on both sides of the issue, but this is merely a guess.

[60] In context, it is clear that "How could I have planned to betray?" is equivalent to "It is unlikely that I planned to betray."

Plato's assertion that "Tisias and Gorgias . . . saw that probabilities should be more honored than truths" (*Phaedrus* 267a); rather, both Sophists recognize the necessity of probability arguments when the truth is otherwise unobtainable. Moreover, the use of probability arguments to defend the innocent Palamedes belies the claim that probability is necessarily at odds with the truth. The Sophists valued the truth but realized that if direct access to it is impossible, they needed to resort to probabilities.

The importance of probability (according to the traditional view of the Sophists) is linked to another axiom of received wisdom, that rhetoric is the art of persuasion.[61] In a famous passage in Gorgias's *Helen* (8–14), the power of *logos* is closely linked to persuasion, as indeed it must be if Gorgias is to show that Helen succumbed to an irresistibly powerful force.[62] But the close identification of *logos* with persuasion and the emphasis on the latter in *Helen,* which provides the justification for Plato's characterization of Gorgias's view of rhetoric as "the craftsman of persuasion" (πειθοῦς δημιουργός),[63] are unique in the writings of the Sophists and are clearly motivated by the needs of Gorgias's argument. Elsewhere in the sophistic fragments, persuasion is mentioned only rarely, often as part of a warning to the jurors that they should not be persuaded by an opponent's deceitful attempts to persuade. Moreover, in *Helen,* Gorgias describes his own *logos* (as opposed to Paris's) as having other aims, and there is good reason to doubt that his purpose in composing the work was to persuade his audience that Helen was innocent. Persuasion may be a goal of some sophistic discourses, but the characterization of rhetoric as simply "the art of persuasion" has distorted our understanding of the Sophists' endeavor by focusing attention on only this one factor and neglecting other important aims of a sophistic *logos,* such as exploring methods of argument.

The emphasis on argument is particularly evident in the *Antilogiae.* Opposed speeches cannot have the aim of persuading the audience. Even if the winning or more persuasive side is indicated, as, for example, in Thucydides' Mytilenean debate, the author's aim is not primarily to persuade his audience.[64] As a rule, however, the winning side is not indicated: the Tetralo-

---

[61] I present the argument in this and the next paragraph more fully in Gagarin 2001b.

[62] Cf. *Helen* 12: "Persuasion, which has the same power . . . as compulsion."

[63] Cf. Lloyd 1990: 86: "The opposition between persuasion and demonstration could be, and was, extensively used by philosophers as a way of contrasting their rivals' work with their own and of course of claiming superiority for the latter."

[64] Thucydides may have believed that Diodotus's speech would persuade the Athenian audience to act, but Thucydides' aim in writing the speech was less to persuade his

gies end with no verdict, and the opposing arguments in the *Dissoi Logoi* are juxtaposed without comment. The Sophists may have composed double *logoi* for many reasons—to shock, to entertain, to dazzle, to enlighten—but rarely to persuade. Indeed, the more sophisticated and intellectually interesting argument may for that very reason be the less persuasive, as perhaps in the Second Tetralogy. Even a single speech like *Helen* seems intended less to persuade others of Helen's innocence (for which purpose other arguments would have been more effective) than to display Gorgias's skills—a stylistic and argumentative tour de force. And the paired speeches in Thucydides seem primarily aimed at clarifying for the reader the forces and motives underlying events and decisions. The focus on rhetoric as persuasion is a Platonic legacy that continues to distort our view of the Sophists.

Finally, if the aim of sophistic *logoi* was at least in part to enlighten, then the new medium of written communication provided an opportunity for more precise and sophisticated forms of analysis than had hitherto been available.[65] As we noted above, Alcidamas takes for granted the greater precision of written composition; his preference for extemporaneous oral discourse is driven by the particular purposes he envisions—ad hoc and practical, not theoretical or analytic. But authors like Thucydides and Antiphon (in his Tetralogies and "sophistic works") understood that the precision of written composition and communication with readers allowed them to carry the analysis of human nature, or causation and responsibility, farther than had hitherto been attempted by their predecessors, such as Gorgias and Herodotus, who still composed primarily for oral communication.

6. RELATIVISM AND HUMANISM

The doctrine most commonly associated with the Sophists is relativism. Although relativism can include a wide range of beliefs, it is Plato's construction of Protagoras's views in *Theaetetus* that has most influenced our understanding of the Sophists' version of relativism as the belief that all truth is relative and therefore no real or absolute truth exists. More specifically, for the Sophists, truth is found in appearances, appearances vary, and therefore everyone's perception or opinion is true and no one can claim to know more than another.

---

readers that this was the best argument than to shed light on Athenian values at the time. See further Woodruff 1994.

[65] The argument of this paragraph is further developed in Gagarin 1999.

As influential as this picture has been, it is doubtful whether it accurately represents the views of Protagoras,[66] and there is no good evidence that the other Sophists held such views. It is true that their travels and inquiries led them to compare political, legal, social, ethical, and religious customs and ideas and to understand that different people had different views on many issues; but at the same time, they seem to have agreed that people everywhere shared certain basic principles. For example, Herodotus's parable (3.38) illustrating the strength of people's beliefs about the treatment of the dead shows both that the specific content of these beliefs differs significantly among different cultures and that all cultures accept the importance of giving due honor to the dead, whether this involves burning them or eating them. The Sophists thus shared a belief in cultural relativism without necessarily denying that there are fundamental norms of human behavior that cut across cultural differences; in fifth-century terminology, they sought in varying ways to mediate the conflicting claims of cultural tradition (*nomos* = "custom, law") and universal human beliefs (*physis* = "nature").[67]

Another factor contributing to the picture of the Sophists as moral relativists is that they devoted themselves more to challenging traditional customs and ideas than to developing positive doctrines of their own,[68] a trait exemplified by Socrates, who portrays himself in the *Apology* as demonstrating that the traditional sources of authority in Athens are wrong while at the same time claiming to have no knowledge of his own. A common interest of Socrates and the Sophists, however, was human behavior and human society, and for this the Sophists have been called the first humanists. Indeed, Protagoras's man-measure saying, which forms the starting-point for Plato's attack in *Theaetetus,* can be read as an affirmation of humanism in response to the abstract authority of Parmenides' Being: "A human being is the measure of all things, of those things that are that they are and of those things that are not that they are not" (1 DK, 15 GW). This assertion seems to be aimed directly at Parmenides' condemnation of the opinions of mortals on logical and ontological grounds; Protagoras, by contrast, posits human beings as the standard for what exists and what does not.

Just how Protagoras elaborated and defended this proposition, if indeed he did,[69] is not clear, but in a related move, he directly criticized the tradi-

---

[66] Woodruff 1999.

[67] Guthrie 1971: 55–134 provides a useful survey of views on *nomos* and *physis*.

[68] Striker 1996.

[69] There is strong evidence that Plato found the man-measure saying in a written text. In *Theaetetus* he quotes it in whole or in part ten times, and each time the word-

tional authority of the gods. Several Sophists held untraditional views of the gods, but Protagoras's is the best known: "Concerning the gods, I am not in a position to know either that they exist or that they do not exist, or what form they might have, for many things prevent our knowing—the obscurity of the subject (*adēlotēs*) and the shortness of human life" (4 DK, 20 GW). This statement is consistent with Protagoras's view that only what is apparent can be known, as expressed in a recently discovered fragment from Didymus the Blind: "It is manifest to you who are present that I am sitting; but to a person who is absent, it is not manifest that I am sitting; whether or not I am sitting is obscure (*adēlon*)."[70] Since knowledge depends on human perceptions, and we do not directly perceive the gods, we cannot know whether they exist. Thus they cannot serve their traditional role of grounding moral values, and human beings must themselves be the authority for knowledge and morality.[71]

I have focused here on Protagoras, since his views are the basis for most discussions of sophistic relativism. If Protagoras is representative, it is not as a relativist but as a humanist—one whose fundamental concern is human beings and who sees in humans the one measure of knowledge and values. Plato indicates some of the difficulties that arise from the man-measure saying, but the Sophists did not necessarily follow the direction of the argument he lays out in *Theaetetus*. It is thus impossible to know in detail what sort of relativism Protagoras and others may have endorsed, but it is clear that the Sophists' primary concern was with human issues, and they looked to humans for the solutions to their problems.

7. CONCLUSION

Shortly after the dissolution of the U.S.S.R., the director of the National Endowment for the Humanities, Lynne Cheney, interviewed Bernard

---

ing is identical or very nearly so. In five of these, he refers explicitly to Protagoras's writings, twice noting that the saying stood at the beginning of Protagoras's *Truth*. On the other hand, the explanation that follows, "As each thing seems to me, so it is for me, and as it seems to you, so, too, it is for you" (152a), is cited twelve times, but with no mention of writing and with varying wording (φαίνεται or δοκεῖ, conditional clause or participle, etc.). Evidently Plato had no text for the relativistic interpretation he claims followed the man-measure saying.

[70] 21 GW; see Gronewald 1968; Woodruff 1985.

[71] One fragment suggests that Protagoras apparently did not accept the supremacy of nature, but put nature and training on an equal level: "Teaching requires natural talent (*physis*) and practice (*askēsis*)" (3 DK, 5 GW).

Knox, the Jefferson Lecturer in the Humanities for 1992. Parts of this interview touch on the Sophists.[72]

CHENEY: You've written about how the rise of democracy led to the humanities.

KNOX: Yes, with the so-called Sophists.

CHENEY: I am just amazed when I read you on the Sophists because you make such a good case for them.

KNOX: Well, a case has to be made for them because Plato blackened their name.

CHENEY: Is it possible that that is a bit of sophistry? Are you making the worse the better cause when you write about the Sophists? . . . It's true, being able to persuade your fellow citizen is essential in democracy, but the worse is still the worse cause. And if you can manage to make the worse seem the better cause, I'm not sure you've done your fellow citizens a favor.

KNOX: Yes, but the same word in Greek that you translate and I sometimes translate "worse" and "better" also means "stronger" and "weaker."

CHENEY: So it's complete relativism, then.

. . . .

CHENEY: Couldn't you look at it another way? That the Sophists had one approach to the humanities and the Platonists another, an approach that emphasized the idea of truth, as opposed to the extreme relativistic stance of the Sophists?

KNOX: If you look at what Plato is actually recommending in the *Republic* . . .

CHENEY: Oh, it's very undemocratic. I understand that.

KNOX: It isn't very humanistic either. Poets are not going to be allowed in the republic unless . . .

CHENEY: They sing the state song.

KNOX: Yes, right. It sounds like something that just collapsed recently on the other side of the world.

CHENEY: That's true.

The enduring success of Plato's hostile portrayal of the Sophists is evident here. The fact that an amazingly good case can be made for them has no apparent effect on Cheney's basic assumptions: they are extreme relativists who oppose the idea of truth and try to persuade their fellow citizens

---

[72] Cheney 1992: 35–36.

that the worse cause is the better one. In this chapter, I have tried to remove the filtering lens of Plato and have presented a rather different picture of their activities and ideas. Although the sophistic movement included a wide diversity of views, so that on most issues generalization is misleading at best, it is useful to keep the traditional designation "the Sophists" to describe the collective intellectual enterprise they were engaged in and some of the interests and approaches that were widely shared among them. Among these are an attitude of skepticism toward traditional ideas and values, a love of competition, and a desire for novelty. The Sophists were pioneers and experimenters, and however we assess the views of individual Sophists, we must appreciate that they provided a crucial stimulus to Greek intellectual life, forcing a reexamination of almost every aspect of traditional culture.

Most Sophists were interested in *logos* in a broad sense, and many taught or wrote about some facets of "the art of *logoi.*" Most thought about the nature and origins of human societies, and justice and right conduct. All were broadly interested in human culture—not just in what we today identify as the humanities, but also in issues today addressed by social and natural sciences. They were the first professional teachers of higher education, and they fostered the close association of education and culture as a whole. These accomplishments notwithstanding, Plato's hostile criticism has prevailed. The Sophists lost the battle to control the discourse about themselves, and even Isocrates, who was strongly influenced by them, rejects the label "Sophist" and repeatedly differentiates himself from them.[73] Like democracy—another product of classical Athens that Plato condemned—the Sophists had few followers in later centuries.[74] Even in the eighteenth century, when democracy first reappeared in the West, the Athenian model of "radical democracy" was largely condemned as extreme and dangerous.[75] A more positive assessment of democracy and the Sophists did not emerge until the middle of the nineteenth century, when George Grote rewrote the history of classical Athens, in part to further the cause of liberalism in England.[76] Grote's brief drew, and still draws, some support, but reactions against it and

---

[73] Generally, for Isocrates, a Sophist is one who engages in forensic oratory.

[74] The significant exception to this was the period ca. 60–230 C.E., known as the Second Sophistic, when rhetoric, particularly in the form of public declamation, achieved an exceptional prominence in the Greco-Roman world in both public life and education.

[75] Roberts 1994. There were some exceptions among French writers during the revolution.

[76] Grote 1869. Grote did have certain precursors, notably Hegel's 1831 lectures.

support for the traditional Platonic view have continued to dominate—thanks to Plato's intellectual and artistic genius and to the almost complete loss of direct evidence for the Sophists.

On the other hand, the ideas championed by the Sophists, if not the Sophists themselves, have steadily gained ground since Grote. Athenian democracy, then viewed as extreme, is today more often criticized for its narrow franchise than for its radicalism. The idea (if not always the practice) of free inquiry is more widely accepted around the world than ever before, and public discourse about human society and human conduct, and about human culture in general, has never been more widespread, even if much of this discourse has moved from the academy to newer forums like television and radio talk shows and other mass media. It is important to appreciate just how much the Sophists did to further the kinds of ideas and ways of thinking that most of us now take for granted, even those for whom the Sophists are still identified with complete relativism. Despite the negative overtones of the name, "sophistic" views have survived Plato's attack (as have poetry and democracy, the other objects of his attacks) and have become an accepted part of modern Western culture.

The remainder of this study will show how one important but hitherto neglected Sophist, Antiphon, helped shape the sophistic views I have sketched here, then drew on these views specifically to advance the study and practice of forensic oratory, which in fourth-century Athens became a major form of cultural discourse.

II. ANTIPHON: LIFE AND WORKS

Two contentious issues have long stood in the way of a full appreciation of Antiphon's accomplishments. First, ever since antiquity there have been those who wished to divide Antiphon into (at least) two different Antiphons, "the orator"[1] (Antiphon of Rhamnus), who wrote forensic speeches, and "the Sophist," who wrote the treatises *Truth* and *Concord.* The main reason for this division in antiquity was apparently stylistic, for the language of the "sophistic works," especially *Truth,* is noticeably different from that of the court speeches. Twentieth-century separatists, on the other hand, have argued primarily from doctrinal differences: the orator was a conservative adherent of law and an aristocratic believer in class differences, whereas the Sophist was a radical egalitarian anarchist. But stylistic differences are not surprising in works of different genres with different audiences and purposes, and, as we shall see, the supposed doctrinal differences stem largely from unwarranted assumptions and from a mistaken supplement of the papyrus text. In fact, the pictures we have of the orator from Thucydides and others and of the Sophist from Xenophon and from the surviving fragments of the sophistic works are similar enough that if they had been drawn from two different men living at roughly the same time and place, then Xenophon would have needed a much clearer means of differentiating the two. Thus Xenophon's epithet "the Sophist" could not have served to designate a different individual from the orator portrayed by Thucydides, who would fit comfortably into the general image of a fifth-century Sophist as outlined in the preceding chapter.

The second division concerns authorship of the Tetralogies. During the last century, opinion has been divided whether the person who wrote the

---

[1] The term "orator" (*rhētōr*) for Antiphon is late and inaccurate, since as an adviser and logographer Antiphon did not himself speak in court except at his own trial in 411; see further Introduction, note 6, and below, note 23.

court speeches also wrote the three Tetralogies preserved in our manuscripts of Antiphon. The primary reason for denying the authenticity of the Tetralogies, which as far as we know was never questioned in antiquity, is that they do not adhere in every particular to Athenian law. Several other concerns have also been raised, including stylistic differences and uncertainties of dating. But stylistic differences and legal discrepancies can all be attributed to differences in genre, audience, and purpose; and once these concerns are removed, it will be clear that the Tetralogies are products of the sophistic thinking of the latter part of the fifth century, and, moreover, that they fit well with Antiphon's other interests. There is no reason, then, not to accept that they were written by him.

On both these issues, the dominant view through most of the twentieth century was separatist, with the result that scholars studied either the court speeches, or the Tetralogies, or the sophistic works, but not all of them together. Recent scholars are more inclined to accept the unity of both the person and his works, but apart from short, encyclopedia-type notices, there still exists no study of the whole of Antiphon's work.[2] The following review of the unitarian case on both points (identity and the authenticity of the Tetralogies) is intended to provide the basis for such a study. On both points, the evidence at our disposal is insufficient to allow for certainty; nonetheless, the preponderance of considerations clearly favors the case for unity, and contemporary scholars are increasingly coming to realize this.

I. ORATOR AND SOPHIST

Antiphon[3] was a common name in Greece,[4] but the most famous Antiphon was the son of Sophilus from the deme Rhamnus, who was probably

---

[2] A hint of the possibilities is given in Zimmermann 1997, whose entry on Antiphon of Rhamnus begins with the issues raised in *Truth* and then considers all six surviving speeches.

[3] Some of the points in this section are discussed at greater length in Gagarin 1990c, which was in part a response to Pendrick 1987b. Although I disagree with Pendrick's conclusions, he raises valid issues and is helpful on many details. The reader should consult these papers, together with Pendrick 1993, for further details.

[4] Pauly-Wissowa's *Realencyclopädie* and its supplement volumes list eighteen Antiphons, some of whom may be the same person. The orator is number 14, the Sophist number 15. Of the others, the most notable are a tragic poet, who was put to death by Dionysius of Syracuse in the early fourth century, and the Antiphon who was put to death by the Thirty in 404/3 (Xenophon *Hellenica* 2.3.40).

born around 480, and was publicly tried and executed for his role as a leader of the short-lived oligarchic revolution of the 400 in 411. He was apparently the only prominent Antiphon in Athens during the decade or two preceding his death, since he is twice mentioned by name without demotic or patronymic by Aristophanes in his *Wasps,* produced in 422. Once someone is said to be "as hungry as Antiphon" (1270), perhaps a reference to his reputed appetite for money, and a little later he is included in a group of "those around Phrynichus" who were present at a banquet where Philocleon behaved outrageously (1301–2). Since Phrynichus was another leader of the coup in 411, this Antiphon is almost certainly the Rhamnusian. Other comic poets, according to late sources, attacked Antiphon for "being clever *(deinos)* in forensic cases and for selling for a high price speeches that run counter to justice" (Philostratus *Vitae Sophistarum* 499), and for "love of money" *(philargyria,* [Plutarch] *Moralia* 833c). These comic allusions, relatively small in number, indicate that Antiphon was known to the public but perhaps was not prominent in public life.

This changed in 411, when Antiphon joined with other Athenian oligarchs in a temporarily successful coup. According to Thucydides (8.68): "The man who planned the course of the entire affair and who gave it the most thought was Antiphon; of all the Athenians of his day he was second to none in integrity *(aretē)* and was best able to think and to speak knowledgeably. He did not come forward in public or enter any dispute willingly, but was regarded with suspicion by the multitude because of his reputation for cleverness *(deinotēs).* However, for those involved in a dispute in court or in the Assembly, he was the one man most able to help whoever consulted him for advice." [5] After the restoration of democracy, Antiphon was tried and, Thucydides adds, "of all the men up to my time . . . he seems to me to have made the best defense in a capital case." [6]

---

[5] ὁ μέντοι ἅπαν τὸ πρᾶγμα ξυνθεὶς ὅτῳ τρόπῳ κατέστη ἐς τοῦτο καὶ ἐκ πλείστου ἐπιμεληθεὶς Ἀντιφῶν ἦν ἀνὴρ Ἀθηναίων τῶν καθ᾽ ἑαυτὸν ἀρετῇ τε οὐδενὸς ὕστερος καὶ κράτιστος ἐνθυμηθῆναι γενόμενος καὶ ἃ γνοίη εἰπεῖν, καὶ ἐς μὲν δῆμον οὐ παριὼν οὐδ᾽ ἐς ἄλλον ἀγῶνα ἑκούσιος οὐδένα, ἀλλ᾽ ὑπόπτως τῷ πλήθει διὰ δόξαν δεινότητος διακείμενος, τοὺς μέντοι ἀγωνιζομένους καὶ ἐν δικαστηρίῳ καὶ ἐν δήμῳ πλεῖστα εἷς ἀνήρ, ὅστις ξυμβουλεύσαιτό τι, δυνάμενος ὠφελεῖν. This and the other ancient texts concerning the life of Antiphon are conveniently translated in Morrison 1972: 114–29.

[6] ἄριστα φαίνεται τῶν μέχρι ἐμοῦ . . . θανάτου δίκην ἀπολογησάμενος. A fragment of this speech is preserved and will be discussed below (section 6.5). Antiphon is briefly mentioned twice more in Thucydides 8.90.

Thucydides' portrait does not identify this Antiphon as either orator or Sophist, but his description of Antiphon's strong intellect and ability to speak, his reputation for cleverness (*deinotēs*), which made him suspect in the eyes of the general public, and his ability to help those who sought his advice with regard to disputes in court or in the Assembly would naturally make contemporary readers associate him with other intellectuals of the period to whom the designation "Sophist" was applied. Clever speaking was a hallmark of a fifth-century Sophist,[7] and an Athenian intellectual who could speak well and whose reputation for cleverness aroused suspicion would surely attract this label. On the other hand, Thucydides also suggests the career of a logographer when he describes someone who gave helpful advice to those engaged in disputes in court. Thucydides' description thus suggests that this Antiphon could be considered both a Sophist and a logographer, and furthermore that rather than treat these as two separate careers, we should accept that there was a large degree of overlap between the roles of logographer and Sophist at this time.[8]

The next evidence for Antiphon's life comes about twenty years later in Xenophon's *Memorabilia* (1.6), where Socrates is reported to have had three conversations with "Antiphon the Sophist," who "wished to attract some of his [Socrates'] followers."[9] In these discussions, which, like the other episodes in this work, are largely fictional, Antiphon maintains that Socrates' poverty makes him a poor model for his students to imitate (1.6.2–10); that Socrates' teaching must be worthless because he charges no fee (1.6.11–14); and that Socrates should not teach others about political life without engaging in it himself (1.6.15). There is some suggestion in the first discussion that Antiphon himself possesses the wealth that Socrates lacks, and although Xenophon nowhere directly implies that Antiphon charges fees or is involved in

---

[7] At the beginning of Plato's *Protagoras*, Hippocrates says first that a Sophist is "one who knows wise things" and then, when pressed, adds that a Sophist knows how "to make people clever at speaking" (τοῦ ποιῆσαι δεινὸν λέγειν, 312c–d). Cf. the description of two Sophists in Plato's *Euthydemus* (272a) as "writing speeches suitable for delivery in court," and *Clouds* 1313–14, where the chorus predicts that Pheidippides will soon prove himself "skilled in arguing (*deinos legein*) for opinions contrary to justice."

[8] See Plato's *Euthydemus* 272a, cited in preceding note. Apollodorus recounts (Demosthenes 59.21) Neaira's experience with "Lysias the Sophist," using this designation apparently without malice, for Lysias's behavior in the episode is quite respectable (so Carey 1992: ad loc.). The identification of the Sophists with those who engage in forensic argument is common in Isocrates; see especially 13 (*On the Sophists*).

[9] πρὸς Ἀντιφῶντα τὸν σοφιστήν . . . ὁ γὰρ Ἀντιφῶν ποτε βουλόμενος τοὺς συνουσιαστὰς αὐτοῦ παρελέσθαι.

politics, his introductory remark that Antiphon wishes to attract Socrates' followers may suggest that unlike Socrates, Antiphon does charge fees for teaching and does take part in public affairs.

Pendrick (1987b) argues that Xenophon's picture of Antiphon does not fit what we know of Antiphon of Rhamnus and that therefore the designation "the Sophist" must be intended to distinguish this Antiphon from the more famous orator. On the first point, however, the features implicitly attributed to Xenophon's Antiphon do seem to fit the Antiphon of Thucydides and the comic poets quite well. These fifth-century sources tell us that he advised others about speaking in court or in the Assembly, charged high fees for his logography, loved money, and was directly involved in politics, at least at the end of his life. As for being a teacher, he is referred to as a teacher of rhetoric by Plato in his only mention of Antiphon (*Menexenus* 236a) and is called a teacher in many later sources.[10] This evidence does not prove that Thucydides' Antiphon was a teacher, let alone that he was precisely the kind of teacher Pendrick infers from Xenophon's text. But nothing in our sources is incompatible with Antiphon's being teacher, charging fees, or being a rival of Socrates. In short, Xenophon's picture of "Antiphon the Sophist" is at the least not inconsistent with our other information about Antiphon, and there is no reason why he could not be describing the same person. Whether or not Antiphon of Rhamnus ever called himself a Sophist or was commonly known as such, the designation "Sophist" was applied broadly enough in the fourth century that it could certainly have been used of him, as it was of Lysias,[11] even if he was not normally known as such.

In other words, a contemporary reader of Xenophon would probably assume that "Antiphon the Sophist" designated the Rhamnusian unless another Antiphon also lived in Athens at about the same time who was well known as "Antiphon the Sophist." We have no evidence, however, that any fifth-century thinker called himself or was routinely called by others "the Sophist."[12] Rather, all the Sophists are identified by other means, usually

---

[10] See especially the passage from Hermogenes (second century c.e.) cited below, where he says, "I am told by many that Thucydides was the pupil of Antiphon of Rhamnus."

[11] See above, note 8. Note also that Aeschines (1.173) refers to the Athenian people executing "Socrates the Sophist"; and according to Aelius Aristides (46, 2.407 Dindorf), Lysias called both Plato and Aeschines Socraticus Sophists.

[12] In fact, in Plato's portrayal (*Protagoras* 316d–317c), Protagoras says that other Sophists have always avoided being identified as such, and that his own acceptance of the name is exceptional.

by city of origin, and it is hard to see why Xenophon would have chosen the designation "the Sophist" rather than some other (ethnic or demotic or patronymic) that would make the identity absolutely clear.

On the other hand, if Xenophon is representing Antiphon the Rhamnusian in this passage, we may wonder why he calls him "Antiphon the Sophist."[13] Antiphon is the only person whom he identifies as a Sophist, though he introduces Prodicus as "the wise" (ὁ σοφός, *Memorabilia* 2.1.21; *Symposium* 4.62).[14] Xenophon's practice in naming people varies; in general, most individuals are introduced only by their names without any extra designation,[15] and the designations he uses vary widely, for reasons that are not easy to fathom; in some cases there seems to be no good reason.[16] So we cannot maintain that Xenophon necessarily felt a need to distinguish this Antiphon from any particular other Antiphon. He may have wished only to suggest that the issues Antiphon raises were commonly raised in discussing Socrates' relationship to the Sophists. Or he may be trying to prejudice his readers against Antiphon.[17] Or he may also have used the designation "Sophist" to distinguish this Antiphon from one or more other Antiphons who were clearly not intellectuals. Possible candidates would include the Antiphon whom Xenophon tells us was put to death by the Thirty in 404/3 (*Hellenica* 2.3.40; cf. [Plutarch] *Moralia* 833a–b), or the tragic poet, who died sometime before 367 and thus was almost certainly active when Book 1

---

[13] A separate question is why he gives these conversations with Socrates to Antiphon, rather than to another "Sophist." As contemporary Athenians with many aristocratic friends, Socrates and Antiphon must have been acquainted, at least, and as one of the very few Athenian Sophists, it may be that Antiphon would be seen as more of a threat than other Sophists to attract Socrates' followers.

[14] Callias addresses Antisthenes as ὦ σοφιστά in Xenophon's *Symposium* (4.4). Other Sophists are introduced in various ways, e.g., "Hippias of Elis" (*Memorabilia* 4.4.5).

[15] Whitehead (1988: 146) calculates that only 8% of the roughly 395 historical persons in the *Hellenica* are given extra designations of any kind (besides the name).

[16] Whitehead (ibid.: 147) suggests personal acquaintance with the individual or with an unmentioned homonym may account for the presence of a patronymic. The closest parallel to "Antiphon the Sophist" may be "Kallistratus the public speaker" (ὁ δημηγόρος, Xenophon *Hellenica* 6.2.39, 6.3.3), who, Whitehead suggests (1988: 146–47), "is so called simply because that is what he was (and despite the fact that Xenophon passes over, without comparable comment, many others of equal celebrity)."

[17] The fact that Antiphon was a member of the oligarchic government of the 400 does not necessarily mean that the oligarchic sympathizer Xenophon had a favorable view of him. The fifth-century sources give a picture of Antiphon that may well have offended more traditionally minded Athenians, such as Xenophon.

of the *Memorabilia* was composed (ca. 380). These and other Antiphons would clearly be excluded by the designation "the Sophist" in a way that the Rhamnusian would not.

The lives and writings (if any) of these other Antiphons were quite different from the intellectual activity of the orator-Sophist, and so it is always clear, either from the context or from some additional designation, when a fourth-century source is referring to one of these others. By contrast, the orator-Sophist is almost always simply "Antiphon." Aristotle uses "Antiphon" without further specification both for Thucydides' Antiphon and for the Antiphon who devised a solution to the problem of squaring the circle and speculated on the material nature of things;[18] but he does make certain to distinguish this Antiphon from the tragedian Antiphon, whom he always designates either "the poet" or the author of a named tragedy.[19] Other classical authors who refer to a historically significant Antiphon normally make it clear by the context that this is some other Antiphon,[20] not the Rhamnusian.[21] If the reference is to Antiphon's writings or ideas, there is no designation of a specific Antiphon unless the reference is to the poet, in which case either he is so designated or a specific play is mentioned.

The implication of this practice is that any writings or ideas mentioned by ancient writers as belonging to a classical Antiphon are the product of one of two Antiphons, either the tragedian, who is always designated as such explicitly or by context, or the orator-Sophist, who generally gets no special designation. The only author whose treatment is an exception is Xenophon,

---

[18] Aristotle refers to Antiphon *simpliciter* to designate the member of the 400 (*Ath. Pol.* 32.2, *Eudemian Ethics* 1232b), the intellectual who squared the circle (*Physics* 185a, *Sophistici Elenchi* 172a), and the theoretician about the nature of matter (*Physics* 193a). Aristotle is also reported to have mentioned "Antiphon the diviner" (ὁ τερατοσκόπος) in Book 3 of his *On Poetry* (Diogenes Laertius 2.46 = Aristotle fr. 75 Rose).

[19] Antiphon "the poet": *Mechanica* 847a; *Rhetoric* 1385a; named play: *Eudemian Ethics* 1239a; *Rhetoric* 1379b, 1399b.

[20] Xenophon *Hellenica* 2.3.40 (the Antiphon put to death by the Thirty); Demosthenes 18.132 and Dinarchus 1.63 (an Antiphon who was executed during the struggle against Philip). Hippocrates (*Epidemics* 1.15) identifies a patient as Antiphon the son of Critobulus. In Andocides 1.15, the name Antiphon appears on a list of those accused of revealing the mysteries in 415; this is probably not the Rhamnusian (see MacDowell 1962: ad loc.).

[21] In addition to the works already cited of Aristophanes, Thucydides, and Aristotle, Lysias also refers to the Rhamnusian as simply "Antiphon" without qualification (12.67, where the context makes the identity clear; cf. Lysias's lost speech "Concerning Antiphon's Daughter," which probably refers to a different Antiphon).

who adds the epithet "the Sophist." [22] Antiphon is never called "the orator," since during this period this term is only used of one who actually speaks in public. [23] Thus, the only possible suggestion in all these sources that there was a fifth-century intellectual named Antiphon who was not the man described by Thucydides is Xenophon's epithet, and, as I have argued, he most likely calls Antiphon "the Sophist" precisely in order to designate Thucydides' Antiphon, whose activity would have fit the common image of a Sophist well. Indeed, it seems hardly possible that anyone at this time would use "the Sophist" to distinguish another Antiphon from the famous Rhamnusian. Even if there was an Antiphon in Athens in the fifth century who was more of a Sophist (so to speak) than the Rhamnusian, he would be more clearly distinguished from the Rhamnusian by a patronymic or demotic than by the designation "the Sophist," which in Xenophon's time would simply not be distinctive enough. [24]

The next major stage in the ancient tradition visible to us is the second-century (C.E.) treatise *On Style* by Hermogenes (*Peri Ideon* 399–400 Rabe = 87A2 DK).

> Anyone discussing Antiphon must first note that, as Didymus the grammarian and a number of others have said, and as my investigation has revealed, there have been many Antiphons whom we must consider, two of whom engaged in sophistic activity (*sophisteusantes*). One of these is

---

[22] In addition to an Antiphon "from Rhamnus" (*Menexenus* 236a), Plato identifies two other Antiphons as relatives of people mentioned in his dialogues: Antiphon "from Cephisia," for the father of one of Socrates' students (*Apology* 33e); and Adeimantus's half-brother, who is given a full family tree (*Parmenides* 126).

[23] See Introduction, note 6. In Plato's *Euthydemus* (305b–c), Socrates asks about an unnamed person, "Is he one of those who is skilled in (legal) contests, an orator (τῶν ἀγωνίσασθαι δεινῶν ἐν τοῖς δικαστηρίοις, ῥήτωρ τις), or one of those who send such people (to court), a composer of speeches (ποιητὴς τῶν λόγων) used by the orators in their contests?" to which Crito answers, "Certainly not an orator, by Zeus; I don't think he himself has ever spoken in court, but by Zeus they say he knows the business and is clever and skilled at composing speeches (δεινὸν εἶναι καὶ δεινοὺς λόγους συντιθέναι)." This passage is cited by Grote (1869, 7:260 n. 1), who suggests Plato may have Antiphon in mind.

[24] In a work of about the same time, Plato writes, "Since they are so close to each other, sophists and rhetors (σοφισταὶ καὶ ῥήτορες) are mixed up in the same area and about the same thing (ἐν τῷ αὐτῷ καὶ περὶ ταὐτά), so that they don't know what to make of themselves, and other people don't know what to make of them" (*Gorgias* 465c, trans. Irwin).

the orator (*rhētōr*) to whom are attributed the homicide speeches and
public addresses and similar works; the other, who is also said to have
been a diviner and dream-interpreter, is the one whose works are said to
be *On Truth, On Concord,* and the *Politicus.* I am persuaded, because of
the difference in style of these works, that there were two Antiphons (for
there is really a large discrepancy between the work *On Truth* and the
rest); but on the other hand, because of what is reported by Plato and
others, I am again not persuaded. For I hear that many say Thucydides was a student of Antiphon of Rhamnus; and since I know that the
Rhamnusian is the one to whom the homicide speeches belong and that
Thucydides is very different [from these] and quite similar in style to the
work *On Truth,* again I am not persuaded. In any case, whether there
was one Antiphon employing two such different styles of writing, or in
fact two, one using one style and the other another, we must treat each
separately. For as we have said, there is a great difference between them.[25]

Hermogenes evidently had available many more works of Antiphon
than we do today, as well as the writings of the first-century B.C.E. scholar
Didymus and others, who had determined that only two of the many Antiphons could be considered Sophists, and these two were different men.
The only reason Hermogenes gives for thinking these are two different
people is that one man is unlikely to have written in two such different
styles. Hermogenes also gives a stylistic argument for unity: the connection

---

[25] περὶ δὲ Ἀντιφῶντος λέγοντας ἀνάγκη προειπεῖν, ὅτι, καθάπερ ἄλλοι τέ φα-
σιν οὐκ ὀλίγοι καὶ Δίδυμος ὁ γραμματικός, πρὸς δὲ καὶ ἀπὸ ἱστορίας φαίνεται,
πλείους μὲν γεγόνασιν Ἀντιφῶντες, δύο δὲ οἱ σοφιστεύσαντες, ὧν καὶ λόγον
ἀνάγκη ποιήσασθαι· ὧν εἷς μέν ἐστιν ὁ ῥήτωρ, οὗπερ οἱ φονικοὶ φέρονται λόγοι καὶ
⟨οἱ⟩ δημηγορικοὶ καὶ ὅσοι τούτοις ὅμοιοι, ἕτερος δὲ ὁ καὶ τερατοσκόπος καὶ
ὀνειροκρίτης λεγόμενος γενέσθαι, οὗπερ οἵ τε Περὶ τῆς ἀληθείας εἶναι λέγονται
λόγοι καὶ ὁ Περὶ ὁμονοίας [καὶ οἱ δημηγορικοὶ] καὶ ὁ Πολιτικός. ἐγὼ δὲ ἕνεκα μὲν
τοῦ διαφόρου τῶν ἐν τοῖς λόγοις τούτοις ἰδεῶν πείθομαι δύο τοὺς Ἀντιφῶντας
γενέσθαι (πολὺ γὰρ ὡς ὄντως τὸ παραλλάττον τῶν ἐπιγραφομένων τῆς Ἀληθείας
λόγων πρὸς τοὺς λοιπούς), ἕνεκα δὲ τοῦ καὶ παρὰ Πλάτωνι καὶ παρ' ἄλλοις ἱστο-
ρουμένου πάλιν οὐ πείθομαι· Θουκυδίδην γὰρ Ἀντιφῶντος εἶναι τοῦ Ῥαμνουσίου
μαθητὴν ἀκούω πολλῶν λεγόντων, καὶ τὸν μὲν Ῥαμνούσιον εἰδὼς ἐκεῖνον, οὗπερ
εἰσὶν οἱ φονικοί, τὸν Θουκυδίδην δὲ πολλῷ κεχωρισμένον καὶ κεκοινωνηκότα τῷ
εἴδει τῶν τῆς Ἀληθείας λόγων, πάλιν οὐ πείθομαι. οὐ μὴν ἀλλ' εἴτε εἷς ὁ Ἀντιφῶν
ἐγένετο, δύο λόγων εἴδεσι τοσοῦτον ἀλλήλων διεστηκόσι χρησάμενος, εἴτε καὶ δύο,
χωρὶς ἑκάτερος ὁ μὲν τοῦτο ὁ δὲ ἐκεῖνο μετελθών, ἀνάγκη χωρὶς περὶ ἑκατέρου
διελθεῖν· πλεῖστον γάρ, ὡς ἔφαμεν, τὸ μεταξύ.

of Antiphon with Thucydides, whose style resembles that of *Truth*. We cannot know whether Didymus or Hermogenes' other sources presented any evidence bearing on the issue of unity apart from stylistic considerations. If anyone did, Hermogenes evidently did not consider it decisive, for otherwise he would surely have mentioned that there were other grounds for deciding the issue in favor of one or two Antiphons, rather than leaving the historical issue in doubt on stylistic grounds alone.[26]

Hermogenes' description of the two styles follows (400–401 Rabe). He informs us that since the Rhamnusian Antiphon, to whom the homicide speeches are attributed, wrote for the public,[27] his style was clear and persuasive. But Antiphon fell short of his successors, since (it is said) he was first to practice this style, he discovered this kind of practical (*politikos*) oratory, and he was the oldest of the ten orators. By contrast, Hermogenes tells us nothing about the career of "the other Antiphon" (*ho heteros Antiphōn*), but speaks only of his style, which was "not at all for the public" (πολιτικὸς μὲν ἥκιστα). Hermogenes thus has information about the career of "Antiphon of Rhamnus," but apparently knows nothing about the life of this hypothetical "other Antiphon." And since he has read Didymus and other scholars on the subject and has carried out his own investigation, it seems unlikely that these predecessors knew much (if anything) about the career of this hypothetical other Antiphon either.

Much of our evidence for Hellenistic and later scholarship is now lost, but we know something of the history of Antiphon's works beginning in the third century B.C.E., when they were catalogued together with works of the other orators in the library at Alexandria, probably first by Callimachus.[28] Callimachus was not especially careful about assigning authorship and apparently included many spurious works among those of the orators he catalogued,[29] but the inclusion of treatises like *Truth* together with speeches in his collection of Antiphon is notable. All the other works he included in

---

[26] Wooten's translation (1987: 122–23) wrongly removes any doubt from Hermogenes' text (contrast Morrison 1972: 114–15). Wooten also twice identifies the person Hermogenes calls "the other Antiphon" (see below) as "Antiphon the Sophist," though this expression occurs nowhere in Hermogenes.

[27] The term *politikos* can mean "involved in public affairs," but the context shows that Hermogenes is characterizing Antiphon's writing, not his life.

[28] In grouping Antiphon together with true orators like Demosthenes, Callimachus was probably the first to use the term *rhētōr* of him and other logographers.

[29] Including perhaps seven speeches by Apollodorus among those of Demosthenes (Trevett 1992).

this canon were speeches (or peripheral works, like letters), which he must have found either previously attributed to one of the ten orators or without attribution, deciding in the latter case to which of the ten it belonged. In Antiphon's case, however, Callimachus can only have found the nonrhetorical works, *Truth* and *Concord*, among the works previously attributed to Antiphon; if he found them without attribution, he would have had no reason to attribute them to any orator, let alone Antiphon. Thus the inclusion of sophistic and rhetorical works together must go back to some time before the third century.[30]

Of the scholars who worked on Antiphon after Callimachus, the most important is Caecilius of Cale Acte (first century B.C.E.). Caecilius wrote on the life of Antiphon, questioned the attribution of twenty-five of the sixty works assigned to him[31] (on what grounds we do not know), discussed his style at some length, and quoted in full the decree passed in 411 prescribing a public trial for Antiphon and the sentence of death that was voted at that trial. Unlike his contemporary Didymus, Caecilius apparently did not discuss the identity of a separate Sophist.[32]

The next important scholar is the second-century C.E. lexicographer Harpocration, whose *Lexicon* includes ninety-nine citations from Antiphon. The majority are attributed to a specific work, and of these, almost one-third come from the nonrhetorical works. Harpocration takes for granted the identity of orator and Sophist, citing the sophistic works in exactly the same form as the rhetorical works.[33] And his entry under the name "Anti-

---

[30] Separatists might argue that Callimachus may have found the nonrhetorical works with the designation "Antiphon" (i.e., "the Sophist") and mistakenly included them with those of the Rhamnusian, but anyone preserving the works of a separate Antiphon would surely have some way of differentiating their author from the better-known logographer. Callimachus did not include tragedies in his collection, even though these were known to be the work of an Antiphon.

[31] In the nineteenth century, it was common to count each Tetralogy as four speeches, making fifteen extant speeches in all, and Blass (1887: 102 n. 2, cited by Edwards 1998: 90 n. 38) maintains that ancient authors never use the name "Tetralogy" and must therefore have counted the speeches individually. But there is ancient evidence on this point, namely Hermogenes' reference to a word in the third speech of Tetralogy 1 as "in the second" (see below, note 55). This shows conclusively that for him, Tetralogy 1 as a whole was the second speech in the collection, as it is in the surviving manuscripts.

[32] At least pseudo-Plutarch, whose life of Antiphon is heavily drawn from Caecilius, gives no hint of this issue (*Moralia* 832b–834b).

[33] Harpocration notes one word (*diathesis*) that is used by Antiphon in his speech against Callias and by "the same person" in *Concord*.

phon" reads simply, "One of the ten orators, the son of Sophilus, from the deme Rhamnus." For Harpocration, the speeches and nonrhetorical writings are the work of a single man. Harpocration is thoroughly familiar with all the works of Antiphon and the other orators that were extant in his time. He is concerned about authenticity and questions that of two of Antiphon's speeches (and many of those by other orators). He is also said to have written another work on Antiphon's style, and he cites works by Didymus and Caecilius. In view of his own interests, we would expect that he knew their studies of the orators especially. It is hard to imagine that he was unaware of the stylistic debate recorded by Hermogenes, or that he would ignore good evidence, if he knew of any, for assigning Antiphon's sophistic works to a different author.

Similar evidence is provided by another second-century lexicographer, Pollux, who cites Antiphon's works nearly fifty times. Although he rarely gives the title of the work cited, six of his citations are words found in the speeches of the logographer, and two citations are said to come from *Truth*.[34] It thus appears that Pollux also did not distinguish the author of the speeches from that of the nonrhetorical works. Other ancient scholars from the same period (e.g., Galen) and later (e.g., Stobaeus) also cite passages from both the speeches and the nonrhetorical works without any indication of authorship besides "Antiphon." We hear nothing more of "Antiphon the Sophist" until the sixth-century Aristotelian commentator Simplicius, nearly 1,000 years after Xenophon, who once uses this designation.[35] The only other occurrence of this label is in the entry on Antiphon in the tenth-century dictionary, the *Suda*, which is even more confused than most accounts of Antiphon.[36] Thus, even ancient scholars who may have accepted the separate authorship of the speeches and the nonrhetorical works almost never attributed the latter to "the Sophist." This may be because, like Hermogenes and apparently Didymus before him, both Antiphons were thought to be "engaged in sophistic activity," so that the epithet "the Sophist" would not

---

[34] Pollux (6.143) also labels one citation as "in the *rhētorikai technai*—but these seem not to be authentic." Modern scholars assign the remaining fragments to either lost speeches or sophistic works on the basis of their content; some are assigned uncertainly to both.

[35] *Commentary on Aristotle's Physics* 9.273. There is no obvious reason for this designation; in eight other cases, Simplicius simply says "Antiphon."

[36] The *Suda* describes three Antiphons: (a) an Athenian diviner, verse-maker (*epopoios*), and Sophist, also known as a "word-cook" (*logomageiros*); (2) the Rhamnusian (with a few brief facts about him); (3) an Athenian dream-interpreter.

serve to specify a different Antiphon than the Rhamnusian.[37] By comparison, Apollodorus's designation of the logographer Lysias as "Lysias the Sophist" (Demosthenes 59.21) is echoed four times in later scholarship.[38] In this case, it appears that the epithet serves to emphasize a specific aspect of the logographer's work or convey a certain opinion of him rather than to differentiate him from any contemporary homonymous writer.

This brief survey of ancient references to Antiphon gives us no reason to accept the separatist view that there were two different fifth-century intellectuals named Antiphon. To sum up the main points: First, Xenophon's designation of an interlocutor of Socrates as "Antiphon the Sophist" very likely refers to the same Antiphon described by Thucydides. Although we cannot prove that Thucydides' Antiphon was a teacher or a rival of Socrates, both of these activities (which may or may not be implied by Xenophon's portrayal) are fully compatible with what we know of the Rhamnusian. In fourth-century usage, the term "Sophist" is applied so broadly to different intellectuals, including Lysias and Socrates, that it would be unremarkable to use it of the logographer Antiphon; thus it could not serve to differentiate some other Antiphon from him. If Xenophon had had another Antiphon in mind, he must have known something else about him that could more clearly differentiate the two.

Second, the only reasons we are given in antiquity for believing in two separate Antiphons are stylistic. To be sure, our main source, Hermogenes, is primarily interested in style, but if other ancient scholars, like Didymus, had presented good, nonstylistic arguments for the separatist position, Hermogenes must have known what these were (since he made his own investigation), and it is impossible to explain why he would leave the whole matter in a state of uncertainty ("on the one hand . . . on the other hand") and make no mention of nonstylistic arguments that could settle the issue, if there were any. It is very likely, therefore, that the sole criteria by which later scholars distinguished two Antiphons were stylistic, grounds that most modern scholars now recognize as inadequate for this purpose.

---

[37] Thus we have the title of a second-century (C.E.) book by Hephaestion (of unknown contents) entitled *On the Antiphon in Xenophon's Memorabilia;* if the title of this work were *On Antiphon the Sophist,* it would not be so clear what the subject was.

[38] Once in Athenaeus (13.593f, referring to Apollodorus's speech), once in Proclus (*Commentary on Plato's Parmenides* 632, referring to Plato's *Phaedrus,* where Lysias is not explicitly called "the Sophist"), and twice in Synesius (*Dion* 14, once referring to Plato's *Clitophon,* once to *Phaedrus*).

Third, the nonrhetorical works of Antiphon were collected under his name in the library at Alexandria, probably by Callimachus in the first half of the third century. These are the only nonrhetorical works collected under the names of the ten Attic orators (except for peripheral works, like letters). This suggests that all the works of Antiphon, rhetorical and sophistic, were already assigned to one author by the end of the fourth century at the latest, and thus that if there were in fact two separate writers, "the Sophist" had lost his bibliographical identity quite early.

Fourth, if there was a separate "Antiphon the Sophist," he also lost his biographical identity almost immediately, for throughout antiquity nothing is reported about the life of this hypothetical figure.[39] We have various descriptions of the life of the logographer Antiphon, some of them clearly confused and unreliable;[40] but some basic information is common to most of them, in particular his patronymic and demotic: Antiphon, son of Sophilus, of the deme Rhamnus. If "the Sophist" was Athenian, surely at least some such identifying information would appear about him somewhere and would then serve as a clear means of differentiating these two figures. And if he was not Athenian, then like all the other non-Athenian Sophists, including such minor figures as Evenus of Paros, he would be known by his city of origin, which similarly would then be used to differentiate him from the Athenian Antiphon. The fact that even fourth-century sources like Xenophon and Aristotle omit any biographical particulars when they mention "the Sophist" is a strong indication that this was not a separate figure. If these sources do not need to distinguish this person from the well-known Antiphon, then biographical particulars are unnecessary, for his biography is simply that of the logographer.

In view of the unreliability of stylistic considerations, particularly for works of very early Attic prose, modern separatists have based their case primarily on the content of the sophistic work *Truth*. Before the discovery of two substantial papyrus fragments of *Truth* early in the twentieth century, little attention was paid to Xenophon's "Antiphon the Sophist."[41] With little discussion, most modern scholars accepted the view that he was a dif-

---

[39] If Hephaestion's work *On the Antiphon in Xenophon's Memorabilia* (above, note 37) contained any biographical information about a separate Antiphon, this information did not make its way into any source that now survives.

[40] But cf. Edwards 1998.

[41] He rates only a footnote in Grote (1869, 8:153 n. 2), who adds that it is uncertain whether this is the Rhamnusian. The main nineteenth-century study is Sauppe 1867.

ferent person from the logographer;[42] and although Blass's attempt to assign what we now call "the Anonymus Iamblichi" to Antiphon's *Concord*[43] generated more interest in the assumed Sophist, he was considered strictly a minor figure.[44] The publication of papyrus fragments of *Truth* in 1915 (*POxy* 1364) and 1922 (*POxy* 1797) changed this dramatically. For most scholars, the content of these revealed a strong proponent of natural forces (*physis*) against the claims of human law and custom (*nomos*). Especially telling was the second part of *POxy* 1364, which was restored as a criticism of class distinctions: "We revere and honour those born of noble fathers, but those who are not born of noble houses we neither revere nor honour. In this we are, in our relations with one another, like barbarians, since we are all by nature born the same in every way."[45] Since it seemed hardly conceivable that the oligarchic politician Antiphon of Rhamnus could have been an opponent of class distinctions, a consensus developed in favor of two Antiphons.[46]

The main dissenter during this period was Morrison, who insisted on including all the speeches and fragments of the orator in his 1972 translation of the testimonia and fragments of the Sophist in Diels-Kranz.[47] About this time, the pendulum began to swing back to the unitarian side, as scholars challenged the traditional interpretation of the papyrus as showing Antiphon's commitment to immorality or anarchy (or both).[48] This more neutral reading of the fragments of *Truth,* together with both a generally accepted

---

[42] E.g., Jebb 1875, 1:2 n. 3; Blass 1887: 94. Smith (1844: 207) distinguishes between the Sophist in Xenophon and another Sophist who wrote on the quadrature of the circle and the nature of matter.

[43] On the attribution, see Cole 1961: 156 n. 1.

[44] E.g., Gomperz [1896] 1901, 1:434–37.

[45] Freeman's translation of Diels-Kranz's German version (Freeman 1948: 148); cf. Moulton 1972: 343–44.

[46] E.g., Bignone 1938; Luria 1963.

[47] Morrison 1972; cf. Morrison 1963.

[48] E.g., Moulton (1972) argues that Antiphon is only presenting views in order to refute them; Saunders (1977–78) sees Antiphon (the Sophist) as "a kind of conservative fundamentalist" (230) trying to bring law closer to nature; and Barnes (1979, 2:207–14) concludes that the papyrus is just analyzing various issues and views and "contains no moral or political recommendations at all." Most recently Lugenbill (1997: 165) has argued that the papyrus text uses the *nomos-physis* antithesis to refute a prodemocratic definition of justice and that *Truth* is thus "pro-oligarchic propaganda."

date of the 420s for this work[49]—well within the Rhamnusian's creative years—and a historical examination of the Rhamnusian's career, which reveals connections with the Sophists, further strengthened the unitarian position.[50] And most important, the publication of a small scrap of papyrus in 1984 (*POxy* 3647), which could be joined to *POxy* 1364, supplies a few additional letters at the beginning of the passage cited above. These letters decisively invalidated previous restorations that had implied criticism of class distinctions and undercut the strongest separatist argument drawn from the content of the work.[51]

None of this, of course, amounts to conclusive proof of the unitarian position, but the arguments in its favor are, at the very least, strong enough that we may take it as a working assumption. The examination in the following chapters of all the works that survive in Antiphon's name shall, in my view, provide the strongest support for a single Antiphon. But before turning to the works, we must consider the other main issue dividing Antiphon, the authenticity of the Tetralogies.

2. THE AUTHENTICITY OF THE TETRALOGIES

The medieval manuscripts of Antiphon preserve six forensic works, all concerned with cases of homicide. Three are single speeches for delivery in an Athenian court (1, 5, 6) and three are Tetralogies (2, 3, 4), each with four speeches, two for the prosecution, two for the defense. Whatever the purpose of the Tetralogies (see below), they certainly were not written for delivery in court in an actual trial. In antiquity these six works were included in the corpus of Antiphon's works collected at Alexandria. The works were apparently grouped by subject,[52] with homicide speeches coming first, per-

---

[49] There is no external evidence for dating *Truth*. Scholars argue primarily from the fact that the Sophists' interest in *nomos* and *physis* seems to reach a peak in this decade; but we cannot exclude possible dates any time during the last three decades of Antiphon's life (i.e., 440–411).

[50] E.g., Ostwald 1986: 359–64, at 364.

[51] Avery 1982 summarizes the unitarian position just before the publication of *POxy* 3647. Among recent adherents are Narcy 1989; Eucken 1996; Zimmermann 1997; Lugenbill 1997; and Zinsmaier 1998. Pendrick (1987b, 1993) is currently the strongest separatist voice.

[52] Compare the speeches of Isaeus. Although he wrote for many different kinds of case, only a group of inheritance speeches survives in full; presumably these were grouped together in the manuscripts.

haps because they were the most highly regarded.[53] Harpocration cites nearly 100 words or phrases from Antiphon, most of which are attributed to a specific sophistic treatise or to a speech that no longer survives.[54] However, one word that occurs in Tetralogy 1 is attributed to "Antiphon in the second."[55] This citation indicates not only that the Tetralogies were part of the corpus of Antiphon at this time,[56] but also that the present order of the speeches was fixed, with Tetralogy 1 coming second in order, as in the surviving manuscripts.[57] Ammonius, a grammarian of the first and second centuries c.e.,[58] also cites a phrase from Tetralogy 1 (2.3.10) as found "in the homicide speeches" (171).[59] In short, as far as we can tell, Antiphontean authorship of the Tetralogies was taken for granted in antiquity.

During the nineteenth century, some scholars questioned the authenticity of the Tetralogies because of their sophistic arguments, though most accepted them.[60] At the end of the century, however, in two influential articles, Dittenberger forcefully challenged the assumption that the Tetralogies were

---

[53] Hermogenes (see above) speaks of "the orator to whom are attributed the homicide speeches and public addresses and other similar works"; see Blass 1887: 107. That the homicide speeches came first is suggested by their survival and proved by Harpocration's reference to Tetralogy 1 (see below, note 55).

[54] Harpocration marks two speeches with the qualification "if genuine." Neither survives.

[55] ἐν τῷ β'. The word is ἀγνεύετε, which occurs in 2.3.11.

[56] Another word, ἀναγινωσκόμενος in the sense "persuade," is cited as in Antiphon without further specification, but the only occurrence of the word in this sense in our extant speeches is in 2.2.7.

[57] The citation also confirms that each Tetralogy was numbered as a single work in antiquity (see above, note 31).

[58] Little is known about this Ammonius (*Thesaurus Linguae Graecae* no. 708), who wrote a work "On Similar and Different Words," of which a later epitome survives. He was once thought to be a Byzantine scholar (see *RE* no. 17), but see Nickau 1966.

[59] Ammonius cites one other expression from Antiphon's *Technē* (437). The citations in Pollux (second century c.e.) generally give no titles, but the seven citations that occur in existing speeches come almost equally from the Tetralogies (2.13, 2.119, 8.21) and the court speeches (2.57, 3.138, 8.24, 9.13).

[60] This includes the main nineteenth-century editor, Maetzner, who has no doubts on the matter (1838: 148–49). See also Smith 1844: 206; Müller 1858: 103–13. Blass (1887: esp. 150–54) reviews the issues; although he recognizes that the question cannot be decided for certain with the evidence we have, he is inclined to accept the Tetralogies as genuine, and in any case accepts that they were composed in Athens in the fifth century.

by Antiphon.[61] Dittenberger's main argument was that they presupposed a system of law significantly different from Athenian law, and that since they were, in his view, exercises intended to help train young men to speak in court, they could not have been written by an Athenian for an Athenian audience. In a rebuttal, Lipsius accounted for most of the alleged discrepancies, but Dittenberger held his ground, especially on "the law prohibiting just and unjust homicide" (see below).[62] Although most of Dittenberger's arguments no longer carry much weight, his attack stimulated further scrutiny of the Tetralogies for discrepancies between them and Antiphon's court speeches, leading many to find other reasons for denying their authenticity.[63] Current opinion is more inclined to accept Antiphon as author,[64] but as with the question of identity, conclusive proof is impossible without further evidence.

Those who deny the authenticity cite legal, linguistic, and historical considerations.[65] The main legal issue is "the law prohibiting just and unjust homicide," cited in Tetralogies 2 and 3; this is incompatible with Athenian law, which recognized a category of lawful homicide. Another discrepancy is the frequent and complex use of arguments concerning pollution in the Tetralogies; these occur rarely in court speeches, and when they do, they take rather different forms. Less significant discrepancies, such as the relative absence of narrative or witnesses in the Tetralogies, are also sometimes cited.

Before considering these legal objections, we must understand that the Tetralogies differed from court speeches in several important ways. A court speech has a clear purpose: to present the strongest possible case to the jurors. The prosecution generally includes a narrative of the relevant events

---

[61] Dittenberger 1896, 1897.

[62] Lipsius 1904; Dittenberger 1905.

[63] Sealey (1984) gives the most thorough review of the arguments.

[64] Decleva Caizzi (1969) presents the most thorough case for authenticity. Carawan (1993: 235) speaks of an "emerging consensus" in favor of authenticity (which he opposes), though he may be overstating the situation.

[65] Carawan (1993) raises several new objections, but these seem to me to rely on dubious assumptions about such matters as the nature of homicide procedure, the purpose of the Tetralogies, and the early history of rhetoric. For example, because Tetralogy 1 largely eschews the evidence of witnesses in favor of arguments from probability, Carawan (267) claims (1) that it "assumes that the evidentiary proof is virtually meaningless," and (2) that such a case would likely be composed "only when the cynical abuses of the traditional procedure were notorious," that is, in the fourth century. As should be clear from my discussion below and in chapter 6, I see no reason to accept either of these claims.

(the defense can reduce or eliminate this if the prosecution has already presented the facts), presents witnesses or other evidence supporting its position, and assembles all the supporting arguments it can devise within the time allowed. Often a wide variety of issues and arguments are combined in one speech. Without a judge to decide matters of law, the only control on the litigants' presentation of their case was the jurors' verdict, which was necessarily based on all the points, factual and legal, raised by both sides. There were no precise rules, such as our rules of evidence,[66] constraining either litigant's construction of his case, and broad considerations, such as the rule that one should stick to the issue, were only loosely followed. Such rules, in any case, could only be enforced, if at all, by the jurors, for whom such considerations might (or might not) influence their verdict. The surviving speeches make it clear that litigants had considerable leeway in constructing their speeches; as Demosthenes reminds the jurors in the proem to his most famous speech, *On the Crown* (18.2), "You should allow each of the contestants to adopt both the order and the line of defence which he has chosen and preferred" (trans. Usher).

By contrast, the Tetralogies are fictional creations, focused on a narrow set of issues or arguments, in which all four speeches are the work of a single author. They belong to the sophistic tradition of *Antilogiae* or opposing arguments (see above, 1.4–5), in which the author's methods and purpose may differ widely from those of a single court speech. Persuasion cannot be the main purpose of a Tetralogy, since the arguments on one side rebut those on the other, and even the individual speeches may not be primarily intended to persuade. The author may, for instance, be most interested in constructing an implausible argument that is novel and clever. Or one speech may be framed primarily to set up issues for the opposing speech that follows. *Antilogiae* may be intended to display and develop skill in argument, or to explore new ways of thinking about ethical, legal, and political issues. Works like this could also be intended to teach others in the broad sense of fostering their intellectual development, but they are not intended to teach in the sense of conveying methods or techniques directly usable in an actual court case. Thus the Tetralogies might contribute to a liberal education, but not directly to a program of professional training.[67]

---

[66] Athenian law had no fixed "rules of evidence," either in the common-law sense of rules governing what kind of evidence is allowed in court, or in the civil-law sense of rules determining the relative weight that should be given to different kinds of evidence.

[67] On the audience and purpose of the Tetralogies, see further below, section 5.1.

For this purpose, Antiphon would naturally have given his works a general Athenian background, but he would be under no obligation to adhere strictly to the facts, procedures, or arguments of any particular case, or to the precise details of Athenian law. The general legal context of the Tetralogies is certainly Athenian,[68] but there are clear differences in the methods and strategies employed by the litigants.

First, the Tetralogies are primarily interested in methods of argument and theoretical issues. The factual background of each case is minimal, with the result that there is no need for an extensive narrative; for the most part, the necessary facts are revealed or implied in the arguments. Witnesses and other evidence are sometimes alluded to but are never actually presented to the (hypothetical) court, for Antiphon's interest is not in the actual testimony but in different arguments a speaker can construct concerning witnesses and other external evidence. Furthermore, the format of opposing speeches allows him to match argument against argument in a way that was undoubtedly rare in actual speeches, where a litigant may not always have been able to or even wanted to respond to every point raised by his opponent. And some of the issues and concerns elaborated in the Tetralogies may not have been of much interest to actual litigants.

These differences between the Tetralogies and real court speeches affect any consideration of the legal objections raised by Dittenberger, the most important of which concerns the reference in Tetralogies 2 and 3 to the *nomos* "prohibiting unjust and just homicide."[69] This *nomos* appears to allude to and then reject the Athenian category of justified (*dikaios*) homicide—that is, homicide that was not punished by law. What Dittenberger failed to observe was that if we take "just" (*dikaios*) and "unjust" (*adikos*) in a legal sense, as "lawful" and "unlawful," then a law prohibiting unjust (unlawful) homicide is tautological, and a law prohibiting just (lawful) homicide is self-contradictory. Such a *nomos*, in other words, could not exist in any legal system. Thus, it cannot be used as an argument against an Athenian legal background for the Tetralogies, for in that case it would argue against every other background as well; rather, it must be understood as something other than a statement or paraphrase of an actual legal statute.

---

[68] This includes, among other points, the structure of four speeches in a homicide case with the defendant being allowed to go into exile before his second speech, the penalties envisioned in case of conviction, the distinction between intentional and unintentional homicide, and the provision that a doctor cannot be held liable for the death of his patient.

[69] μήτε ἀδίκως μήτε δικαίως ἀποκτείνειν, 3.2.9; cf. 3.3.7, 4.2.3, 4.4.8.

This raises several further considerations. First, the word "just" (*dikaios*) has a broad range of meanings, of which "lawful" is only one. It is often used in a moral sense ("right"), in which case it may, of course, reflect various moral concepts. It may be *dikaios* to crush your enemy, or to give your enemy a fair hearing. The various meanings of *dikaios* and other evaluative terms were of great interest to the Sophists in the second half of the fifth century, and it would not be surprising to encounter intentionally ambiguous uses of *dikaios* in a work like the Tetralogies. We must also note that *nomos* often means a "rule" or "principle," not an actual legal statute, and this ambiguity, too, may be at play here. If so, this "law" may be a nonlegal or extralegal rule, external to and perhaps critical of a legal system that recognized a legal category of lawful homicide.

These ambiguities open up several possible understandings of the "law prohibiting just and unjust homicide." It could be seen as a moral or religious "rule" that even homicide that is "just" according to the law is morally wrong and must be prohibited. Or it could be a legal "statute" prohibiting a morally "just" homicide (in Athens, this might refer to unintentional homicide, which was punishable).[70] In either case, the implication of the *nomos* would be that the Athenian legal system is at odds with a moral or religious rule or principle. One reason for introducing this *nomos* might then be to raise questions about the relation of moral and legal rules, and about the potentially conflicting moral and legal uses of a term like *dikaios*. It would be inappropriate, of course, to suggest such questions in an actual court speech, but no such difficulty arises in the quasi-fictional world of the Tetralogies that is sometimes called Sophistopolis.[71] And indeed, the possibility that words like *dikaios* may have self-contradictory meanings is raised in other sophistic works of the period, most notably in the work *Truth,* which I shall consider in detail in Chapter 3.

From another perspective, we can put aside the question of the law's meaning and consider instead its function. Eucken has recently shown that in Tetralogies 2 and 3, this *nomos* is used to eliminate potential arguments that might arise if the case were argued strictly in terms of Athenian law:[72] in Tetralogy 2, it might be argued that the killing is justified because it took

---

[70] The fact that in Tetralogy 2 the terms imply "unintentional" and "intentional" (see Gagarin 1978b) lends support to this interpretation.

[71] Innes (1991) takes the term from Donald Russell, who coined it to describe the world of declamations in the Second Sophistic.

[72] Eucken 1996.

place during an athletic competition,[73] and in Tetralogy 3, it might be argued that the killing was justified because it was an act of self-defense. However, the author wants to exclude these traditional lines of argument so that
he can concentrate instead on other issues—in Tetralogy 2, the question of
agency (who is the real agent of the death?), and in Tetralogy 3, the question of causation (who is the ultimate cause of the death?). This concentration of focus on a narrower range of issues is typical of the Tetralogies;
Tetralogy 1, for example, is devoted almost exclusively to arguments from
likelihood (*eikos*). In Tetralogies 2 and 3, the law prohibiting just and unjust homicide makes the arguments intellectually more sophisticated: by
excluding the argument that the immediate agent of the death should be
automatically absolved of liability, Antiphon can raise new questions—in
Tetralogy 2, the victim's role in his own death, and in Tetralogy 3, the operation of a chain of causal events.

The *nomos* prohibiting just and unjust homicide, in demanding strict requital for homicide, reflects an attitude characteristic of the religious world
of Greek myth and tragedy—a world where Oedipus and others must pay
for their deeds no matter what an Athenian court would have ruled.[74] Also
from this same world of myth and tragedy comes the strong sense of pollution found in the Tetralogies, which similarly requires that the killer be
punished or else the whole community will be infected with his pollution.
The Tetralogies carry the idea of pollution further than anything we find in
tragedy when they argue that even the victim's relatives and the jurors can
become polluted if they convict the wrong man. Like the law prohibiting
just and unjust homicide, this strict sense of pollution is unlike anything
that existed in actual Athenian law; it is likely that both ideas are drawn
from the world of myth and tragedy.

But in drawing on these older ways of thinking, the author of the Tetralogies is not returning to the moral or legal thinking of an earlier generation; rather, he is using certain general rules or ideas from this tradition as
a means of directing moral and legal arguments to new issues. His purpose
appears to be, in part at least, to restrict the discussion to certain specific issues, and conversely to force the argument away from issues that may have

---

[73] Eucken (ibid.: 76) suggests that even if, in fact, the killing did not take place ἐν
ἄθλοις in the strict legal sense, the case would probably be argued as such in a real Athenian court.

[74] Ibid.: 79–81. In Oedipus's case, we can only speculate, but I suspect that if he had
been tried in fifth-century Athens, he would have been convicted of homicide but not
of patricide (if this crime were legally punishable, which is questionable).

arisen in actual legal discourse at the time and into new areas of argument. We cannot conclude that the author was an especially religious person or believed strongly in conservative values; his motive was more likely to allow the works to focus more narrowly on certain issues that had begun to enter the discourse of the Greek sophistic community. The effect is clearly to push the argument in new, and sometimes surprising, directions, an effect that would of course fit well with the spirit of the sophistic period in Athens.

All this further confirms that the main purpose of the Tetralogies cannot have been specific training in techniques of Athenian legal discourse; for this purpose, arguments about the justifications for homicide that were recognized by Athenian law would be more relevant. But the Tetralogies could still have originated in an Athenian legal context, particularly in the sophistic period of intellectual experimentation. In such a context, they could provide a demonstration of innovative methods of argument that would not be entirely useless to someone preparing to enter public life, though it would not be aimed specifically at preparing him to write a court speech or speak in public. And a young man who wanted to be on the cutting edge of intellectual activity might seek out a teacher like Antiphon, attracted more by ideas that were innovative and experimental than by any desire to rehearse specific arguments from contemporary legal discourse.

Linguistic considerations have also entered the question of authenticity. Differences between the language of the Tetralogies and that of the court speeches are evident. In particular, Dittenberger and others have noted the anomalous presence in the Tetralogies, which are written predominantly in the Attic dialect, of certain apparent Ionicisms.[75] Most often cited are Ionic forms like οἴδαμεν (for Attic ἴσμεν), or words that have meanings that are found in Ionic but not in Attic, like ἀναγιγνώσκειν in the sense of "persuade." Some scholars have taken these as evidence of Ionian authorship, perhaps an Ionian Greek living in Athens. Against this, Dover noted that the Ionic touches occur in such common words and expressions that they can hardly be accidental on the part of someone whose native dialect was not Attic, but must rather indicate that the author is drawing on or alluding to an earlier genre or work in Ionic dialect.[76]

---

[75] The basic sources for Ionic prose are Herodotus and the works of the Hippocratic corpus. Dover's discussion of Ionic features in early prose (1997: 81–95) reminds us that Greek dialects were complex and continually changing, and that inconsistencies in the practices of individual authors are not uncommon.

[76] Dover 1950: 57–58.

We know very little about Greek prose, Attic or Ionic, before the publication of Herodotus's *Histories* around 430. In particular, we possess no early works with opposing arguments, such as Protagoras's *Antilogiae,* and so we cannot be certain that Protagoras wrote this or other works in Ionic (or partly in Ionic).[77] But it is a reasonable supposition that much, if not most, early prose was written in Ionic, and that the Tetralogies were composed against this background. As sophistic exercises, these would be directed at an audience of both Athenians and foreigners, for whom the Ionic dialect would be appropriate. The Tetralogies are certainly among the earliest Attic prose works we possess.[78] We may never know why their author included some evident Ionicisms in his work, but it is clear that authors at the time were not bound by considerations such as their city of origin to write in a single consistent dialect.[79] The court speeches, on the other hand, had a different audience. Any litigant or logographer addressing an Athenian jury would speak (or write) in Attic, even if that were not his native dialect,[80] and so the discrepancy between the dialects of the court speeches and the Tetralogies is not good evidence for different authorship.

Other differences between the language of the two groups can be similarly explained by the difference between the intended audiences—an international audience of intellectuals versus a group of ordinary Athenian jurors. Moreover, the Tetralogies, unlike the court speeches, were written for others to read and study and were not intended primarily for oral presentation.[81] Features such as the greater syntactic complexity of the Tetralogies

---

[77] Protagoras's few surviving fragments are in Attic, but this does not necessarily mean that they were originally written in this dialect, since the few lines that we have could easily have been transformed from Ionic to Attic. A later example of opposing arguments, the *Dissoi Logoi,* is written in Doric.

[78] The fragments of Pherecydes of Athens, who probably wrote his *Genealogies* in the first quarter of the fifth century, have come down to us in a prose dialect very close to Attic, but ancient scholars like Dionysius of Halicarnassus testify that they were originally written in Ionic, and most scholars accept this; see Jacoby 1947: esp. 34–36; Fowler 1999: esp. 14–15. The one surviving work of Attic prose (aside from inscriptions) that may be earlier than the Tetralogies is the so-called Old Oligarch (= [Xenophon] *Constitution of the Athenians*). Suggested dates for this treatise range from about 450 to 404, though most scholars incline toward a date around 430.

[79] Dover 1997: esp. 85–87.

[80] Dinarchus, for example, was born and raised in Corinth and only moved to Athens in his twenties, but his speeches are written entirely in Attic.

[81] Gagarin 1999.

may also be related to this difference in modes of communication. We have no external evidence that the Tetralogies were primarily intended to be read, but such a purpose could account for the greater complexity of both their syntax and their argument, as well as for other stylistic differences that have been noted. For example, certain expressions common in the court speeches but absent from the Tetralogies, like τοῦτο μέν . . . τοῦτο δέ, help to demarcate an antithesis for a listening audience.[82] Similarly, αὐτὸς οὗτος (only used twice in the Tetralogies) adds emphasis and immediacy to the court speeches. Conversely, the relatively frequent use of single or double τε in the Tetralogies would probably distance them from normal spoken Attic; and the abundance of adverbial participles, often in complex combinations, which the Tetralogies use "to a greater extent than any other Greek prose whatsoever"[83] but which are rare in the court speeches, is more suitable for written communication than for an oral performance.[84] In sum, though there are clear differences in the language and style of the Tetralogies and the court speeches, these do not constitute evidence for separate authorship.

Finally, historical concerns have been raised in connection with dating the Tetralogies, which could affect the question of authorship. Sealey has argued, for instance, that an expression at the beginning of Tetralogy 2 echoes the distinction between a law (*nomos*) and a decree (*psēphisma*) that was not formally incorporated into Athenian law until 403.[85] But Sealey's interpretation of the Greek is questionable, and in any case, *nomos* and *psēphisma* could be paired before the two were legally distinguished in 403.[86] The other main consideration affecting the date of the Tetralogies is the defendant's claim in Tetralogy 1, in a long list of his civic benefactions (2.2.12), that he has contributed much to many *eisphorai* (special levies on the rich, usually in time of war). Since the list as a whole seems to represent an unrealistically large degree of public benefaction—more than any actual person could normally claim—we may take this particular argument as an ex-

---

[82] As Dover (1997: 95) reminds us, however, the use of expressions like this may also vary simply according to individual preference.

[83] Dover 1950: 57.

[84] For Antiphon's language and style, see further Gagarin 1997: esp. 32–35.

[85] 3.1.1: ὑπό τε τοῦ νόμου . . . ὑπό τε τῶν ψηφισαμένων (Sealey 1984: 80–84); for the form and meaning of the participle, see Gagarin 1997: 146–47.

[86] E.g., Aristophanes *Thesmophoriazusae* 361–62 (produced in 411). A decree from Erythrea (an Athenian colony), dated before 454 (*IvEr* 2.A.21–22), has the expression κατὰ νόμους καὶ ψηφίσματα ("according to the laws and the decrees"). See, in general, Hansen 1978: 316–17.

aggeration. However, if Thucydides is correct when he writes (3.19.1) that in 428/7 the Athenians "then for the first time raised an *eisphora* of 200 talents," and if he means that this was the first *eisphora* ever, not just, as some scholars understand,[87] the first to raise as large a sum as 200 talents, then the Tetralogies would have to be dated after 428. This would eliminate the possibility that the Tetralogies are early works of Antiphon, as many have suggested, but it would not rule out Antiphon as their author.

The conclusion we may draw from all these considerations is that although the Tetralogies clearly differ from the court speeches in several important respects, these differences can be related to the different natures and purposes of the two sets of works and do not constitute evidence that they should be attributed to different authors. Without new evidence, we may not be able to prove for certain that Antiphon of Rhamnus wrote these works, but there is no good reason why we should not abide by the manuscript tradition and the opinion of ancient scholars and accept them as his. The spirit of the Tetralogies, moreover, is consistent with what we know of Antiphon's career and interests. Indeed, they are thoroughly in the spirit of legal, rhetorical, and philosophical activities of the second half of the fifth century in general, and of Antiphon of Rhamnus in particular.

---

[87] E.g., Hornblower 1991: 403–4.

III. *TRUTH*

Two major sophistic works are ascribed to Antiphon, *Truth* (*Alētheia*, in two books) and *Concord* (*Homonoia*). The former has attracted more scholarly attention, especially since the discovery of substantial papyrus fragments early in the twentieth century, which contain the longest continuous texts and are of great philosophical interest (44 DK, 90–92 M).[1] *Concord* is of less philosophical interest but is still important for the full understanding of Antiphon's work. In addition, the little that is known about Antiphon's work on dreams suggests an attitude of inquiry and skepticism similar to that of *Truth*. This chapter will examine the fragments of *Truth; Concord* and Antiphon's views on dreams will be the subject of chapter 4.

I. THE PAPYRUS FRAGMENTS

Before examining the text of *Truth* (see full text of 44 in appendix A), we must consider briefly the identification of the papyrus fragments. Since their publication virtually all scholars have accepted that *POxy* 1364 (44A and B), together with the recently discovered scrap from the same papyrus

---

[1] I follow Diels-Kranz in assigning these fragments the number (44) Diels assigned to the relevant citation from Harpocration (see below, note 2) in his 1903 edition. However, I cite the text of Decleva Caizzi 1989, because it includes the most recent papyrus fragment (*POxy* 3647), published by Funghi 1984. Decleva Caizzi follows Funghi in reversing Diels-Kranz's ordering of the first two fragments; thus the numbers 44A, 44B, and 44C in her text correspond to 44B, 44A, and 44 (or 44C) respectively in Diels-Kranz and other older editions. As Lugenbill notes (1997: 170 n. 29), the case for reordering is not strong (it is based on the discoloration of part of the papyrus), and he prefers the traditional order. Nothing in the discussion that follows hinges on this ordering. The translations are slightly modified from Gagarin and Woodruff 1995: 244–47. Disputed points of text and translation will be treated at relevant points in the discussion.

(*POxy* 3647), comes from Antiphon's *Truth,* and most have agreed because of similarities in content that *POxy* 1797, found together with 1364 but written in a different hand, is also from this work, though perhaps from a different book. The first identification is based on a citation from Harpocration (A7, s.v. *ἄγοι*), who quotes Antiphon as using the verb *agō* in an unusual sense "in his work on Truth." [2] The expression Harpocration attributes to Antiphon, "he considered (*agoi*) the laws important," appears verbatim, including the third-person present optative form of the verb, in the papyrus text of 44B (1.16–20). This would seem conclusive proof of Antiphontean authorship, but since Bilik has recently challenged this conclusion, we must consider the matter in greater detail.[3]

Bilik argues that the content of the papyrus fragments is incompatible with either a unitarian or a separatist view of Antiphon; for this reason he seeks to show (1) that Harpocration's citation is in error, (2) that the contents of the papyrus do not fit what we know of *Truth* or *Concord,* (3) that the stylistic differences between the papyrus text and the fragments from *Concord* are so great that if the papyrus fragments belonged to *Truth,* Hermogenes (and his predecessors) could not have grouped *Truth* and *Concord* together stylistically, and (4) that the contents of the papyrus fragments are so different from that of *Concord* that they are not likely to be the work of the same author. Bilik's solution to these difficulties is that Harpocration's original text referred the citation to *Concord,* not *Truth,* but in any case, he was not citing the text of this papyrus but a different text from that work that no longer survives and that just happened to use the same common phrase. Bilik concludes that the papyrus fragments have nothing to do with Antiphon but are the work of an unknown author of around the same time.

Our examination of the papyrus text below will make clear that I do not consider its content incompatible with Antiphon's other work, but even if there are serious discrepancies, the grounds for challenging its Antiphontean authorship are weak. (1) Although *agō* in the sense "consider" is not uncommon in classical prose and poetry, it is unlikely that the four-word phrase "consider the laws important," especially with the third-person present optative form, would occur verbatim anywhere else.[4] Bilik notes that in

---

[2] Ἀντιφῶν δ' ἐν τῷ περὶ ἀληθείας φησὶ "τοὺς νόμους μεγάλους ἄγοι" ἀντὶ τοῦ ἡγοῖτο.

[3] Bilik 1998.

[4] Bilik (ibid.: 42) cites an anonymous comic fragment (726 Kock) as identical except that the verb is a first-person singular indicative (ἄγω instead of ἄγοι). But Kassel and Austin (1995: 511) more plausibly take these words (cited without attribution in a schol-

all his other references to *Truth,* Harpocration designates this work by the simple noun, *Truth* (*alētheias*), rather than a prepositional phrase, *On Truth* (*peri alētheias*); from this he infers that Harpocration's original reference was to *Concord,* which he always denotes with a prepositional phrase (*peri homonoias*), and that this was later changed by a scribe.[5] But Harpocration's other references are not completely consistent, the variation between the simple noun and a prepositional phrase is frequent elsewhere in references to Antiphon's works (as in Hermogenes, above, 2.1), and rewriting Harpocration's text simply to conform to an alleged standard[6] is a desperate and unnecessary remedy. This entry (A7) is longer and more complex than most of Harpocration's other entries, where reference to Antiphon comes at or near the beginning and he is usually the only author cited. Thus, that Harpocration uses a different form of reference here is no reason to doubt his text.

As for content (2), it is evident from other surviving fragments that *Truth* dealt with different subject matter from *Concord. Truth* is a "scientific" work that treats many of the main intellectual issues of the day; *Concord* is more concerned with common human behavior and seems addressed to a more general audience. This difference could also account for the stylistic differences (3) between the papyrus text and fragments from *Concord,* which are closer stylistically to Antiphon's court speeches. Hermogenes' information that stylistically Antiphon's *Truth* resembles Thucydides suggests that he is aware that stylistically *Truth* differs from Antiphon's other works (including *Concord*). Finally (4), differences in content between *Truth* and *Concord* simply indicate different purposes and perhaps different audiences. In short, denial of Antiphontean authorship is a desperate solution to a nonexistent problem.

2. *NOMOS* AND *PHYSIS*

It is most convenient to examine the fragments topically, beginning with the most prominent issue, the relationship of *nomos* and *physis.*[7] This issue

---

ion to Euripides) as a reference to the Antiphon text with the original form of the verb altered to the more common first-person indicative.

[5] Bilik (1998: 43) implausibly suggests that a reference to *Alētheia* "immediately before" (in Keaney's 1991 edition, fourteen lines intervene) led the scribe to change *Homonoias* to *Alētheias.*

[6] For the sake of uniformity, Bilik (1998: 42 n. 40) also wants to add the title *Alētheias* in two other entries of Harpocration where only the name, Antiphon, is given.

[7] Outside the papyrus, none of the fragments of *Truth* discusses *nomos* and *physis,* though *physis* is the general subject of 15 DK on the composition of matter. Thus, be-

seems to have been of special interest to several Sophists in the last third of the fifth century, though relatively little direct evidence for their views has survived.[8] Antiphon is usually classed among the upholders of *physis*, but it is best to examine the papyrus fragments without reference to other discussions of this issue. I shall consider first *physis*, then *nomos*.

44 (A2) ⟨The laws [the gods?] of nearby communities⟩[9] we know and respect, but those of communities far away we neither know nor respect. We have thereby become barbarian toward each other, when by nature (*physis*) we are all born in all respects equally capable of being both barbarians and Greeks. We can examine those attributes of nature that are necessary in all humans and are provided to all to the same degree, and in these respects none of us is distinguished as barbarian or Greek. For we all breathe the air through our mouth and our nostrils, and we laugh when our minds are happy **(A3)** or weep when we are pained, and we receive sounds with our hearing, and we see by the light with our sight, and we work with our hands and walk with our feet.

In 44A, *physis* clearly has the concrete sense of those physiological qualities necessarily present "by nature" in all humans: we breathe through our mouth and nose, cry when we are hurt, and so forth. No one can choose to act differently: it is impossible, for example, to breathe through one's ears. These qualities are the same for Greeks and barbarians, but we now ignore these natural similarities and "barbarously" treat Greeks and barbarians differently. Antiphon may have proceeded to describe how different people came to have different laws and customs (*nomoi*),[10] so that differences that

---

fore 1915, scholars treated Antiphon's views differently; for example, Gomperz ([1896] 1901, 1:434–37) does not mention *nomos* or *physis*. And although the complete text of *Truth* was available to ancient scholars, in what survives, none of these scholars cites Antiphon's views on *nomos* and *physis*.

[8] See the survey in Guthrie 1971: 55–134 (107–13 on Antiphon), and also Ostwald 1986: esp. 250–73. Guthrie's division into upholders of *nomos*, realists, and upholders of *physis* may be misleading. Plato's vivid portrayals of Thrasymachus, Polus, and Callicles as thinkers for whom *nomos/physis* was a primary concern has led (perhaps misled) modern scholars to consider this issue a primary sophistic concern.

[9] The intelligible papyrus text begins in mid-sentence. Only a few letters survive from column A1, and the translation gives just one possible supplement, though "gods" (*theous*) has been suggested as an alternative for "laws" (*nomous*).

[10] The fragmentary lines of A4 are supplemented as follows by Decleva Caizzi (only the underlined letters survive): κα(5)τὰ τὸ ἀρέ[σκον συν/εχώρη]σαν / ἑκαστοι[. . . / καὶ τοὺς νόμ[ους ἔθεν/το· ("Each group agreed to their satisfaction . . . and enacted

now exist by convention (*nomos*), are now considered more important than natural similarities. Whatever the continuation, the basic sense of *physis* is established here as those features common to all humankind.

The second and longest papyrus fragment seems to pick up the argument shortly afterwards:

44 (B1) Justice (*dikaiosynē*) therefore is not violating the rules (*nomima*) of the city in which one is a citizen. Thus a person would best use justice to his own advantage if he considered the laws (*nomos*) important when witnesses are present, but the requirements of nature (*physis*) important in the absence of witnesses. For the requirements of the laws are supplemental, but the requirements of nature are necessary; and the requirements of the laws are by agreement and not natural, whereas the requirements of nature are natural and not by agreement. (B2) Thus someone who violates the laws avoids shame and punishment if those who have joined in agreement do not notice him, but not if they do. But if someone tries to violate one of the inherent requirements of nature, which is impossible, the harm he suffers is no less if he is seen by no one, and no greater if all see him; for he is harmed not in people's opinions (*doxa*) but in truth (*alētheia*).

My inquiry into these things is prompted by the fact that most things that are just according to law are hostile to nature. For rules have been made for the eyes what they should (B3) and should not see, and for the ears what they should and should not hear, and for the tongue what it should and should not say, and for the hands what they should and should not do, and for the feet where they should and should not go, and for the mind what it should and should not desire. Thus the things from which the laws dissuade us are in no way less [more?] congenial or akin to nature than the things toward which they urge us. For living and dying belong to nature, and for humans, living is the result of advantageous things, whereas dying is the result of disadvantageous things. (B4) The advantages laid down by the laws are bonds on nature, but those laid down by nature are free. Thus things that cause pain do not, according to a correct account (*orthos logos*), benefit nature more than things that cause joy. Nor would things that cause grief be more advantageous than things that cause pleasure; for things that are in truth advantageous must not harm but benefit. Thus things that are advantageous by nature. . . .

---

laws"). If this is the sense (and it is far from certain), Antiphon may next have described the *nomoi* that were imposed on the original state of *physis*.

and those who (**B5**) defend themselves when attacked and do not themselves begin the action, and those who treat their parents well even when they have been badly treated by them, and those who let their opponent swear an oath when they have not sworn one themselves.[11] One would find many of the things I have mentioned hostile to nature; and they involve more pain when less is possible and less pleasure when more is possible, and ill treatment that could be avoided. Thus, if the laws provided some assistance for those who engaged in such behavior, and some penalty for those who did not but did the opposite, (**B6**) then the tow-rope of the laws would not be without benefit. But in fact it is apparent that justice (*to dikaion*) derived from law is not sufficient to assist those who engage in such behavior. First, it permits the victim to suffer and the agent to act, and at the time it did not try to prevent either the victim from suffering or the agent from acting; and when it is applied to the punishment, it does not favor the victim over the agent; for he must persuade the punishers that he suffered, or else be able to obtain justice by deception. But these means are also available to the agent, ⟨if he wishes⟩ to deny . . . (**B7**) . . . the defendant has as long for his defense as the plaintiff for his accusation, and there is an equivalent opportunity for persuasion for the victim and for the agent.

44B directly juxtaposes *nomos* and *physis*. We are first told (B1–2) that in the absence of witnesses, the most advantageous use of justice is to heed "the requirements of *physis*,"[12] for these are necessary, natural, not by agreement, impossible to violate, and the cause of true harm to anyone who violates them, whether he is seen by others or not. This follows logically from the description of *physis* in 44A: if one tries not to breathe through one's mouth, one suffers harm even if no one else observes it, and in fact, it is impossible to violate this requirement and breathe differently. Later (B2–3) Antiphon explains that rules have been set by *nomos* (*nenomothetētai*) for what the eyes should or should not see, and similarly for the ears, tongue, hands, feet, and mind (*nous*). In other words, *physis* determines the physi-

---

[11] It was common in Athenian law to challenge the other party to swear an oath concerning a disputed point or to offer to swear an oath oneself; the oath was not sworn unless both sides agreed, which was rarely the case (Mirhady 1991). The point here seems to be that offering an oath to an opponent who is willing to swear falsely gives him an advantage if you cannot also swear an oath.

[12] The Greek says literally "the things of nature" (τὰ τῆς φύσεως), and later, "the things of the laws" (τὰ τῶν νόμων). Other interpretations are, of course, possible.

cal composition and function of the human body, but rules governing the proper or accepted use of these organs are set by *nomos*.

These rules set by *nomos* are introduced as evidence that "most things that are just according to law (*nomos*) are hostile (*polemios*) to nature (*physis*)" (B2.26–30). It is not that *nomos* is directly opposed to *physis*, for *physis* does not set different rules for what we should see with our eyes; it sets no rules at all. It simply does not concern itself with what we see, as long as we see it with our eyes. Thus, *nomos* imposes supplemental (*epitheta*) requirements on *physis*. *Nomos* is hostile in the sense of restricting the freedom of action allowed by *physis*, but it does not necessarily contradict *physis* or require us to violate it. Thus, to follow the requirements of *physis* in the absence of witnesses, as Antiphon suggests in B1, may, but does not necessarily, mean violating *nomos*. Rather, the force of *nomos* is limited since, because it is sanctioned only by the other members of the community, it can be ignored with impunity when no one else is present. In short, *nomos* imposes rules on matters that *physis* leaves unregulated, and thus "the advantages laid down by the laws are bonds on nature, but those laid down by nature are free" (B4.1–8).

After giving examples of restrictions imposed by nature, Antiphon continues to explore the realms of *nomos* and *physis* (B3.18–25): "The things from which the laws dissuade us are in no way less [more?] congenial or akin to nature than the things toward which they urge us." A few letters are missing in the text, making it uncertain whether the sense is "not less congenial" or "not more congenial";[13] but in either case, the force of the negative comparison is that the positive requirements and the negative prohibitions of *nomos* are equally foreign to *physis*, which is not concerned with what the eyes see, where the feet go, etc. The prescriptions of the laws, in other words, are hostile to nature not because they run counter to prescriptions of nature but because they prescribe in areas nature leaves unregulated.

This relationship between *nomos* and *physis* may also underlie Aristotle's report (*Physics* 2.1, 193a10–16 = 15 DK, 83 M) that Antiphon said that if you

---

[13] The sentence begins, [   ]ν οὖν οὐδὲν τῇ φύσει φιλιώτερα οὐδ᾽ οἰκειότερα. Traditional supplements (e.g., Diels-Kranz's [οὐ μέ]ν) produce the meaning "[not] more congenial," whereas Decleva Caizzi thinks the context requires [ἧττο]ν ("[not] less"); but see the sensible remarks of Hoffmann (1997: 193 n. 72). In any case, we should not understand "not more" as "less" (or "not less" as "more"); if Antiphon meant to say, "Things prohibited by the laws are less congenial to nature than things prescribed by them," then he would use this positive expression rather than a negative periphrasis (see Pendrick 1987a: 127, with references).

plant a piece of bed in the ground and it rots and then gives out a shoot, the shoot would be wood, not bed. Aristotle takes this to mean that the true nature of things is matter, but Antiphon may have meant rather that the basic unrestricted *physis* that is wood is made into a bed by *nomos,* the creative human custom of modifying nature to suit human desires. *Nomos* imposes restrictions on the *physis* of the bed, for without *nomos* it would simply be wood, but when a bed rots, its original *physis* reasserts itself. This example shows that the impositions of *nomos* on *physis* are not in themselves harmful or evil, and indeed, nowhere in 44 does Antiphon condemn *nomos* in general; he only criticizes specific instances of *nomos* that are harmful. This more neutral understanding of the realm of *nomos* is consistent with the fact that the realm of *physis* is also neutral. It can be either advantageous or disadvantageous, for it includes both living and dying (B3). True, the advantages that result from *physis* are free, whereas those resulting from *nomos* restrict nature (B4), but evidently both realms have advantages,[14] and disadvantages, too (such as death). Thus, advantage and disadvantage are independent of *nomos* and *physis.*

Similarly, pain and pleasure are apparently independent, not only of the *nomos/physis* polarity but also of advantage and disadvantage (B4): "Things that cause pain do not . . . help nature more than things that cause joy," and "things that cause grief" are not more advantageous than "things that cause joy." "Things that cause grief" (and joy) may not be precisely the same as pain (and pleasure), but they belong to the same realm of human experience, a realm that is apparently disconnected from advantage, from nature, and probably from law, too. Finally, the neutrality of both realms is further indicated by the use of negative comparisons ("not more than," cf. "no less congenial" in B3 above); positive comparisons would privilege one or the other realm, but Antiphon's language adheres to a more neutral assessment, according to which both realms have advantages and disadvantages.

Antiphon begins B5 with three examples of behavior that evidently accords with *nomos* but in many cases is "hostile to nature": not acting first to forestall an attack, treating parents well, and letting an opponent swear an oath. Each involves more pain and less pleasure than is necessary. Such conduct, as we saw earlier (B2), is not regulated by *physis,* but rules are imposed on *physis* by *nomos,* which is described as "hostile to *physis.*" In other words, *nomos* adds constraints in matters to which *physis* is indifferent, constraints that in these cases are disadvantageous.

---

[14] Something more was said at the end of B4 about "things that are advantageous by nature," but a gap in the papyrus at this point prevents us knowing what it was.

This is all that the papyrus says about the realm of *physis*, which Antiphon has described as the realm of physical elements and constraints affecting all humans alike. *Physis* does not regulate, and indeed is indifferent to, other aspects of human conduct. From this one can perhaps infer that we should treat others more like ourselves rather than privilege differences between, say, Greeks and barbarians, which are caused by *nomos*, but we cannot infer an obligation, say, to treat parents well or badly. *Physis*, in other words, is the basic—perhaps the original—human condition, to which *nomos* applies restrictions. The nature of these restrictions and the advantages and disadvantages they bring make up the realm of *nomos*, to which we now turn.

Antiphon's view of *nomos* may be foreshadowed in 44A, which begins in mid-sentence: ". . . we know and respect; but those of communities far away we neither know nor respect." Antiphon is almost certainly presenting a contrast here between people living nearby and those living far away, but the reference of "those" (*tous*) is lost. If we accept Funghi's suggestion to fill the gap with "laws" (*nomous*),[15] then Antiphon is apparently describing a relativist view of laws rather like that portrayed in Herodotus 3.38, where Greeks and Indians each insist on their own burial custom while denouncing the custom of the other, and the external observer (Herodotus, the reader) perceives the similarity of commitment to one's own *nomos* underlying the opposition of the two different *nomoi*. Even if Antiphon did not write *nomous* here, A4 may have contained an account of the historical differentiation of the two groups by means of *nomoi*.[16] And even if it did not, the fragment as a whole still suggests a similar coexistence of the opposition between Greek and barbarian that results from *nomos* and the fundamental identity of the two according to *physis*.

Many scholars[17] understand the thrust of Antiphon's remarks to be that the natural similarity of all people is more real than differences in law and custom, though some have argued[18] that Antiphon intends to give equal weight to both similarities and differences. But there is a further consideration: Antiphon also asserts that "we [Greeks] have become barbarian (*bebarbarōmetha*) toward each other," indicating that the original *physis*-based identity of people, on which *nomos* imposed an opposition between Greek and barbarian, has again become an identity: both Greeks and barbarians are

---

[15] Funghi 1984: 4; see above, note 9.
[16] For Decleva Caizzi's proposed supplements, see above, note 10.
[17] E.g., Furley 1981: 90.
[18] E.g., Ostwald 1990.

now barbarians because of the way they treat one another. Thus, an original unity of all people has divided into opposites (Greek and barbarian) and then recombined into a new unity (we have all become barbarized). Antiphon does not explain this "barbarization," but there may here be an allusion to the ambivalence of current Greek views of barbarians as both better and worse than Greeks.[19] I shall return to this pattern of unity and opposition below (3.6).

The first certain occurrence of *nomos* comes at the beginning of 44B,[20] where Antiphon concludes[21] that justice is adherence to the laws of one's city. We do not know what led him to this conclusion, or whether it is his own view, but from this definition he proceeds to conclude, logically, that the most advantageous use one could make of justice would be to treat the laws as important in the presence of witnesses but to value "the requirements of *physis*"[22] in the absence of witnesses. He explains that the requirements of the laws are supplemental and by agreement; a violation brings no punishment unless someone else sees it, and in that case the punishment is in part shame, which is a matter of opinion, not truth. In other words, violating *nomos* can bring disadvantages, though these are in part (but only in part) only the opinions of others and could theoretically be ignored.

As we have seen, although *nomos* regulates many aspects of human life in ways that restrict *physis,* dictating, for example, what the eyes can see, the restrictions imposed on *physis* can be "advantages laid down by the laws" (B4); moreover, these restrictions may equally well be congenial to nature (B3). Whatever Antiphon originally said about the advantages of *nomos* at the end of B4,[23] we have no reason to think they are not genuine advantages.

---

[19] Cf. Euripides *Orestes* 485–86, where the same verb (*bebarbarōsai*) is used with evident irony as the presumed difference between the two categories is called into question (Tyndareus accuses Menelaus of having become "barbarized" because he continues to support his nephew Orestes, whereas Menelaus replies that it is Greek to honor one's family). See the interesting discussion in Cassin 1992.

[20] The initial noun is the neuter adjective *nomimon* (B1.8), which suggests the sense "custom, traditional rule" as distinct from "law, legal statute," but *nomos* occurs soon afterwards (B1.18–19) in a way that suggests that Antiphon is using the two terms as virtual equivalents in this passage. The letter traces before the word "justice" (B1.6) are consistent with the word *nomimon* (see below, note 25), but this restoration is just a guess, and even if it were certain, we have no further context at this point. On the possibility of restoring *nomos* in A4, see above, note 10.

[21] Almost all scholars restore οὖ]ν in B1.7.

[22] For this expression, see above, note 12.

[23] See above, note 14.

Up to this point, then, Antiphon has provided a rather complex assessment of the advantages and disadvantages of *nomos* and its relation to *physis*. This is not a radical attack on *nomoi,* but rather an analysis that treats *nomoi* as secondary to *physis,* though nonetheless capable of bringing advantages.

The end of 44B, however, explores apparent disadvantages of *nomos:* not attacking first but waiting to be attacked, treating parents well despite being mistreated by them, and letting an opponent swear an oath (B5–7). Such conduct is "hostile to nature" (which, as we saw, does not regulate these areas) and may bring unnecessary pain. Such actions are disadvantageous because the law does not provide any assistance to people in such situations (B5–6). It does not defend a victim against an assault, and in any subsequent litigation the victim and his assailant are on equal terms. In some respects, then, the law is ineffective; it does not protect people from harm, even when they follow its precepts, and the legal system gives the criminal the same rights and opportunities as the victim (B6–7). Thus a person derives no advantage from obeying the law. Antiphon implies that the laws could be more advantageous if they were improved, but at this point the papyrus breaks off, and the third fragment (44C) has nothing significant to say about *nomos* or *physis*.

3. JUSTICE

Just as Antiphon is often seen as a critic of *nomos,* so the views expressed in these papyrus fragments are generally considered critical of justice, which in 44B is always linked to the judicial system and to obedience to the law (*nomos*).[24] Here, too, although he criticizes some aspects of justice, Antiphon's overall view, to the extent that it can be determined, is more ambivalent, and his discussion seems directed more at analyzing the implications of popular views of justice than at condemning justice per se or establishing his own positive doctrine.

Justice is not mentioned in 44A, but the first complete word in 44B[25] is "justice" (*dikaiosynē*), which is defined as not violating the rules of one's community. *Dikaiosynē* is the common word for "justice" in Plato and other philosophers, but it is relatively rare in the fifth century and is overshad-

---

[24] There is no hint in 44 of any "natural justice" apart from *nomos;* see Hoffmann 1997: esp. 191–200.

[25] Four letters (νομι) can be read at the end of line 5. Decleva Caizzi supplements these to produce νόμιμον (*nomimon,* "lawful"), but other supplements are possible. For the sense of *nomimon,* see above, note 20.

owed by both the poetic form *dikē* and the neuter adjective with a definite article, *to dikaion* (literally "the just").[26] Its use here in what appears to be a definitional statement is thus notable. As in several Herodotean passages, such as the description of Deioces, who "practiced justice" (1.96), it should designate a continuing pattern of behavior; *dikaiosynē* is not an absolute virtue that can override other considerations, but rather a type of conduct that one uses for a certain purpose. Deioces practices *dikaiosynē* during his successful quest to become king of the Medes; twelve Egyptian kings employ *dikaiosynē* in order to preserve their kingdoms (2.151); and Glaucus's reputation for *dikaiosynē* (6.86) is the reason he receives a large deposit on faith, though he seriously contemplates violating *dikaiosynē* and keeping the money. In a similar vein, Antiphon speaks of *dikaiosynē* as a kind of conduct a person would "use" to his own advantage by obeying rules selectively depending on whether or not one is observed. Antiphon does not explicitly counsel this course of action, but his explanation and justification for such a course may suggest approval. As noted above, his advice is not that one ought to violate the law in the absence of witnesses, but only that when unobserved, a person can let his actions be determined by *physis,* which may or may not lead him to violate the law.

Antiphon returns to the discussion of justice in B5, with examples of conduct approved by the laws but disadvantageous, such as not attacking first. If the law assisted those who are disadvantaged by following *nomos,* he continues (B5–6), its restrictions would confer some benefit. But in fact, "justice (*to dikaion*) derived from law (*ek nomou*)" does not help; it only intervenes after the fact, and its intervention, moreover, is impartial, giving victim and offender equal rights and resources. In B7 Antiphon's criticisms become very specific: plaintiff and defendant have an equal amount of time and thus an equal opportunity to persuade the jurors. This is not a blanket condemnation of the judicial process as a whole, for it suggests that improvements are possible, such as perhaps allowing defendants more time.

The text then breaks off, and we next hear about justice in 44C.

44 (C1) To testify truthfully for one another is customarily thought (*nomizetai*) to be just (*dikaios*) and not less useful in human affairs. And yet one who does this will not be just if indeed it is just not to wrong (*adikein*) anyone, if one is not wronged oneself; for even if he tells the truth, someone who testifies must necessarily wrong another somehow,

---

[26] Fifth-century uses of *dikaiosynē* are surveyed by Havelock 1969.

and will then be wronged himself, since he will be hated when the testimony he gives causes the person against whom he testifies to be convicted and lose his property or his life, all because of this man whom he has not wronged at all. He wrongs the person against whom he testifies for this reason, namely, that he wrongs someone who is not wronging him; and he is wronged by the person against whom he testified, in that he is hated by him (C2) for having told the truth. And it is not only that he is hated but also that for his whole life he must be on guard against the man against whom he testified. As a result, he has an enemy who will do him whatever harm he can in word or deed.

Now, these things are clearly no small injustices (*adikēmata*), neither those he suffers nor those he inflicts. For it is impossible that these things are just and that the rule not to do wrong and not to be wronged oneself is also just; on the contrary, it is necessary that either only one of these be just or that they both be unjust. Further, it is clear that, whatever the result, trying cases, giving verdicts, and holding arbitration proceedings are not just, since helping some people hurts others. In the process, those who are helped are not wronged, while those who are hurt are wronged.

44C introduces two commonly accepted principles of justice—one should testify truthfully, and one should not wrong anyone if[27] one is not wronged by him—and argues that these are in conflict and cannot both be valid. The first rule, to testify truthfully,[28] is used to represent any form of participation in the legal system, as we see at the end of C2: "trying cases, giving verdicts, and holding arbitration proceedings." Any participation in the system will hurt one of the parties. The second rule is not part of the legal system but a rule of traditional Greek morality, which more generally sanctions helping friends and harming enemies. Most discussion of 44C has aimed at deciding which of these rules, if either, represents Antiphon's own view,[29] but this is perhaps the wrong question. We must first examine more closely the argument of 44C.

---

[27] The negative μὴ indicates that ἀδικούμενον ("not being wronged") must have a conditional sense here, and this sense is reinforced by the argument that follows. The difference between this and the rule "not to do or suffer wrong" (C2.19–21) will be considered below.

[28] This rule is as old as Hesiod (*Works and Days* 282–85).

[29] See Hoffmann 1997: 208–16 (with references). He thinks Antiphon would support a rule of mutual nonaggression but would not call it justice.

Antiphon begins[30] by noting a contradiction: testifying truthfully is considered just, but someone who testifies truthfully will not be just if indeed it is just "not to wrong anyone if one is not wronged oneself." For, he explains, a witness testifying truthfully will necessarily injure someone who has not injured him, and will then suffer retaliation. The meaning of the verb *adikein,* "to wrong," is obviously equivocal. Etymologically, it means "commit injustice" (*adikia*), but the meaning of "injustice" can shade into "injury." Antiphon plays on this ambiguity: a person's behavior that is just by the rules of the legal system has the consequence that it injures someone who has done them no harm. Thus, in a manner reminiscent of Socrates, Antiphon demonstrates contradictions that result from juxtaposing two popular views.

The matter is further complicated by the fact that someone who testifies truthfully will in turn be wronged by the person against whom he testifies. This second "injustice" is allowed according to the rule not to wrong anyone if one is not wronged oneself, since it will be committed in retaliation; but (we may infer) it will probably violate the rules of the legal system.[31] This inference is spelled out in C2: "These things are clearly no small injustices (*adikēmata*), neither those he suffers nor those he inflicts." The sense of *adikēmata* here is not specified. It almost certainly suggests in the first place violation of the legal system ("unlawful acts"), but it also suggests a more general idea of injustice without specification, that is, without reference to either of the specific rules of justice with which the fragment begins. And this must be the sense a few lines later, when Antiphon raises the possibility that both systems of justice might be "unjust" (see below).

At this point there is an important (and unsignaled) shift to a different version of the traditional rule: "For it is impossible that these things[32] are

---

[30] The letters before our text (C1.1–2) include the words *tou dikaiou.* A common speculation is that these lines originally read "when [if, since] justice is taken seriously" (τοῦ δικαίου [σπουδ]αίου δοκοῦν[τος]).

[31] The possibility that the person who testifies truthfully will suffer retaliation links this discussion to B5, for it provides another example of conduct that accords with the law but is against one's own interest.

[32] I.e., the witness's testimony and his victim's retaliation. Most scholars take "these things" (*tauta*) to refer only to testifying truthfully, but since *tauta* in the sentence immediately preceding refers to both the wrongs the witness inflicts and those he suffers ("These things are clearly no small injustices, neither those he suffers nor those he inflicts"), the second *tauta* must designate the same pair of wrongs (Hoffmann 1997: 208–16, esp. 211 n. 113, with references).

just and that the rule not to do wrong and not to be wronged oneself is also just; on the contrary, it is necessary that either only one of these be just or that they both be unjust" (C2.17–25). At first glance this may seem a restatement of the rule not to wrong anyone if not wronged oneself (and in Greek they appear even closer),[33] but the first is a single prohibition ("Do not do wrong") with a condition attached, whereas the second is a double prohibition ("Do not do or suffer wrong") without conditions, where the second prohibition has little force. Since a person cannot necessarily control what others do to him, the second is more a description of an ideal life ("Live your life so that you neither do nor suffer wrong").[34] The same conflict is present in either version between this traditional rule of conduct and the legal obligation to testify truthfully, but it may seem greater in the second version because two rules (do not do harm, do not suffer harm) appear to be violated.

The next sentence pursues the consequences of this conflict: "It is necessary that either only one of these [views of justice] be just or that they both be unjust." This is as far as the argument goes in the surviving text. Since he has criticized both views already, it seems likely that if Antiphon reaches a conclusion, it will be that neither of these views is just, but where (if anywhere) he might take the argument from there is impossible to know. In the few lines of remaining text, he proceeds instead to extend his observations on giving testimony to the whole judicial process: "Whatever the result, trying cases, giving verdicts, and holding arbitration proceedings are not just, since helping some people hurts others." Thus any conduct required by the legal system may be unjust by the standard of justice derived from a traditional view, that justice is doing no harm.

Traditional Greek morality was based in large part on personal and family relationships: your treatment of someone depended on your relationship with that person, which was determined by your past dealings with him and by relations between the families and friends of the two parties.[35] A legal system, on the other hand, enforces a set of rules that apply impersonally: "if someone (*tis*) does *X* to someone." But however impersonal and abstract the rules might be, personal considerations clearly affected the actual operation of Athenian law. Litigants commonly recite the history of their rela-

---

[33] The shift is from *mē* with a participle to *mēde* with an infinitive.

[34] This kind of "polar expression," in which the second element often has little or no independent force, is popular in Greek. Sinclair (1967: 79 n. 1) observes that the formulation "not to do or suffer wrong" also occurs in interstate treaties at the time.

[35] Blundell 1989: esp. 26–59.

tions with their opponent (and his family and friends) in an effort to show that any wrong they may have done their opponent was the result of wrong that they have suffered and that their opponent has repeatedly wronged them without any provocation. Witnesses, moreover, were often friends or relatives of the litigant for whom they testified. The Athenians took for granted that personal relations had a proper role in the legal process. Even so, in Antiphon's time, the legal system may have been seen as a relatively recent institution that in some ways impinged on these more traditional standards of personal conduct. A conflict of this same sort between institutional and personal justice is dramatized in Sophocles' *Antigone,* and Antiphon's analysis may have ended with no more indication of a solution to the conflict than does Sophocles' dramatization.

Fragment 44 as a whole thus notes three shortcomings of justice in the sense of conduct in accordance with the law (*to ek nomou dikaion,* B6.6 – 7). First, it is not always advantageous to follow justice, since if no witnesses are present, one can violate justice with impunity. Second, justice does not adequately assist victims of wrongdoing. Third, conduct in accordance with the law results in injustice by a more traditional standard of justice. All three criticisms are based on traditional standards of conduct: that one should serve one's own best interest and the interest of family and friends, and that wrongdoers should be punished and victims of wrongdoing compensated. Since both the legal system and these traditional standards would be considered *nomoi,* by setting the public institution of justice in the form of the legal system against traditional standards of conduct, Antiphon is exploring inconsistencies and contradictions within the realm of *nomos. Physis,* it seems, does not provide any rules or standards for behavior beyond basic physiological functions, and so is apparently irrelevant to issues of justice.

If there is a solution to this dilemma, it probably comes in the realm of *nomos* in the form of some larger idea of justice, such as is implied in C2, where Antiphon seems to refer to a more all-encompassing standard of justice when he designates both the legally just act of testifying truthfully and the traditionally just act of retaliation as "injustices." But it may be more likely that *Truth* did not provide a more positive theory of justice, but rather left the reader with the aporia with which the surviving text ends.

4. ADVANTAGE AND DISADVANTAGE, PLEASURE AND PAIN

In connection with *nomos* and *physis,* Antiphon several times refers to two pairs of values, advantage/disadvantage and pleasure/pain. These do not have a large presence in the fragments, but they seem to offer a less equivocal standard for behavior than justice, law, or nature. As Thucydides' *History* testifies, during this period advantage, or self-interest, was considered by many the most important and often the only justification for human action, and it is tempting to think Antiphon shared this view. In fragment 44, however, he does not seem to attach much importance to either advantage or pleasure. They and their opposites occur in the course of his argument about more important issues, but their role is limited, and they are not presented as ends in themselves.

Advantage is first mentioned in B1, where Antiphon advises how best to use justice "advantageously (*xympherontōs*)." He explains that violating the laws in front of witnesses can lead to shame and punishment, which are evident evils, but he says no more here about advantage per se. Later (B3) he observes that "living and dying belong to nature, and for humans, living is the result of advantageous things, whereas dying is the result of disadvantageous things." The advantageous and disadvantageous things that lead to living and dying appear to be features of *nomos*. Life and death are also caused by *physis*, but Antiphon's concern here seems to be how they are affected by *nomos* even though they exist in the realm of *physis*. *Nomos* may preserve life (perhaps by deterring crime) or may cause death (perhaps as punishment for violating *nomos*). "The advantages laid down by the laws," are thus "bonds on nature" (B4), since laws interfere with the natural processes of life and death, even if they do so with the goal of preserving life.

Just as advantage is not a standard grounded in *physis*, neither is pleasure, for "things that cause pain" are not more beneficial to *physis* than "things that cause joy" (B4). Moreover, pleasure and pain are equally advantageous: "Things that cause grief would not be more advantageous than things that cause pleasure; for things that are in truth advantageous must not harm but benefit" (B4.14–22).[36] This seems to imply that any painful restrictions *nomos* might impose are no more helpful to nature and thus no more advantageous than any pleasure it might bring. Thus the two values, pleasure and advantage, seem to be independent of each other and of *nomos* and *physis*. Laws may bring pleasure or pain, advantages or disadvantages, but the consequences for nature are not predictable.

At the end of B4, Antiphon turns to "things that are advantageous by nature," but the papyrus breaks off before we learn what he says about them.

---

[36] The argument seems to require that pain (τὰ ἀλγύνοντα) and grief (τὰ λυποῦντα) be equivalents, and also joy (τὰ εὐφραίνοντα) and pleasure (τὰ ἥδοντα). This is not a certainty, but there is no apparent distinction between the two pairs.

He may have claimed that the advantages of nature do convey benefit and are truly advantageous, but since the last three comparisons in B3–4 are negative ("not more than"), it is perhaps more likely that Antiphon presented the advantages of nature as equally likely to bring pleasure or pain.

In B5–7 Antiphon gives examples of behavior that accords with *nomos* but is hostile to nature, such as not being the first to attack. Such behavior involves more pain and less pleasure than one would otherwise have. Here again, pain and pleasure are effects brought about by *nomos,* which is hostile to *physis* in that it attempts to impose restraints on what *physis* leaves unrestrained. But as before, *physis* apparently remains unaffected, and the main purpose of the discussion seems to be to find ways to make the law less painful (and more beneficial).

In sum, advantage and pleasure and their opposites are throughout seen as attributes or consequences of *nomos* or, less often (in the surviving text, at least), of *physis.* There is no hint that either might function as an objective value. Antiphon's interest is primarily in *nomos, physis,* and justice, and only secondarily in these attributes.

5. THE SENSES AND THE INTELLECT

Truth dealt with many other issues besides *nomos, physis,* justice, and advantage, which are the main subjects of 44. In fact, without the chance discovery of this particular piece of text, we would have a very different impression of *Truth,* since the other fragments give almost no hint of these issues.[37] *Truth* apparently began with words cited by Galen (1 DK, 67 M), who prefaces his citation by noting that, like Critias, Antiphon "differentiates the intellect (*gnōmē*) from the senses (*aisthēseis*)."[38] The text of Galen's citation is clearly corrupt and must be emended to yield any sense. Most scholars now accept Morrison's version as more intelligible and palaeographically easier than that of Diels-Kranz, though substantial difficulties remain.[39]

For someone who says one thing, there is not in fact one mental concept (*nous*), nor is there for him one thing, neither one of the things he who

---

[37] See above, note 7.

[38] ἀντιδιαιρῶν ταῖς αἰσθήσεσι τὴν γνώμην (Galen *In Hippocratis librum de officina medici commentarii* 18.2, 656 Kühn). Morrison (1972: 213) translates ἀντιδιαιρῶν "opposing," but the word need not imply opposition.

[39] Morrison 1963; Hoffmann 1997: 246–47.

sees best sees with his sight (*opsis*) nor one of the things he who knows best knows with his intellect (*gnōmē*).[40]

The sense appears to be that a single word does not correspond either to a single thought or to a single "thing," whether the thing is perceived by the sight or known by the intellect. The second part of the sentence provides the differentiation of sight (*opsis*) and intellect (*gnōmē*) that interested Galen, but the first part, challenging the ability of language to represent thought or reality unequivocally, may be more important.

Morrison and Diels-Kranz see an analogy in the Hippocratic treatise *On the Art*, in which the eyes (*ophthalmoi*) and the intellect (*gnōmē*) are paired: "I don't know how anyone could think things do not exist that can be seen to exist by the eyes and thought to exist by the intellect. This cannot be so, but things that exist are always seen and comprehended, and things that do not exist are neither seen nor comprehended."[41] The Hippocratic author proceeds to argue that language is applied by convention to this reality, which is both seeable and knowable. Antiphon, too, is interested in the relation between language and things. It is not clear whether he took any stand on the question of whether names are conventions, but his assertion that no single word corresponds to a single mental image or to a single thing has important ramifications for his view of language and reality (below, 5.6).

With respect to sense perception, most scholars agree that Antiphon (like the Hippocratic author) is opposing the Eleatics, who denied that sense perception is a guide to reality. He is also distancing himself from Gorgias's view, expressed in *On Not-Being*, that even if something did exist, we could not know it; Gorgias is apparently skeptical of both sense perception and in-

---

[40] ἐν τῷ (perhaps better ἕν τοι) λέγοντι οὐδέ γε νοῦς εἷς, ἕν τε οὐδὲν αὐτῷ οὔτε ὧν ὄψει ὁρᾷ ⟨ὁ ὁρῶ⟩ν μακρότατα οὔτε ὧν γνώμη γιγνώσκει ὁ μακρότατα γιγνώσκων. The text of the two οὔτε clauses seems fairly secure, but there is uncertainty about the first line, and even about where the fragment begins. To illustrate the variations that are possible, I quote the beginning of Freeman's translation of Diels-Kranz's text (1948: 144): "If you realise these things, you will know that there exists for it (*the mind*) no single thing of those things which . . ." Note that there is no word for "thing" in the Greek, but it serves to translate neuter pronouns: "one thing" translates *hen* ("one"), and "the things (which)" translates a neuter-plural relative pronoun.

[41] *Peri Technēs* 2: οὐκ οἶδ' ὅπως ἄν τις αὐτὰ νομίσειε μὴ ἐόντα, ἅ γε εἴη καὶ ὀφθαλ-μοῖσιν ἰδεῖν καὶ γνώμη νοῆσαι ὡς ἐστιν· ἀλλ' ὅπως μὴ οὐκ ᾖ τοῦτο τοιοῦτον· ἀλλὰ τὰ μὲν ἐόντα αἰεὶ ὁρᾶταί τε καὶ γινώσκεται, τὰ δὲ μὴ ἐόντα οὔτε ὁρᾶται οὔτε γινώσκεται.

tellect as means of knowing an object,[42] but Antiphon appears not to question the validity of sense perception[43] as a means to knowledge; his concern is rather the uncertain nature of language (see below). On the other hand, fragment 1 implies that there is a kind of knowledge that is attained through the intellect, rather than through perception.

Fragment 1 gives little indication that perception and intellect are related, but it would be reasonable to assume that the intellect uses data received by the senses to attain knowledge. Two other fragments are compatible with this understanding of the relation between *opsis* and *gnōmē*.[44] The first is often considered a rhetorical fragment, but Morrison more plausibly assigns it to *Truth* (68 M = 35 Th): "People consider things they see with their sight more credible than things for which an examination of the truth leads into the unseen."[45] Sight is not necessarily unreliable, but the search for truth requires more than sight, though most people are reluctant to go beyond what they have perceived with sight. Sight is a means of acquiring information, but it is not enough for knowledge, which requires the intellect, as Antiphon suggests in 2 DK (70 M), which Galen cites immediately after fragment 1: "In all people the intellect (*gnōmē*) leads the body to health and disease and all other things."[46] That the intellect leads the body implies that it has a more important role in the body's physical operation than the senses do. None of these three fragments directly addresses the re-

---

[42] "Things we see are no more likely to be the case than things we have in mind" (Gagarin and Woodruff 1995: 208 = [Aristotle] *De Melisso, Xenophane, Gorgia* 980a15–16; cf. Sextus *Adversus Mathematicos* 7.81).

[43] Recall that in 44A2–3, sense perception (seeing with the eyes, etc.) is a common feature of all humans.

[44] *Gnōmē* or a cognate form occurs in three other fragments besides 1 and 2: 24a, 104, 106a.

[45] οἱ γὰρ ἄνθρωποι ἄττα ἂν ὁρῶσι τῇ ὄψει πιστότερα ἡγοῦνται ἢ οἷς εἰς ἀφανὲς ἥκει ὁ ἔλεγχος τῆς ἀληθείας. The fragment is cited by the *Suda* to illustrate the rare form ἄττα. Although the *Suda* first cites a sentence from a court speech and adds "and again" (καὶ αὖθις), followed by this sentence, this wording does not mean that the two citations must be from the same work, or even from the same genre. Two other fragments from *Truth* (7 and 24a) are cited together with examples from forensic works. Morrison (1972: 214 n. 107) argues that the last two words, τῆς ἀληθείας, do not belong to the quotation but indicate its source ("from *The Truth*"), but it is more natural to take them with ὁ ἔλεγχος ("examination" [of the truth]).

[46] πᾶσι γὰρ ἀνθρώποις ἡ γνώμη τοῦ σώματος ἡγεῖται καὶ εἰς ὑγίειαν καὶ νόσον καὶ εἰς τὰ ἄλλα πάντα.

lationship between sense perception and intellect, but they all imply that both are valid paths to knowledge, though intellect is superior.

Several other fragments of *Truth* also seem to indicate that although sense perceptions are valid, the intellect can make use of and go beyond the knowledge gained by the senses.[47] For example, Antiphon attempted to square a circle by inscribing inside it a series of polygons or triangles with increasingly more sides, which gradually approach closer to filling the circle (13 DK, 81 M). By Aristotle's time, it was known that a regression like this will never succeed in completely filling the circle, but Aristotle still considered Antiphon's attempt notable. And if Antiphon believed the polygon would eventually be perceived as a circle, he may have taken this as an example of how the senses provide valid but limited data from which the intellect can determine the truth, that the polygon is not a circle no matter how much it may appear so to the senses. The same idea may underlie the report that Antiphon said time was a thought (*noēma*) or a measure (*metron*), which would suggest that the intellect can go beyond the perception of time to a better understanding of it as a measure (9 DK, 77 M).[48] Finally, several fragments from *Truth* (including 22–37) concern cosmology, meteorology, and zoology; some of these, at least, suggest that the intellect is able to go beyond the power of sense perception.[49] Although these fragments give us only a general sense of Antiphon's views on perception and intellect, they consistently imply that both are valid, though the latter is superior.

Finally, it is tempting to speculate that Antiphon's views on this subject,

---

[47] That the power of the senses is limited is also suggested by a fragment (71 Th, 162 M) attributed to "The Rhetorical Arts (*Rhētorikai Technai*)": "It is natural for us to perceive things present, at hand and beside us. It is unnatural to keep a clear impression (*typos*) of them when they are out of our way" (trans. following Morrison) (τὸ μὲν τὰ παρόντα [ἔφη] καὶ τὰ ὑπάρχοντα καὶ τὰ παρακείμενα αἰσθάνεσθαι κατὰ φύσιν εἶναι ἡμῖν, παρὰ φύσιν δὲ τὸ φυλάττειν αὐτῶν ἐκποδὼν γενομένων ἐναργῆ τὸν τύπον).

[48] Dunn 1996 defends the authenticity of the fragment.

[49] 29 DK (101 M), for example, says that hail results from the compression of raindrops by the wind. Gorgias may similarly suggest that astronomers go beyond sense perception: "Astronomers . . . replace opinion with opinion: displacing one but implanting another, they make incredible and invisible matters apparent to the eyes of opinion" (*Helen* 13). In addition, some of Antiphon's very short fragments (many only one word) may have treated issues of cosmogony and zoogony (93–116 M, 22–43 DK). It is possible that in these, Antiphon was exploring hidden truths and exposing inconsistencies in popular beliefs, but these fragments are too scanty to support anything more than a guess.

like his title *Truth* (below, 3.6), were influenced by Protagoras's view that when one person perceives a wind as hot and another as cold, both perceptions are valid (Plato *Theaetetus* 152b–c). Although most people are content with their perceptions, the intellect can lead a person beyond these perceptions to an understanding of the truth.

6. LANGUAGE AND TRUTH

As we noted, fragment 1 denies any direct, one-to-one correspondence between words and thoughts or "things": "For someone who says one thing, there is not in fact one mental concept, nor is there for him one thing." The threefold repetition of "one" suggests that Antiphon is specifically rejecting a one-to-one mapping of language on reality. The implication of this assertion for Antiphon's view of truth can best be understood against the background of Hesiod's famous passage on *eris*, or "strife" (*Works and Days* 11–26).[50] Hesiod observes that there is not, after all, one *eris* but two, one good, the other evil, but that these opposing forces (which we might call "striving" and "strife") have the same name. In Antiphon's terms, we could say that one word, *eris*, does not correspond to one thought or one thing, but corresponds instead to two thoughts and two things, good *eris* and bad *eris*. As Hesiod's description proceeds, however, the opposition between the two *erides* collapses (20–26), as it becomes evident that they can become similar, even indistinguishable. Thus, *eris* is both double and then again single, though the single *eris* is still in a sense also double. And this ambivalence of *eris* in the real world, where striving and strife, constructive and destructive competition, compete but also merge into one another, corresponds to and is accurately represented by the verbal ambivalence of the word *eris*. In this context, Antiphon's fragment may be denying not the correspondence of language and reality, but the singularity or "univocality" of both.

Some of the Presocratics, of course, notably Parmenides, had rejected any connection between sense perception (and hence ordinary language) and reality, but the Sophists seem to have had little sympathy for Parmenides' logic. Gorgias's *On Not-Being* was certainly aimed at Parmenides and his Eleatic successors, as was most likely Protagoras's *Truth*, which began with his man-measure statement. If, as Plato indicates in the *Theaetetus*, Protagoras's *Truth* contained the example of a wind that one person perceives as warm and another as cold, this could be taken in the context of Hesiod's analysis of *eris* to mean that a single word "wind" corresponds to a real thing,

---

[50] This point is argued more fully in Gagarin 1990a, 2001a.

a wind, but that this thing is ambivalently both a warm wind and a cold wind. Protagoras may also have extended this perspective to moral judgments, understanding words like "justice" as ambivalent: "justice" would be the same word for different people but would be realized in different, even opposed, acts (such as acquittal and conviction). Such a view would be consistent with Protagoras's claim that there are two *logoi* on every matter, and with his invention of the form of opposed *logoi,* or *Antilogiae.* There is wide disagreement, of course, about just what Protagoras meant by his man-measure saying,[51] but taken together with his idea of opposing *logoi,* it suggests a theory of the ambivalence of language that I am suggesting also underlies Antiphon's fragment—that language corresponds to reality, but not in the sense of one word corresponding to one thing.

The first part of Parmenides' poem is called the "Way of Truth" (1.27–29, 2.2–4). Protagoras's work was entitled *Truth,*[52] but also has an alternate title, *Kataballontes* (sc. *Logoi*), or *Overthrowing Arguments.* This metaphor is from wrestling and suggests that *logoi* are continually competing against each other. If each *logos* corresponds to a certain reality—for example, "the wind is hot" and "the wind is cold"—then (on the view proposed here) not only could each of these be true, but there could be a further truth—e.g., that "the wind is both hot and cold"—that would incorporate both initial *logoi.* Whatever Protagoras's precise views, ideas such as these are discernible in his work, and it is reasonable to suppose that Antiphon had Protagoras's book in mind when he gave his own work the title *Truth.*[53]

What, then, is truth for Antiphon? Three times in 44C he speaks of "testifying truthfully" (1.3–4, 1.17–18, 1.38–2.2), where truth is simply the

---

[51] Hoffmann (1997: 12–34) has a thorough discussion with reference to previous work.

[52] The title *Alētheia* is given only by Plato (*Theaetetus* 161c, etc.). Since it clearly serves Plato's purpose in the context of the *Theaetetus,* it has been argued that the title is Plato's own invention (Untersteiner 1961–62, 1:72). But Plato's persistent mocking of the title *Alētheia* can also be taken as evidence for its authenticity; otherwise Plato's use of it would be perverse (Heitsch 1969).

[53] We cannot be certain that the title goes back to Antiphon. Some titles given to works of the Presocratics are certainly not original, but with the increasing use of writing by the Sophists, it seems more likely that Protagoras and his successors gave their works titles and that these would be preserved. The variety of titles recorded for the Sophists, some of which at least (like Protagoras's *Truth*) are not derivable from the opening words of the work, suggests that titles served to identify their works (Schmalzriedt 1970: esp. 126–27 n. 21 on Antiphon). We have no good evidence for the dates of Protagoras's and Antiphon's treatises, but Protagoras's work is very probably the earlier.

straightforward correspondence between a witness's *logos* and what really happened. But elsewhere in 44 Antiphon gives evidence that he viewed the reality to which any truth might correspond as ambivalent. The ambivalence of truth emerges in connection with three issues: Greek and barbarian, *physis* and *nomos,* and justice.

The first indication that for Antiphon language is not simple comes in his remarks on Greek and barbarian (A2): "We have thereby become barbarian toward each other, when by nature we are all born in all respects equally capable of being both barbarians and Greeks. We can examine those attributes of nature that are necessary in all humans and are provided to all to the same degree, and in these respects none of us is distinguished as barbarian or Greek." By Antiphon's day, "Greek" and "barbarian" were firmly engrained in Athenian thought as value-laden, mutually exclusive categories of language and reality. But Antiphon observes that at some level of reality, which is our physiological composition, no one is Greek or barbarian, for we are all the same in *physis.* Greeks have created this duality by *nomos,* and in so doing they have become barbarian. In other words, by creating in both language and reality a duality, Greek/barbarian, out of an original unity, Greeks have also reaffirmed that unity, for Greeks are now barbarians. Thus language corresponds to reality, but not in any straightforward way, since "barbarian" can truthfully designate the unity of all people (we are all barbarians), as well as one half of the polarity, Greek versus barbarian.

The opposition between *nomos* and *physis* also seems to break down; though the two realms do not merge, they seem to grow more similar as Antiphon's argument progresses. The opposition is established in B1: "The requirements of the laws (*ta tōn nomōn*)[54] are by agreement and not natural, whereas the requirements of nature (*ta tēs physeōs*) are natural and not by agreement."[55] But as the text continues, the opposition between *nomos* and *physis* is modified; the two continue to exist as separate realms, but they are seen to have common elements. "Most things [not 'all things'] that are just according to law are hostile to nature" (B2.26–30) may imply that some

---

[54] It might make the argument clearer if "realm" were used rather than "requirements" to translate the expressions (literally) "the things of the laws" and "the things of nature," but I keep "requirements" for the sake of consistency.

[55] The opposition of *nomos* and *physis* is also linked to the traditional opposition of opinion (*doxa*) and truth (*alētheia*): "He [who violates *nomos* and is caught] is harmed not in people's opinions but in truth" (B2.21–23). Here "truth" seems to have the same sense as in "telling the truth" in 44C, namely correspondence to reality, and "in truth" is equivalent to "in reality."

things are consistent with both. "The things from which the laws dissuade us are in no way less [more?] congenial or akin to nature than the things toward which they urge us" (B3.18–25) implies an open relationship between the two rather than an opposition. And although specific information about the advantages of the laws has been lost from the text at the end of B4, it is clear that nature, like justice, includes advantage and disadvantage. Antiphon's complete argument is not entirely clear, but interspersed among indications that *nomos* and *physis* are opposites are several indications of their similarities. Thus, wherever Antiphon's argument might lead, he is bringing *nomos* and *physis* closer together as he proceeds.[56]

The third opposition concerns justice, which, like Hesiod's *eris,* is a single word designating (at least) two realities, the justice of a legal system and the justice of traditional retaliation. Someone who acts justly according to the first view does injustice according to the second, and vice versa (C1–2). The two justices are not designated good and bad, like Hesiod's two *erides,* but their differences amount to an opposition in which much of the conduct required by one justice is prohibited by the other. We cannot tell how far Antiphon took this analysis, but it appears at the end as if he may be appealing to a third, more general standard of justice than either of the two he has been discussing.[57] This third standard of justice makes each of the other two kinds of justice unjust. Thus we may have here the first step of an analysis that, as in the two preceding cases, begins with an opposition (between two senses of justice), proceeds to make each of the members ambivalent (each is both just and unjust), and then indicates how a larger justice might encompass them both.

Since we cannot see Antiphon's complete discussion of any of these three oppositions (and in what we can see, he approaches each one differently), we can only speculate what conclusions (if any) he might have reached, but it appears that his view of truth was complex and ambivalent in the tradition of Hesiod's *eris.* He accepts the validity of perceptions and of traditional views but shows how they can lead to conflicting conclusions on specific issues. To resolve such conflicts and understand the complexity of things, one must rely on the intellect (*gnōmē*), although most people put more trust in

---

[56]Cf. Ostwald (1990: 303): "It rather looks as if Antiphon's theme was to delineate the advantages that accrue to a human being from following, respectively, the dictates of society and those of nature. Partial truth is to be found in both." Cassin (1992) also denies that Antiphon considered nature primary.

[57]"These things are clearly no small injustices, neither those he suffers nor those he inflicts"; see above, 3.3.

their perceptions. Antiphon's method is to direct the reader's attention to the conflicting views that result from perception, and then try to reveal the basic similarities that are present together with these differences but are not so apparent. Greek and barbarian, *nomos* and *physis,* legal justice and traditional retaliatory justice all conflict in some respects, but in other respects the terms in each pair also share certain similarities. A better appreciation of this complexity can only be gained through *logos*—speech and reasoning—which is itself ambiguous, but which can lead to greater understanding. Antiphon's truth is thus complex and may have remained ambiguous even at the end. But he holds out the hope that *gnōmē,* human intelligence, using *logos,* can achieve understanding, not by rejecting popular perceptions and conceptions, but by building on them to create a better, more complex truth.

7. STRUCTURE AND STYLE

Truth has attracted notice for its unusual style ever since antiquity. Hermogenes (above, 2.1) notes that "there is really a large discrepancy between the work *On Truth* and the rest," and also that "Thucydides is very different [from Antiphon's homicide speeches] and quite similar in style to the work *On Truth.*" [58] The stylistic description that follows is directed primarily at the style of *Truth.*

> The other Antiphon, to whom is attributed the discourse *Truth,* did not write in a style suitable for the public; [59] rather, his style is solemn and weighty in several ways, especially because he composes all his statements in a manner that is dignified and aims at grandeur, in diction that is elevated and harsh, making it almost austere. He amplifies his words rather indiscriminately, which is why his discourse is often confused and unclear. He constructs his sentences carefully and enjoys creating balanced expressions (*parisōsis*). The man is not concerned with character (*ēthos*)

---

[58] One small trait *Truth* shares with Thucydides is using the old Attic form ξυν- for συν- (in Decleva Caizzi's proposed supplement [see note 10, above], she should have written ξυν/εχώρη[σαν). Otherwise, the dialect of *Truth* is fairly standard classical Attic (though ἥδοντα in B4.17–18 is considered Ionic by some [Pollux 3.98; see Pendrick 1987a: 135]).

[59] Literally, "was not at all *politikos*"; in other contexts this would mean "was not a public figure," or "did not practice oratory," but here it is used of style; see above, chapter 2, note 27.

or with creating an impression of truthfulness, and one would say that he cares about the appearance of cleverness but not about truly being clever.[60]

On the basis of the surviving text, any general judgment of style, such as "dignified" or "unclear," must remain tentative, and in any case, such judgments are only a starting point for a useful assessment of style. We can, however, note specific stylistic features of the fragments we have. We may begin with the observations of Dover, who demonstrates, using a rather complex method for counting words, that one feature of 44C1–3 is "the intensive use of a comparatively small vocabulary."[61] Dover does not relate this to the nature of the argument in these columns, his interest being primarily in historical change from early prose authors like Antiphon to fourth-century oratory;[62] but it is not surprising that in an argument that assesses two views of justice each in terms of the other, a relatively few words, like *dikaios* ("just"), will be used intensively.

Other features of style can also illuminate the nature of Antiphon's argument. First, Antiphon keeps the reader aware that this work is an intellectual inquiry by several references outside the argument: "we can examine" (A2.15–16); "my inquiry into these things is prompted by the fact that" (B2.23–26); "according to a correct account" (B4.10–11); "one would find many of the things I have mentioned" (B5.13–16). The language of his argument, moreover, is logical: *oun* ("therefore") indicates that a conclusion is being drawn (eight times, plus twice in the negative form *oukoun*),[63] and *gar* ("for") shows that an explanation is being offered (eleven times). In addition, eight conditional ("if") clauses give structure to the argument; in two cases, the conditional clause is followed by a participle expressing the

---

[60] Ὁ δ' ἕτερος Ἀντιφῶν, οὗπερ οἱ τῆς Ἀληθείας εἰσὶ λεγόμενοι λόγοι, πολιτικὸς μὲν ἥκιστά ἐστι, σεμνὸς δὲ καὶ ὑπέρογκος τοῖς τε ἄλλοις καὶ τῷ δι' ἀποφάνσεων περαίνειν τὸ πᾶν, ὃ δὴ τοῦ ἀξιωματικοῦ τε λόγου ἐστὶ καὶ πρὸς μέγεθος ὁρῶντος, ὑψηλὸς δὲ τῇ λέξει καὶ τραχύς, ὥστε καὶ μὴ πόρρω σκληρότητος εἶναι. καὶ περιβάλλει δὲ χωρὶς εὐκρινείας· διὸ καὶ συγχεῖ τὸν λόγον καὶ ἔστιν ἀσαφὴς τὰ πολλά. καὶ ἐπιμελὴς δὲ κατὰ τὴν συνθήκην καὶ ταῖς παρισώσεσι χαίρων. οὐ μὴν ἤθους γέ τι οὐδ' ἀληθινοῦ τύπου μέτεστι τῷ ἀνδρί, φαίην δ' ἂν ὡς οὐδὲ δεινότητος πλὴν τῆς φαινομένης μέν, οὐ μὴν οὔσης γε ὡς ἀληθῶς (*Peri Ideon* 401 Rabe).

[61] Dover 1997: 133; his main discussion of *Truth* is on 131–33 and 138–39.

[62] It might be more valid to compare the style of *Truth* to that of philosophical passages in Plato and Aristotle rather than to orators composing for oral public delivery.

[63] Twice (C1.15–16, C2.22) a result is said to be necessary (*ananke*).

contrary condition.[64] But Antiphon is far more likely to use a paratactic construction, adding a clause that draws a conclusion or offers an explanation rather than using a subordinate conditional or causal ("since") clauses.

There are many signs of this paratactic style. The connective *kai* ("and") occurs forty-nine times; almost two-thirds of these are paired with *te* ("and") or with another *kai* (twice there are six in a row). *Te* itself occurs fourteen times; in twelve of these it is paired with *kai* or another *te*. And the negative pair *oute . . . oute* ("neither . . . nor") occurs three times. The high number of pairs among these connectives indicates a high degree of parallelism.[65] Words, phrases, and whole clauses take parallel forms, whether in conjunction or in antithesis; the latter is usually indicated with *men . . . de* ("on the one hand . . . on the other hand"), which occurs eight times.[66] These stylistic features are also present in the other fragments from *Truth* (besides the papyrus text) that are more than a few words long.[67] It should be noted, of course, that these features occur in other texts of the time, notably in the passage from the Hippocratic treatise *Peri Technēs,* cited above (note 41).

Parallelism is evident throughout, often as *parisōsis* (as Hermogenes notes), or the balancing of equal phrases or clauses. For example, toward the end of B3, Antiphon observes that "living and dying belong to nature," and continues, "and for humans, living is the result of advantageous things, whereas dying is the result of disadvantageous things." *Parisōsis* is a feature of sophistic style especially associated with Gorgias, who adds numerous verbal effects, such as rhyme, to emphasize the parallelism. Antiphon seems more intent on creating a clear argument characterized by logical and thorough reasoning buttressed by supporting evidence. With a fragmentary text it is difficult for us to see what his ultimate aim is, but the sense of each specific step in the argument is in most cases quite clear.

Two other features should be noted. The first is a tendency to abstraction, characteristic of sophistic writing. Antiphon creates abstract expressions primarily with the neuter-plural pronoun *ta* ("things") followed by an

---

[64] εἰ μετὰ μὲν μαρτύρων . . . μονούμενος δὲ μαρτύρων (B1.16–22); εἰ ἂν λάθῃ . . . μὴ λαθών (B2.5–10).

[65] There are also two instances of ἤ . . . ἤ ("either . . . or").

[66] This includes the opening of A2, where *men* almost surely occurred in the lines immediately before the surviving text. One other antithesis takes the form *ou . . . alla.*

[67] 67 M (1 DK, above, note 40) has *te* as a single connective, a paired *oute . . . oute,* and *parisōsis;* 68 M (above, note 45) and 70 M (2 DK, above, note 46) both have *gar* as a connecting particle, and the latter has a triple *kai;* and 162 M (above, note 47) has paired *kai* and a *men . . . de* antithesis.

adjective, as in *ta anankaia* ("things that are necessary, necessities"); by a noun in the genitive, as in the expression we already noted, *ta tōn nomōn* ("the things of the laws," perhaps "legal requirements"); or by a participle, as in *ta xumpheronta* ("things that are advantageous, advantages"). And in C1–2 he twice uses an expanded articular infinitive to express the sense of a rule or principle: *to mē adikein mēdena mē adikoumenon auton* (literally, "the not to wrong anyone if not being wronged oneself," i.e., "the rule that one should not wrong anyone if one is not being wronged oneself"), and *to mēden adikein mēde auton adikeisthai* ("the not to wrong and not to be wronged oneself"). These features are picked up and taken even further by Thucydides, who (as we have noted) was said to have been Antiphon's student.

Finally, a significant and unusual feature, already noted, is Antiphon's fondness for negative comparison, such as "not less than" instead of "more than." There are five examples,[68] including one where the comparandum is not expressed (C1: "To testify truthfully for one another is customarily thought to be just and not less useful in human affairs"; presumably it is not less useful than to testify falsely). This type of expression makes the argument less assertive and more tentative in its analysis. To say that the law's prohibitions are "no less congenial" to nature than its commands is to make a weaker claim than it would be to say they are "more congenial." I note this feature in particular because it is a small indication of the exploratory nature of Antiphon's argument. The clear, logical deductions do not point obviously to a single overall conclusion. To demonstrate contradictions or inconsistencies between two views of justice does not resolve the issue in favor of either view or of some third view. Several scholars have suggested that Antiphon may not be giving his readers his own answers.[69] If more of the text were preserved, of course, answers might appear, but the text we have points rather to the conclusion that Antiphon was more interested in asking questions and challenging established views, in particular views about justice and the law, than he was in propounding his own view.

8. CONCLUSION

The traditional understanding of Antiphon is that he, like Plato's characters Thrasymachus and Callicles, is a critic of the human institution of

---

[68] This includes the expression in B3, "in no way less congenial" (discussed above, 3.2), where the text is in doubt.

[69] E.g., Kerferd 1957.

nomos: people have no reason to adhere to the law if they can get away with violating it, for what is truly important is *physis.*[70] But Antiphon seems much less assertive in his presentation of arguments than either of these two, and more focused on specific details of an argument. He establishes a number of clear logical deductions, supported by unquestionable, rather mundane facts (such as that we see with our eyes), but with a rather limited scope. At the beginning of B1, he seems to establish a definition of justice as obeying the laws of one's city, but, particularly since he treats a different view of justice in C1–2 as equally valid, we cannot be certain whether the first definition, and the conclusions he draws from it, are truly his own, or whether, as seems more likely, he presents them as a step in the argument that will be superseded as the argument progresses. Many considerations, from details of style (such as negative comparisons) to the general spirit of the sophistic age and of Antiphon's other work, suggest to me that the underlying attitude of *Truth* is one of questioning and challenge, of ambivalence and ambiguity, not one of affirmation and certainty.

---

[70] See most recently Winton 2000: 97–99.

IV. *CONCORD,* DREAM-INTERPRETATION

I. *CONCORD:* CONTENT

Antiphon's other well-attested, sophistic work was entitled *Concord* (*Homonoia*). Of the twenty-nine fragments usually assigned to it (45–71 DK, 117–145 M), only fourteen are explicitly attributed to it; none of these is longer than two lines, and nine are single words or very short phrases.[1] The other fifteen fragments are generally longer; most are preserved in Stobaeus's fifth-century C.E. anthology, where they are attributed simply to "Antiphon." They are traditionally assigned to *Concord* on the basis of content and style, and there seems no good reason to question this decision. Even so, I shall first examine the fragments explicitly assigned to *Concord.*[2]

The title might be a guide to the contents of the work, if in fact it is original.[3] But the term *homonoia* is not securely attested before the end of the fifth century, when, apparently as a result of the revolution of the 400, of whom Antiphon was a leading member, it suddenly becomes prominent in the political sense of reconciliation between opposing factions.[4] After this event, *homonoia* rapidly became a political catchword expressing the ideal that all citizens, especially those from opposed political factions, could live together. The link between the word and the coup of the 400 tempts one

---

[1] The nine, which I do not discuss, are 45, 46, 47, 67, 67a, 68, 69, 70, 71. All are from Harpocration. I take the genuine text of 70 DK (144 M) to be only the single word "easiest on the reins." Morrison thinks the entire sentence that follows ("One who is gentle and moderate and does not cause trouble is 'easy on the reins'") is Antiphon's, but most editors, including Diels-Kranz, take these words as Harpocration's.

[2] A text and translation of all the fragments from *Concord* except those listed in note 1 can be found in Appendix B.

[3] Cf. above, chapter 3, note 53.

[4] See de Romilly 1972. Thucydides (8.93) describes how the 400 persuaded their opponents to put away their arms until an Assembly was held to discuss *homonoia*.

to think the title was assigned by Antiphon himself and that the work was somehow connected with the political program of the 400, but none of the preserved fragments has any direct connection with political harmony. Of course, we have only a very small portion of the whole work, and a few fragments offer advice that might be relevant to the general idea of concord. But if the title is original, then *Homonoia* must have been written at the very end of Antiphon's life, at a time when he was primarily occupied with politics, of which there is little trace in these fragments. So it is perhaps more likely that the title was assigned at a later date by someone who was aware of Antiphon's association with *homonoia* and thought it an appropriate title for this work.[5]

The five substantial fragments explicitly assigned to *Concord* are:

48: Man, who claims to be of all creatures the most godlike.

52: It is not possible to take back one's life like a checker-piece.

55: To delay where there is no need to delay.

63: But knowing the arrangement, they listen.

65: Many people have friends and do not know it, but they make acquaintances who flatter wealth and fawn on good fortune.

These few fragments do not shed much light on *Concord* as a whole, but they reveal an attitude (shared by many Sophists and Presocratics) implicitly critical of certain beliefs or ways of behaving.[6] The implication of several of these fragments, moreover, is similar to a fragment from *Truth* (68 M),[7] in which Antiphon chides people for relying on their perceptions rather than using their minds to go beyond perceptions. 65 criticizes people for trusting their perceptions of flatterers and not having the intelligence to know who their true friends are. 48 may imply that people see statues of gods and think humans look like them, and 52 seems to criticize people who act with-

---

[5] It is no easier to conclude that a separate "Antiphon the Sophist" wrote *Concord* and gave it this title after 411, for such a person would surely know the word's history and its connection with the Rhamnusian, with whom he would probably not want to link his work.

[6] Even 63 may come from a context in which Antiphon is criticizing most people for not making clear an arrangement, perhaps the arrangement of speeches they write, with the result that their audience does not listen or understand.

[7] "People consider things they see with their sight more credible than things for which an examination of the truth leads into the unseen." See above, chapter 3, note 43.

out thinking and later regret their actions. Finally, in all five fragments it is possible that Antiphon's criticism formed the starting point for more positive advice urging people to use their intelligence more. In other words, these fragments are consistent with the view of *Truth* that by using their intellect, people can attain a better understanding, though many do not go beyond the information they receive through their senses.

The fifteen fragments assigned to Antiphon but not explicitly to *Concord*[8] include several that share this critical attitude toward popular beliefs. 53 and 54 criticize the view that prosperity lies in possessing material wealth; some people love to accumulate possessions but cannot bear to use them (53), but those who store up their money and do not use it derive no more benefit from it than from a stone (54). And 53a may be related if it means that those who store up possessions that they never use are preparing themselves for a different life from the one they actually lead. These fragments may be criticizing people who rely on limited perceptions of wealth and do not use their intellect to understand what true wealth is. More generally along the same lines, 51 criticizes those who claim that "everything is small and weak and short-lived and mixed with great pains." This kind of criticism is easy, says Antiphon, implying surely that it is wrong. This fragment, too, then, criticizes those who perceive only the obvious features of life and do not use their intellect to reach a deeper understanding.

Such criticisms do not necessarily imply that all popular perceptions or beliefs are wrong, but only that they are limited and that people are unwilling to think more deeply about things and understand complexities and ambivalences of the world. This ambivalence is made clearest in regard to pleasure and pain, whose nature is most fully evident in 49, on marriage. At first, marriage is called a contest: it may turn out to be full of pain when one thought one was getting pleasure, or it may be pleasant, in which case nothing is sweeter. But in fact, these are not so separate: "In this same place where pleasure resides, somewhere close by there is also pain, for one cannot traffic in pleasures by themselves, but pains and toils accompany them." This insight may also apply to other fragments. The pleasure wealth brings is accompanied by the pain of parting with it (53), and the pain of entrusting one's money to others may bring compensating pleasures (54).

Thus people's perceptions are not false, but they may often be limited; they need to use their intellect to understand more fully the complexity of things. A man who is sick may see only the benefit of not having to go to

---

[8] 49, 50, 51, 53, 53a, 54, 56, 57, 58, 59, 60, 61, 62, 64, 66 (cf. appendix B, note 6).

work (57); this perception is valid but is only part of the picture. Life may be "mixed with great pains" (51), but (Antiphon implies) it is also mixed with pleasures. Or, from one perspective life may seem insignificant, like a single day (50); but this perspective, too, is balanced by the implicit perspective of life as comprising many days. Finally, the same man may have contrary perspectives at different times, both of which are true, like the man who feels confident in the face of a future danger but is frightened when it is at hand (56). Perhaps he should learn to bring these two feelings together in a more balanced response to present and future dangers.

The complexity of the world and the limitations of human perceptions require the exercise of the intellect, and this in turn requires education, the most important human activity (60). Education must start young because it takes time to shape character (62) and teach order and discipline (61). Just as the strongest bonds of friendship are forged over a long period of time (64), so prudence and orderliness require experience; you cannot simply tell people what they should do, but they must be faced with temptations and eventually learn how to resist on their own (59, cf. 58, end). The moralizing implicit in these fragments is most evident in 58, where it is grounded in a true understanding of a person's own self-interest. One may initially perceive one's self-interest to lie in harming one's neighbor, but this is in fact a false perception and likely to produce the opposite result from what one expected. Someone who has a true understanding of relations between neighbors will not rely on false hopes but will act prudently, will change his mind, and will refrain from harming his neighbor; and the result will be the most advantageous for his own self.

Now, the rather strong traditional morality evident in 58 in particular may seem to contradict the allegedly anarchic, immoral message often read in *Truth,* but this is perhaps to misunderstand the sense of both works. As we saw above (3.2), *Truth* does not simply reject *nomos* and advocate a morality based on *physis,* but rather questions traditional morality and the effectiveness of the legal system and explores some of the conflicting consequences of adhering to *nomos.* Many of the fragments of *Concord* also question traditional beliefs, criticizing in particular the shortsightedness of most people, who do not go beyond their perceptions and have too narrow an understanding of their own interests. In isolation, some statements in *Truth* could lead a reader to reject traditional morality entirely, whereas *Concord* could lead readers to look more favorably on such morality; but the fragments as a whole suggest rather that we read the two works as a pair of opposed *logoi.* The aim of *Truth* is to raise questions about *nomos* and human justice; the aim of *Concord* is to reach more positive conclusions that may, in some cases at least, affirm traditional morality. According to *Truth,* one would best serve one's own interest by ignoring *nomos* when one can get away with it. According to *Concord,* on the other hand, people should not deceive themselves about the possibility that they can benefit from violating *nomos;* in fact, if they try to violate *nomos,* they are more likely to inflict harm on themselves. A reader can accept the conclusion of *Truth,* that "a person would best use justice to his own advantage if he considered the laws important when witnesses are present, but the requirements of nature important in the absence of witnesses," but he must at the same time realize that the act of harming a neighbor will more likely not be in his own best interest. Most people do not use their intelligence enough to understand the likely consequences of their actions; for them, it is better to follow traditional *nomoi* even when they think they might profit from ignoring them.

There is no hint in the fragments of either work that Antiphon argued that a few people have sufficient understanding that they can profit from ignoring *nomos.* And if he had, like Callicles, advocated that those who are truly intelligent should ignore *nomos* and consider simply their own interest, it is hard to imagine that Plato would have let his work pass with so little notice. More likely his position is accurately reflected in *Concord:* criticism of many traditional beliefs, but an underlying acceptance of much traditional morality.

One caution, however: we must bear in mind that the sometimes sententious moralizing of many of the fragments of *Concord* does not necessarily mean that the work as a whole had this nature, for these characteristics may be related to their preservation in Stobaeus and the *Suda,* which are extremely fond of moralizing sentiments. The sample that survives, in other words, may not be representative of the whole. We might note in particular that the information that pain and pleasure are inseparable comes in the course of the longest fragment (49), which was certainly not preserved because of this observation. *Concord* as a whole may have had many more such insights that no longer survive because they did not interest ancient scholars.

2. CONCORD: STYLE

Although the contents of *Concord* and *Truth* can be reconciled, it is apparent that the two works took different approaches to issues. It is thus possible that they were written for different audiences. Stylistically, despite sharing a number of features, the two works also differ. *Concord* is more rhetorical and less intensely analytical; its sentiments are more readily comprehensible; and it addresses popular issues and concerns rather than the concerns of contemporary intellectuals. All this suggests that *Concord* is aimed at a fairly general audience, whereas *Truth* was intended for more intellectual readers. Some of the features of *Concord,* moreover, may suggest that it was written for oral presentation rather than for the more leisurely study afforded by reading, although it has few verbal "sound effects"[9] and is stylistically not so oral as, say, Gorgias's *Helen.*[10]

In some respects, however, *Concord* is stylistically rather similar to *Truth.* These similarities include a generally paratactic style with a moderate amount of balanced phrasing and *parisōsis.*[11] In this regard, *kai* as a connective occurs forty-seven times; in more than half of these occurrences, it is paired with at least one other *kai* or a *te. Te* itself occurs eleven times; in nine occurrences it is paired. *Concord* also has four pairs of negatives (*oute* or *mēte*), and like *Truth,* it often (fourteen times) marks a logical continuation with *gar* ("for").[12]

On the other hand, *Concord* never once allows its author to intrude into the argument, as he intrudes in *Truth.*[13] *Concord* is also less intensely logical than *Truth. Oun* ("therefore") occurs only twice, both times in rhetorical questions toward the end of 49, and there are only four conditional clauses (two of which, in 49, are the same clause repeated). There is also less antithesis, only three instances where antithesis is marked by *men/de,*[14] and little of the abstract vocabulary that is common in *Truth.*[15] Finally, although *Concord* shows many instances of repeated words and even clauses,[16] these generally have a rhetorical effect rather than the more logical effect of the

---

[9] Only perhaps *apousi . . . mellousi* in 56.

[10] In Gagarin 1999 I track stylistic differences between *Helen* and the defendant's first speech in Antiphon's Second Tetralogy, whose style is directed at a reading audience. The differences in style between these two works are much greater than the differences between *Truth* and *Concord.*

[11] For example, 49 has two cases where three prepositional phrases in a row each begin with *hyper te* and each phrase resembles its neighbor.

[12] Since all the fragments from *Concord* taken together have very nearly the same number of words as the papyrus fragments from *Truth,* the figures can meaningfully be compared to those given in 3.7.

[13] There are no references to "things I have mentioned" or "my inquiry," as in *Truth.*

[14] This includes 48, where the *men* was probably followed by a *de* clause. In addition, 53a has *men . . . alla.*

[15] I note only *tōn en anthrōpois* in 60.

[16] Examples from 49 include ἀξιώσαντα καὶ ἀξιωθέντα, ἐκτῆσθαι κτῆμα, λέγωμεν λεγέσθω, and εἴ μοι γένοιτο σῶμα ἕτερον τοιοῦτον, repeated verbatim a few lines later.

intensely concentrated recurrences of word clusters that Dover analyzes in *Truth* but that are rare in *Concord*.[17] Other differences are even more striking, notably the use of vivid similes and metaphors (50, 52, 57, 60; cf. 53, 54, 66), the occurrence of asyndeton in 49 (where the normal connective is omitted),[18] and five rhetorical questions. Finally, there are no negative comparisons in *Concord*.

It is evident that in *Concord* (as in *Truth* and the Tetralogies), Antiphon gave considerable attention to the language and style of his writing. At times, as with asyndeton in 49, he seems to be experimenting with or trying out a feature that he then (to our knowledge) does not use again. The result is rather a mixed bag of features that lacks the polish and smoothness of later authors such as Lysias (for rhetorical prose) or Plato (for philosophical argument) or the easy flow of Herodotus's narrative prose, but retains a forcefulness and elevation that are quite effective. In both thought and style, Antiphon is an innovator and experimenter, probing beyond traditional views and methods of expression without stopping to perfect any particular style or mode of argument.

3. DREAM-INTERPRETATION

Several ancient reports, from Hermogenes to the *Suda*, speak of Antiphon (or an Antiphon)[19] as an interpreter of dreams. The *Suda* also reports that he wrote a book about interpreting dreams (*peri kriseōs oneirōn*), and the existence of a book on dreams may be implied by some of the other reports; but we have no good evidence for the title of a book on dreams, and it seems more likely that Antiphon's views on dreams either were contained in other works or were simply reported by others and then found their way into other authors' books on dreams.[20]

According to a late source, Antiphon defined prophecy as "an intelligent man's conjecture" (*anthrōpou phronimou eikasmos*)[21]—a nicely ambiguous

---

[17] The only similar concentration in *Concord* is the *hēd-* and *lup-* words (for pleasure and pain) in the middle of 49 (τί γὰρ ἥδιον, etc.).

[18] "That day, that night begins a new spirit, a new fate . . . like-minded, like-spirited."

[19] The *Suda* lists a dream-interpreter as the third Antiphon; Hermogenes, apparently following Didymus, reports that *Truth* and *Concord* were written by the dream-interpreter (see above, 2.1).

[20] The evidence is usefully assembled and this issue is fully discussed by van Lieshout 1980: 217–29, 247–51; he concludes that from the evidence, it is impossible to establish the title of Antiphon's work or any general theory of dreams.

[21] A9 DK = *Gnomologia Vindobonensis* 50, p. 14 Wachsmuth.

conjunction of guesswork and intelligence—and he probably had the same view of interpretations of dreams and omens. Cicero (*De Divinatione* 1.39) considered Antiphon's interpretations both highly original, revealing ingenuity (*acumen*), and artificial—the result of the interpreter's intelligence rather than of any actual connection between the dream and reality (1.116). The surviving examples of Antiphon's work confirm this general view. Cicero cites two cases of runners' dreams before a race (2.144). In the first, the runner seems to be riding in a four-horse chariot, and an interpreter takes this to mean he will win his race, since he will run as fast as the four horses. Antiphon, however, takes the dream to mean he will lose, because there are four runners in front of him. Another runner dreams he is an eagle, and again an interpreter takes this to mean he will win, since the eagle is the swiftest bird. But again Antiphon disputes this and says the runner will lose, since an eagle always pursues other birds and so comes in last.

Cicero concludes that dream-interpretation is nothing more than deceiving with one's wits (*eludentis ingenio*), an art that demonstrates only "human ingenuity in drawing now one inference, now another from any sort of similarity."[22] This judgment could well reflect Antiphon's own view, for the two examples just cited seem to serve the function of showing that a clever interpreter can find any meaning he wishes in a dream. More specifically, both these examples of Antiphon's art of dream-interpretation reveal an ability to derive exactly the opposite meaning from that given by some other authority, producing, in effect, an *Antilogiae*—opposing *logoi* interpreting the same phenomenon. In other words, Antiphon is not giving his own true interpretations of these dreams, but rather is demonstrating that he can make a case for the opposite of any interpretation someone else might propose—he can make the weaker interpretation stronger.

We may have other examples of this skill. Artemidorus relates conflicting interpretations of the meaning of soft fish, such as octopus or squid, in dreams (good for criminals but bad for others) and adds that Antiphon mentions this dream. Antiphon may have been arguing (in the manner of the *Dissoi Logoi*) that although these creatures are generally seen as bad signs, they can also be good signs.[23] And Clement reports that when a sow ate her litter and her owner understood this as a bad sign, Antiphon realized that

---

[22] *acumen hominum ex similitudine aliqua coniecturam modo huc, modo illuc ducentium* (*De Divinatione* 2.145).

[23] It is possible that Antiphon only mentioned the last of Artemidorus's examples, the squid, which signifies benefits for runaways since it often uses its ink-jet to conceal its escape.

the man was not feeding the sow enough and told him to be grateful that she had not eaten his children;[24] in other words, what the man had interpreted as a bad sign could also be understood as bringing good news.

Finally, Antiphon is reported to have explained that if a man's right eye has a tick, he will dominate his enemies; if his right eyelid has a tick, success and health will follow; but if the right eyelid of a slave has a tick, an attack is coming; and if that of a widow, she will travel abroad.[25] Here, Antiphon's point seems more general—not that one can derive opposite meanings from dreams, but that almost any sign can mean almost anything one wishes. The evidence suggests, in other words, that far from being an interpreter of dreams himself, Antiphon challenged the whole business of interpreting dreams, cleverly turning around previously rendered interpretations to mean just the opposite, and generally showing that dreams and other supposedly meaningful phenomena could be interpreted to mean almost anything anyone might wish.

We can confidently reject the view that Antiphon was a serious interpreter of dreams, a view that prompted Dodds to doubt that Antiphon the dream-interpreter could be the same person as Antiphon the Sophist, since "it is hard to attribute a deep respect for dreams and portents to the author of *Truth,* who 'disbelieved in providence.'"[26] Few as they are, the fragments and other testimony to Antiphon's activities in this area make it quite clear that, far from showing a deep respect for dreams, his primary aim was to display his sophistic ingenuity in refuting traditional interpretations of dreams and in showing that any dream could yield any meaning to a clever interpreter.

4. OTHER WORKS

Two other theoretical works of Antiphon's are reported by title, a *Politicus* and a *Technē* (*Art*). The former seems to have resembled *Concord* more than *Truth,* though of the six surviving fragments (72–77 DK, 146–51 M), only two are more than a word: 73, "when someone squanders his own property or that of his friends"; and 76, "not to be called 'fond of drink' and, under the influence of wine, appear unconcerned about one's affairs." *Art* is said to

---

[24] A8 DK = Clement *Miscellanies* 7.24.

[25] 81a DK = Melampus *On Palpitations* 18–19.

[26] Dodds 1951: 132–33 n. 100, citing a late report (12 DK, 80 M), which says that Antiphon in the books he wrote *On Truth* "disbelieved in providence (*pronoia*)"; none of the words in this report are Antiphon's, except the title. Dodds infers from Xenophon's report (*Memorabilia* 1.6, above, 2.1) that "Antiphon the Sophist" was not an Athenian.

have consisted of at least three books; [27] it may have been an analytical work, more like *Truth*. One fragment attributed to *Art* (71 Th, 162 M) was noted in our discussion of sense perception in *Truth* (above, chapter 3, note 47); the other four (72–75 Th, 163–66 M) are single words. [28]

These fragments add support to the conclusion that Antiphon investigated almost the entire range of issues that interested thinkers at the time, from squaring the circle to the merits of the legal system, from the meaning of dreams to the nature of language. His approach in general was innovative, secular, and skeptical, but he used the contradictions he found in traditional views not simply to suggest that traditional values or institutions are worthless, but also to force people to consider alternatives and improvements. His arguments, like those of Socrates and the Sophists, can appear eristic and destructive; but the positive potential of *Antilogiae* was not lost on Antiphon, and the contradictions and criticisms he notes often seem to point the way, potentially at least, to a better course.

---

[27] The title is sometimes reported as *Rhētorikai Technai* (*Rhetorical Arts*), but this terminology must be later than Antiphon.

[28] 72 (163 M) reports that Antiphon said that past events are confirmed by *sēmeia* ("signs"), future events by *tekmēria* ("indications").

V. THE TETRALOGIES

Although Antiphon's three Tetralogies take the form of court speeches, they were not written for delivery in court but for a more intellectual audience, perhaps the same audience as that of his more explicitly theoretical works. As already noted (above, 1.5), the Tetralogies fall into the category of *Antilogiae,* or opposed speeches, but are the only examples we know of with two pairs of speeches in each. This unique structure, which replicates an actual Athenian trial, has important consequences that are apparent when we contrast the Tetralogies with Antisthenes' pair of speeches, *Ajax* and *Odysseus,* and with Gorgias's stand-alone speeches, *Helen* and *Palamedes.*

Both of Gorgias's speeches presuppose an agonistic context, but neither makes the opposing *logos* explicit; instead, the case for the prosecution (so to speak) is explicitly (in *Helen*) or implicitly (in *Palamedes*) identified as the poetic or mythological tradition. The general outlines of this tradition were common knowledge to Gorgias and his audience, but the heart of a philosophical argument is in the details, and these are missing from the opposing *logos.* If Gorgias had written the opposing *logos* himself, he would have had to specify these details—precisely what blame allegedly attached to Helen and precisely how and why Palamedes was supposed to have conspired with the Trojans[1]—and this would have forced him to go more deeply into these issues than he does in the single speeches. By comparison, Antisthenes created a pair of speeches in which he explores the claims of the two heroes to Achilles' armor and to the honor of being judged his successor, as well as important general issues, such as the true nature of courage and cowardice,

---

[1] The later speech written by Alcidamas for Odysseus's prosecution of Palamedes (Gagarin and Woodruff 1995: 283–89) suggests some of the possibilities for the prosecution's case. No similar counter-*logos* exists for the more radical arguments in *Helen.*

the value of traditional virtues in contrast to a more flexible "situational ethics," the value of appearance, and even the ability of *logoi* to rewrite and thus reinterpret the story of the past. By setting specific arguments against one another on each point, Antisthenes can probe more deeply into these issues than Gorgias does. For the same reasons, the Tetralogy form allows Antiphon to scrutinize specific issues even more intensely.

The Tetralogies, as we noted earlier (above, 2.2), differ from court speeches in several ways: the narrative is virtually eliminated, and circumstantial detail is kept to a minimum, allowing the author to concentrate all his effort on the arguments. To help shape the argument and set its parameters, moreover, certain artificial factors may be introduced that are absent from court speeches, such as an extreme version of the theory of homicide pollution or a law prohibiting just and unjust homicide. In short, the world of the Tetralogies is a controlled setting, a "Sophistopolis," [2] that allows the author to focus narrowly and intensely on a limited set of issues and to structure the opposing arguments in a direct point-counterpoint format that is virtually impossible in a real courtroom setting. The result is a detailed and thorough exploration of the complexities of an issue that can introduce radically new ways of thinking together with more traditional objections to these novel ideas.

In the court speeches, Antiphon assembles a variety of arguments on different subjects and presents them in whatever order (or disorder) he thinks will be most effective. The Tetralogies, on the other hand, take one issue and pursue it without distraction: the likelihood that the defendant is the killer in Tetralogy 1, and responsibility for an accidental death in Tetralogy 2 and for an unintended death in Tetralogy 3. Although they are set in a courtroom, the cases yield no verdict, and neither speaker wins. Thus certain arguments common in court speeches are absent from the Tetralogies, notably ad hominem attacks on the actions and motives of the speaker's opponents. The brief ad hominem comments in the Tetralogies are directed at the opponent's speech, not at his other conduct or his motive for bringing the case.[3] Other arguments are found only in the Tetralogies, such as the elaborate structure of claims and counterclaims about pollution, which loom large in the prologues and epilogues (below, 5.2). Even these sections, therefore, demonstrate different methods of argument than do the same sections of court speeches.

---

[2] See above, chapter 2, note 71.

[3] E.g., 3.3.1: "In the past he wasn't the least bit disrespectful or daring, but now he is compelled by misfortune itself to make statements I never imagined he would utter."

The purpose of the Tetralogies has been much disputed. I have argued elsewhere that the greater complexity of style and of forms of argument in the Tetralogies is an indication that they were written not for oral delivery, like the court speeches, but for readers who would have the time to think about and assess the arguments.[4] This conclusion is based on a comparison of the defendant's first speech in the Second Tetralogy with Gorgias's *Helen*. Gorgias writes about, and therefore thinks about, the issues of cause and responsibility paratactically, treating one argument in itself and then another; he moves from the familiar and convincing (the gods or physical force are responsible, not Helen) to the unfamiliar and more suspect (*logos* or *erōs* are responsible). Gorgias's reasoning is implicit: if the first of these arguments is valid, then the second, third, and fourth, which are similar in structure, are also valid. Antiphon's *logos* is quite different: he treats the same general situation analytically, building a complex case point by point using logical forms of argument, notably the hypothetical antithesis.[5] The complexity of style and argument strongly supports the conclusion that the Tetralogies were written primarily for a reading audience, though they might also have been performed orally on some occasions.

This reading audience must have consisted primarily of other intellectuals and would-be intellectuals. Among them may have been those we could call Antiphon's "students," though these cannot have been seeking specific training in forensic or logographic techniques,[6] for anyone seeking practical forensic training would not find much help in the Tetralogies: the situations they portray are artificial and would rarely concern most Athenians,[7] and their arguments are not necessarily those that would be effective in court. A young man could perhaps improve his skill in reasoning or argument, but it is more likely that he read the Tetralogies out of general intellectual interest, for the challenge they posed, and perhaps simply for pleasure. A reader

---

[4] Gagarin 1999.

[5] The argument of a hypothetical antithesis is, if a certain factor had been different, then my conclusion would be different; but since it happened this way, then my conclusion is valid. The argument serves to clarify the issue by differentiating closely similar situations from one another (see further below, 5.4).

[6] No young man in Antiphon's time would have planned a career as a logographer, since Antiphon did not begin the practice of logography until late in his life, and it would have been some time before it would be recognized as a career.

[7] Only Tetralogy 3 concerns a situation that was likely to be encountered in real life. The legal issue in Tetralogy 2, though apparently similar to one that is said to have actually occurred (Plutarch *Pericles* 36), must otherwise have occurred very rarely, if at all.

of the Tetralogies was not in the position of a judge or juror whose task was to render a verdict, though he (and probably occasionally she) would surely have thought about the validity of each case and might have looked for counterarguments or further supporting arguments on either side.

A good presentation of opposing arguments, especially one with novel and clever arguments, would be too intense and intellectual for successful oral presentation to Athenian jurors, but would appeal to anyone interested in contemporary intellectual issues. Young men who were eager to participate in the public discussions of the day could find much of interest in the Tetralogies, and we can imagine readers discussing the arguments with each other and perhaps trying their hands at composing further arguments on the issues. So little of the writing of this period survives that we may have the misleading impression that intellectual activity was confined to a few works by the great masters, like Protagoras and Gorgias, but lesser works like the *Dissoi Logoi* or the "Old Oligarch" suggest that anonymous, less original thinkers also contributed to contemporary debates. The Tetralogies may seem idiosyncratic to us, but in the culture of late-fifth-century Athens, many similar works must have been composed that were not preserved.

Other than what can be inferred from their style, we have no information about when the Tetralogies were composed, but they appear to have been conceived as a group. Within the general structure of Athenian legal procedure, specifically homicide procedure, they explore issues that might arise in any kind of case: arguments based on probability, and issues concerning error, responsibility, and causation. It is possible that the three works represented the basic kinds of homicide case tried in different courts, intentional, unintentional, and lawful (see below, 6.1), but the match only works for the first two, since the plea of self-defense in the third was probably not one of the specific categories of lawful homicide heard by the Delphinium.[8] Still, the idea for the first two, at least, may have come from a desire to match the kinds of case heard by the Areopagus and the Palladium.

A more interesting perspective on the relationship among the Tetralogies is the later theory of *stasis* (Latin *status*)—"issue" or "position"[9]—which

---

[8] These include accidental killings (a fellow soldier, an opponent in an athletic contest), the justified killing of a rapist or an adulterer or a highwayman, and special situations like a doctor treating a patient; see Gagarin 1978a. The issue of a doctor's responsibility is raised in Tetralogy 3, but the doctor himself is not on trial.

[9] The hypotheses or brief introductions to the Tetralogies, which were written by later scholars and are preserved in our manuscripts, begin by identifying the supposed *stasis* of the case.

played an important role in Hellenistic and Roman rhetorical theory.[10] This theory analyzes judicial disputes into different "issues" or "positions," such as *stasis stochasmos* (*status coniectura*), a dispute about the facts, and *stasis horos* (*status definitiva*), a dispute about interpretation or definition (do the facts fit the definition of the crime?). The roots of this theory are often traced to Aristotle,[11] and Russell is probably correct to suggest that the Tetralogies prefigure it.[12] No formal *stasis* theory was developed in the fifth century, but *stasis* may nonetheless help us understand the relationship especially between Tetralogies 1 and 2.

Particularly suggestive are the plaintiff's opening words in Tetralogy 2 (3.1.1): "When the facts are agreed on by both sides, the verdict is determined by the laws and by those who voted,[13] who have final authority over our government; but if there is disagreement on any matter, it is your duty, citizens, to decide. In this case I think even the defendant will not disagree with me." The only kind of judicial dispute the plaintiff envisions here is a question of fact: if the facts are not in question, the case is automatically settled by the laws, and the verdict is not in doubt. The jurors are only needed if there is disagreement about the facts. Since in this case the facts are agreed on, the plaintiff confines himself to stating these without argument; he does not expect the defendant to challenge this view, since he cannot envision any other interpretation of these facts. The defendant, of course, does not accept this conclusion, but in an analysis that he admits is subtle and that would probably strike many readers as a typically sophistic challenge to traditional ways of thinking, he argues that these very facts lead to a different verdict. The issue then becomes, given these facts, what verdict does the law require?

The plaintiff's words appear to be an allusion to Tetralogy 1, where the dispute is entirely about the facts: the victim was undoubtedly murdered, and the two sides disagree only on the factual question, by whom? By contrast, Tetralogy 2 is explicitly presented as a case where the facts are not in dispute but the litigants disagree about who bears the legal responsibility. The distinction between questions of fact and questions of law (to use modern terminology that is only slightly misleading) is the most basic division in any *stasis* theory, for however many categories of other issues later theo-

---

[10] Kennedy 1963: 306–14.

[11] There is no evidence that Aristotle had an actual theory of *staseis,* but he does discuss several different issues that may arise in a case (Thompson 1972).

[12] Russell 1983: 17.

[13] I.e., "those who approved the laws in the Assembly"; the text may be damaged.

rists created, the first *stasis* is always the question of fact, and other *staseis* can only be relevant if there is no dispute about the facts. Thus, it appears that in Tetralogy 2, Antiphon signals precisely this division between the issues treated in his first two Tetralogies.

Antiphon may not have been the first to understand this division. Gorgias's two speeches, *Palamedes* and *Helen*, are similarly distinguished:[14] questions of fact in the former—did Palamedes conspire to betray the Greeks?—and questions of interpretation in the latter—accepting the fact that Helen went to Troy, is she to blame? The latter is particularly notable, since Gorgias was probably the first to defend Helen while still accepting the traditional version of the facts, that Helen went to Troy with Paris;[15] previous defenders of Helen, like Stesichorus, argued that Helen was blameless because she never went to Troy. Gorgias does not acknowledge or even suggest that he is introducing a new kind of question into the debate about Helen, nor does he anywhere suggest that the issues in *Helen* and *Palamedes* are different in kind; but it is possible nonetheless that he was aware of the difference and created these speeches as a pair specifically to illustrate it.

Whatever Gorgias had in mind, Antiphon is the first explicitly to acknowledge the division of issues we find in the first two Tetralogies. This raises the difficult question of whether Tetralogy 3 is intended to introduce a third basic issue. The first two Tetralogies concentrate intensely on a single question each—the facts in the first case, legal responsibility in the second—but Tetralogy 3 raises several different issues of both fact and law: Who was the aggressor? If the victim started the fight, is he responsible? Did the doctor cause the death? Are the victim's friends to blame for consulting a bad doctor? This mixture of factual and interpretive issues confounds any attempt to classify Tetralogy 3 in terms of a *stasis*.[16] It seems, then, that Antiphon only envisioned the division of issues into fact and law and illustrated this division in his first two Tetralogies. In that case, Tetralogy 3 may be intended to show that some cases are not limited to a single issue. On this reading, Tetralogy 3 would be intended to balance the artificially narrow fo-

---

[14] The Tetralogies may, of course, have been written before Gorgias's two speeches; and we do not know the order of these latter two works.

[15] We cannot be certain of the date of *Helen*, though it is usually thought to be earlier than 427 (Buccheim 1989: ix). The other early argument for Helen's innocence that accepts the traditional story is Euripides *Trojan Women* 914–65, performed in 415.

[16] The hypothesis, however, calls it an *antengklēma* or "countercharge" (see Kennedy 1963: 312).

cus of the two preceding works with a more complex and realistic mixture of issues.

2. POLLUTION

The one prominent issue that is raised by both sides in all three Tetralogies is the effect of homicide pollution. Like many other peoples, the Greeks believed that events such as birth and death brought about a state of pollution (*miasma*) that required a ritual cleansing or purification.[17] A death caused by homicide was sometimes thought to bring pollution on the killer, though the nature and extent of this belief varied. In Homer, killers are not represented as polluted, but scholars dispute whether this mirrors actual beliefs in eighth-century Greece or is the result of the poet's desire to keep this doctrine out of his story. In the classical period, homicide pollution is most prominent in fifth-century tragedy and emerges again in Plato's last work, *Laws* (after 350). Each of these presents it differently: in tragedy, homicide pollution nearly always results from kin-killing (perhaps because most homicides in tragedy are committed by kin);[18] for Plato, many kinds of homicide bring pollution on the killer, and in a few cases (e.g., 866b, 871b), pollution also comes on someone who fails to prosecute the murder of a relative. Pollution has a relatively minor place in Athenian homicide law; only one litigant in an actual case appeals directly to it (Antiphon 5.82–84), and it is absent from most accusations of homicide, such as Lysias 13. It is most notably absent from Antiphon 1, a prosecution speech alleging a familial homicide. By contrast, in the Tetralogies, although none of the accused killers is (as far as we can tell) a relative of the victim, every litigant mentions pollution, and the idea is more fully elaborated in these works than in any other Greek source.[19]

Specifically, the issue of pollution is raised at the beginning and end of most of the twelve speeches but is absent from the litigants' central arguments. The plaintiff generally begins by noting that the whole community

---

[17] Parker 1983 is the fundamental study (104–43 for homicide pollution); cf. MacDowell 1963: 141–50; Gagarin 1997: 22–23.

[18] Killing someone other than a relative could also bring pollution: Achilles, for example, is polluted for his role in the death of Iphigenia (Euripides *Iphigenia in Aulis* 938–47).

[19] "It seems that the author of the *Tetralogies* has taken the doctrine of pollution to a theoretical extreme some way beyond the level of unease that in practice it created" (Parker 1983: 130).

suffers from the killer's pollution, which causes harvests to fail, the precincts of gods and the tables of men to be fouled, and affairs in general to miscarry (2.1.3, 3.1.2).[20] This pollution stems from the demand of the dead man or his avenging spirit (*prostropaios, enthymios*) for revenge. This demand will not be satisfied, and the pollution will not be removed from the city, until the killer is punished (2.3.10–11). These ideas are generally familiar from tragedies like *Oedipus the King,* although the avenging spirit Antiphon attributes to the victim is more personal than, say, the Erinyes who pursue Orestes in *Eumenides,* who are in one sense Clytemnestra's own spirits of vengeance but who also function independently.

But Antiphon goes further, much further. Starting from the premise that pollution imposes a strict obligation on the relatives of a homicide victim to prosecute the killer,[21] he proceeds logically to extend the reach of this obligation. If the relatives do not prosecute the killer, or if they prosecute someone other than the killer, then the killer's pollution becomes theirs (2.1.3, 2.2.11).[22] Moreover, witnesses who assist in such unjust prosecutions also share in the pollution (4.1.3). The jurors, too, may be involved—or they may not: here we have contrary assertions according to the speaker's needs. A plaintiff tells jurors they will not be polluted by convicting an innocent man, since the plaintiffs will bear this burden (4.1.4), but they will be afflicted by the victim's pollution if they acquit the true killer, namely the defendant (3.3.11–12). A defendant makes the opposite claim, that even if he is the killer, the jurors will not be polluted by mistakenly acquitting him, for the victim's spirit will turn on the plaintiff if their case fails (4.2.8); but if he is innocent and they wrongly convict him, then they, not the plaintiff, will be afflicted with pollution (4.4.10).

Statements such as these show that Antiphon is presenting pollution as an idea that litigants can manipulate to serve the needs of their argument, whether for conviction or acquittal. The artificiality of this manipulation is clear when one defendant says, "If I am wrongly acquitted . . . I will set the dead man's spirit of vengeance on the person who did not inform you,

---

[20] For each type of argument, I cite only the clearest examples. In other passages, these arguments are interwoven in more complex ways.

[21] Draco's homicide law says, "The relatives are to prosecute," implying an obligation, but to our knowledge no legal action was taken against someone who failed to do so.

[22] Thus those who convict the wrong man get two pollutions, the original victim's (because they have not prosecuted the true killer) and the wrongly convicted defendant's (4.4.10).

not on you. But if I am wrongly convicted by you, I will inflict the wrath of his avenging spirits on you, not on him" (4.2.8). An actual litigant might threaten to set his own spirit of vengeance on someone who wrongly caused his death, but it would be preposterous to assert that he could somehow determine which victim someone else's avenging spirit would pursue.

In the Tetralogies, in other words, the idea of pollution is subjected to rhetorical manipulation. Statements about pollution cannot be taken at face value as representing current religious or legal doctrine, and they bear little or no relation to actual forensic argument. Rather, Antiphon seems to be demonstrating the various, sometimes contradictory ways such ideas can be manipulated, depending on the speaker's need. Extreme assertions about pollution reveal the implicit logic of the idea but have no necessary correspondence to ideas in contemporary law or religion. Readers could experiment with further arguments or counterarguments, and in the process could sharpen their general powers of argument and debate, but they could hardly treat these statements as material to be used in an actual trial.

In addition to providing for the manipulation of arguments, the well-established idea that a killer is polluted and that therefore the victim must be avenged also has the important function of restricting the scope of the debates that form the core of the Tetralogies by requiring that the homicide be met with, in Bernard Williams's words, a "whole person response"; in other words, "someone has to be killed or banished." [23] Thus, each case must determine whether the defendant is responsible for the death. Others might be responsible, too, but this would not affect the case. One cannot argue, as the defendant in Tetralogy 1 might otherwise wish to do, that the killer cannot be known; someone must be available to satisfy the avenging spirit. Nor can one argue for partial responsibility, since just as one cannot be only partly polluted, so one cannot be only partly a killer. This is especially important in Tetralogies 2 and 3, where it is arguable that others involved might bear partial responsibility for the death. The plaintiff in Tetralogy 2 is willing to concede that both the victim and the defendant were responsible, but if so, he concludes, both must be fully punished (3.3.10). The defendant, on the other hand, must argue that his son had no share at all in the death, and that the victim was entirely and solely responsible; otherwise his son would have to be found guilty and punished fully.

---

[23] Williams 1993: 61; he finds a similar idea in U.S. tort law (ibid.: 63–67), though some states require that damages be apportioned among the parties according to their share of the responsibility.

The idea of pollution thus creates a world of strict liability or "whole person" responsibility that has its roots in the world of myth and religion.[24] The justification for this worldview is given at the beginning of Tetralogy 3, where the speaker explains that god created humans, and so the killing of a human is a sin against the gods (4.1.2); for this reason, the victim leaves behind an avenging spirit that will bring pollution on the killer (4.1.3). These conditions impose a necessity on the victim's relatives to find and punish the killer, even when they may not have good evidence leading them to him (as in Tetralogy 1), and to ensure the identification and punishment of the true killer in Tetralogies 2 and 3. Thus, however much litigants may manipulate the concept of homicide pollution, it sets important restrictions on the central debates that unfold in the Tetralogies; and these restrictions serve Antiphon's basic aim of concentrating the arguments in each Tetralogy on a narrow set of issues.

3. TETRALOGY I

Tetralogy 1 explores various arguments concerning what is likely or probable (*eikos*).[25] This type of argument becomes particularly important for oratory around the middle of the fifth century when, we are told, it was one of the main interests of the traditional founders of rhetoric, Corax and Tisias.[26] Aristotle (*Rhetoric* 2.24.11, 1402a17–28) attributes a version of a probability argument to Corax: after a fight between a weak man and a strong man, the former argues that he, a weak man, is not likely to have assaulted a strong man. The latter counters with a "reverse-probability" argument, that he, a strong man, is not likely to have assaulted a weak man, since he would immediately be the likely suspect.[27] Since the weak man's argument is a type that can be found in earlier Greek literature, the main novelty of Corax's (or Tisias's) *logos* was probably the reverse-probability argument, which is the sort of clever, turning-the-tables type of argument that was popular with the Sophists. Perhaps for this reason, we find no example of a reverse-probability argument in the extant court speeches, but it is presented (and answered) in Tetralogy 1, along with many other probability arguments.

---

[24] Eucken 1996: 79–81.

[25] See Gagarin 1994 and above, 1.5.

[26] For these two, see Kennedy 1963: 58–61; Cole (1991a) is more skeptical.

[27] Plato attributes to Tisias a different version of the same argument (*Phaedrus* 273b–c). Plato's version presents a less sympathetic picture of Tisias's contribution and is, in my view, more likely a distortion of the original.

No account of the facts is given in Tetralogy I,[28] but we learn in the course of the arguments that the victim was found dead in the street one night and that his attendant, a slave who died almost immediately after being found, reportedly identified the defendant as the killer. Antiphon has thus created a case with some evidence of the defendant's guilt but no conclusive proof. The plaintiff first observes (2.1.1–2) how difficult it is to obtain sure knowledge or proof when an intelligent person has time to plan and carry out a crime. In such cases, the jurors should put their trust in arguments even if they are only likely (*eikos*). This remark signals that he will use probability arguments out of necessity, since sure knowledge is unavailable in a case like this. Thus Antiphon is concerned not only to explore probability arguments, but also to consider the reasons for such arguments and their validity relative to other types of argument.

The plaintiff first uses probability to eliminate other possible suspects or explanations (2.1.4). He then notes that the defendant's previous relations with the victim gave him a strong motive for the crime and make him the likely killer (2.1.5–8). He adds that he cannot present many witnesses since there was only one, but this one implicated the defendant (2.1.9).[29] The amount of space devoted to each argument suggests that the most important concern is motive, and that the attendant's testimony carries less weight than the arguments based on likelihood.

The defendant in turn complains that to prove his innocence, he will have to find the real killer, or at least a more likely suspect, since the plaintiff has been unable to do this (2.2.2, 2.2.4, cf. 2.4.2–3). He introduces the reverse-probability argument that if circumstances appear to make him the likely killer, in fact they make it unlikely, since, knowing that he would immediately be suspected, he would not only avoid killing the man but would prevent others from doing so if he could (2.2.3). He then argues that probability arguments on his side ought to carry as much weight as they do on the other side: if the plaintiff has used the argument that others are unlikely to be the killer as proof of his guilt, then his arguments that someone else is the likely killer ought to prove him innocent (2.2.4). He suggests several likely alternatives to the plaintiff's account (2.2.5–6), and then adds yet another twist on the reverse-probability argument: others who had motives

---

[28] Some text has dropped out at the beginning of 2.1.4. Probably only a few words are missing, but a brief narrative may also have been lost.

[29] The dead attendant is, of course, not actually a witness in court (others report his words), but his testimony resembles that of a witness, though it is more questionable.

for killing the man, even if these motives were weak, were more likely to kill him, because they knew that he, the defendant, would be suspected. He then argues that the attendant is unlikely to have known or spoken the truth and that, as a slave, his testimony is unreliable without the test of torture (2.2.7). Finally, he states, he is unlikely to have killed the man, since the murder would have posed a greater risk than the man did while alive (2.2.8–9).

At the end, the defendant adds the argument that his previous conduct and service to the city are reasons for his acquittal (2.2.12). It was common for litigants to cite their previous service, but as with several other arguments, Antiphon presents an extreme version that no actual litigant could ever match: the defendant has performed every possible service more splendidly than anyone else ever. The plaintiff responds that such service is a sign of wealth, which is a good motive for murder (2.3.8), to which the defendant in turn responds that rich people favor a stable social order and thus do not commit murder (2.4.9). Like most issues in the Tetralogies, this one can be argued both ways, so that on this point, as on others, the *Antilogiae* demonstrate how an argument based on service, which is essentially an argument from likelihood, can be used to support either side.

The second speeches of both litigants are primarily rebuttals. The plaintiff counters the defendant's probability arguments about other killers (2.3.2–3) and about his motive (2.3.5–6) and argues for the credibility of the attendant's testimony. He also neatly counters the defendant's reverse-probability argument by observing that it leads to the logical absurdity that no one would ever kill anyone: however strong or weak one's motive to kill, it would make him to the same degree a likely or unlikely suspect, and this likelihood or unlikelihood would then be an equally strong or weak motive to avoid the crime (2.3.7). Thus, a strong (or weak) motive to kill would automatically be also a strong (or weak) motive not to kill. Similarly, the defendant counters the plaintiff's arguments about other likely killers (2.4.4–6) and about his motive (2.4.9), and he again attacks the credibility of the attendant's testimony (2.4.7).

In the course of his rebuttal, however, the defendant adds a new and unexpected argument that is "not a matter of likelihood but of fact (*ergon*)."[30] He was home on the night in question and all his slaves, whom he offers up for interrogation, will testify to this. Moreover, he recalls specifically that it was the night of an Athenian festival, the Dipolieia. In two of Antiphon's court speeches (1, 6), a previously tendered challenge to interrogation plays

---

[30] οὐκ ἐκ τῶν εἰκότων ἀλλ᾽ ἔργῳ (2.4.8).

a significant role. In both cases, the challenge has been refused by the other side, and the speaker dwells at length on the refusal as an indication of guilt. Here the argument is handled quite differently: the challenge is apparently first made at the trial, which was certainly unusual, though perhaps not illegal in Athenian law,[31] and the speaker simply asserts his alibi and adds a challenge, with no further argument. He then proceeds to a rebuttal on a separate point (2.4.9), a final summary where he claims that the probability arguments support him and the witness's testimony is unconvincing (2.4.10), and a brief epilogue (2.4.10–12). He never returns to the alibi, at least not explicitly.

To understand why Antiphon introduces this rather startling new evidence at this late point, we must see how it fits into the overall aim of Tetralogy 1, which is, in the first place, to explore various manipulations of the argument from likelihood (*eikos*). Antiphon constructs a fairly simple set of facts that cast suspicion on the defendant but provide no solid evidence of his guilt. Both sides then marshal an array of probability arguments and counterarguments, which provide an interesting display but do not give either side a clear victory. These arguments were undoubtedly of interest in and of themselves, but as we noted above, Antiphon signals a second purpose of the work, to assess the relative value of different kinds of argument or proof (*pisteis*). This metadiscourse continues through the Tetralogy: as the two sides marshal their opposing probability arguments, they simultaneously engage in an analysis of the status and validity of this form of argument relative to other kinds of support they might have for their cases.

The plaintiff introduces this issue with his opening words: "It is not difficult to obtain a conviction for crimes (*pragmata*) planned by ordinary people, but when those with natural ability and practical experience commit a crime at that point in their lives when their mental faculties are at their height, it is difficult to get any knowledge or proof of it. . . . You should be aware of this, and even if you accept a point as only likely (*eikos*), you should have confidence in it" (2.1.1–2). Thus Antiphon begins by establishing that arguments from likelihood are necessary in some cases but have less value as proof than direct evidence of the *pragmata*. After presenting these probability arguments and the witness's evidence, the plaintiff returns to this issue (2.1.9), claiming that the defendant is "convicted by probability arguments and by those who were present."[32] No one, he adds, who

---

[31] There is a later instance in Aeschines 2.126–28; see Thür 1977: 190–93.

[32] ἐξελεγχόμενος δ' ὑπό τε τῶν εἰκότων ὑπό τε τῶν παραγενομένων. Note the *paromorōsis* here and in the following note.

plans a crime can ever be convicted "if they cannot be convicted either by the testimony of those present or by arguments from likelihood" (2.1.10).[33] In the plaintiff's first speech, then, Antiphon establishes that all the relevant evidence in this case falls into one of two categories of proof—likelihoods and factual evidence.[34]

The defendant does not respond directly to this claim, since his strategy, at least initially, is to assume that the entire case is a matter of probability arguments; even the witness's testimony is treated as a matter of likelihood: "It is not likely that he recognized the killers, but it is likely he was persuaded to agree with his masters" (2.2.7). He insists that the likelihoods are on his side, "in case anyone thinks arguments from likelihood carry as much weight against me as the truth (*alētheia*)" (2.2.8), but he concludes that even if the likelihoods are against him, this does not mean that he is in fact the killer, and the jurors should still vote to acquit: "Even if it is likely but not a fact that I killed the man, then it is only just that I be acquitted; . . . your proper task is to convict killers, not those who have a reason to kill."[35] In short, Antiphon presents two lines of defense, probability arguments to counter those of the prosecution and a challenge to probability arguments in general: likelihoods are not reliable indications of fact, and jurors should only convict on the basis of fact. At this point he does not claim that the facts are on his side, only that they are uncertain and thus not a basis for conviction.

This metadiscourse about the value of arguments from likelihood continues in the last two speeches. After rebutting the defendant's probability arguments, the plaintiff (not surprisingly) reasserts the validity of likelihood in the absence of factual evidence: "When he says that murderers are not those who are likely to have killed but those who actually did kill, he is correct about those who killed, if it were clear to us who his actual killers were. But if the actual killers have not been revealed, then since his guilt is proven by the arguments from likelihood, this man and no other would be the killer;

---

[33] εἰ μήτε ὑπὸ τῶν παραγενομένων μήτε ὑπὸ τῶν εἰκότων ἐξελέγχονται. The statement is repeated at 2.3.9 with the substitution of "those who testify" (ἐκ τῶν μαρτυρουμένων) for "those who were present."

[34] These categories correspond roughly to Aristotle's *entechnoi pisteis* and *atechnoi pisteis* (*Rhetoric* 1.2.2).

[35] ἀπολύεσθαι δὲ ὑφ' ὑμῶν, εἰ καὶ εἰκότως μὲν ὄντως δὲ μὴ ἀπέκτεινα τὸν ἄνδρα, πολὺ μᾶλλον δίκαιός εἰμι . . . τούς τε ἀποκτείναντας καὶ οὐ τοὺς αἰτίαν ἔχοντας ἀποκτεῖναι ὀρθῶς ἂν καταλαμβάνοιτε (2.2.10).

for such things are not done in the presence of witnesses, but secretly" (2.3.8). To this the defendant responds, as before, that he should not be convicted if it is uncertain who killed: "They call me the murderer simply because they do not know who really killed him" (2.4.2). This time, however, he implicitly acknowledges that the attendant's testimony falls in the category of factual evidence, not likelihood, when he claims that he should only have to defend himself against the attendant's testimony, not show who the real killers are. Despite this acknowledgment, he returns to probability arguments about other likely suspects and merely repeats his assertion that the attendant's testimony is unreliable (2.4.7).

To this point, then, the defendant has presented no factual evidence of his innocence, and it is thus a complete surprise when in 2.4.8 he introduces his alibi as a fact (*ergon*) to set against the likelihoods (*ta eikota*). Strictly speaking, the alibi is not evidence of his complete innocence, only a refutation of the prosecution's claim, supported by the attendant's testimony, that he was present at the murder; he could still be guilty if he had an agent commit the murder. But if true, the alibi directly refutes the attendant's testimony and thus delivers a strong, if not fatal, blow to the prosecution's case. The defendant clearly implies that the factual evidence of his alibi is decisive, but oddly, he does not directly comment on its validity. Even when he returns to the issue of the value of different proofs at the end of his arguments (2.4.10), he comments only indirectly, at best, on the alibi:

> Although they claim to establish my guilt on the basis of likelihood, they then assert that I am the man's killer not in likelihood but in fact.[36] But it has been shown that the likelihood is on my side; moreover, the witness's testimony against me has been proven to be unconvincing, and it cannot be tested. Thus, I have shown that the evidence (*ta tekmēria*) supports me, not him, and that the tracks of the murder lead not to me but to those who are being set free by my opponents.

This conclusion draws on the same two categories of proof, fact and likelihood. The former clearly includes the witness's evidence and probably also the defendant's alibi, to which there may be an allusion in the remark that the witness's testimony has been proven to be unconvincing, and it "cannot be tested." In his first speech, the defendant argued that the witness was unreliable because his evidence had not been tested by torture (2.2.7), and his offer to allow his own slaves to be tortured to confirm his alibi (2.4.8) would

---

[36] οὐκ εἰκότως ἀλλ' ὄντως; cf. οὐκ ἐκ τῶν εἰκότων ἀλλ' ἔργῳ (2.4.8).

present a direct contrast: by asserting that the prosecution's witness cannot be tested, he reminds the jurors that the witnesses for his own alibi can be tested. Thus, the evidence (*tekmēria*) mentioned in the last sentence presumably includes his alibi, in contrast to "the tracks of the murder," which are the probability arguments.

The defendant's conclusion does not speak directly about the relative value of the two kinds of argument, and the reader is thus given no clear guide to judging either the relative value of the two categories or the force of the arguments on either side within each category. Every point made by one side, it seems, is met by an equal argument from the other side. But the alibi is an exception, and it seems qualitatively different, even from the attendant's testimony. No reason for doubting it is suggested; it is supported by the customary offer of slaves for torture; it is confirmed by an unusual detail (the Dipolieia); and finally, since it comes at the end of the last speech, it is never answered. This final point in itself seems to be an indication that the alibi trumps the other arguments. Antiphon could easily have introduced it in the defendant's first speech, where the plaintiff would have had a chance to answer it; placing it at the end can only indicate that no valid response can be made.

In sum, in Tetralogy 1 Antiphon carries on a rather unobtrusive meta-analysis of "proof" (to use the most common translation of Aristotle's general term *pistis*),[37] while at the same time rehearsing a variety of probability arguments and counterarguments. Many of these arguments, including the reverse-probability argument, are pushed to the limit, and in most cases both argument and counterargument seem valid, suggesting (as the plaintiff indicates at the beginning) that probability arguments in general have only a limited validity. This is confirmed at the end by the presentation of an unrefuted and thus, Antiphon seems to imply, irrefutable piece of factual evidence. The importance of probability arguments is thus undeniable but also limited, and on the scale of proofs they must rank below certain kinds of factual evidence. This is the message Tetralogy 1 is intended to convey: the specific arguments and counterarguments match each other, resulting in no firm conclusion, but the reader should have reached a deeper understanding of the nature of this kind of argument.

---

[37] *Pistis,* as used in *Rhetoric* 1.2.2 and passim, overlaps with "argument" and "evidence" as well as "proof"; see Grimaldi (1980: esp. 19–20), who renders *pistis* as "evidentiary material of a specifically probative character with respect to the subject matter."

4. TETRALOGY 2

As noted above (5.1), Tetralogy 2 quickly differentiates itself from Tetralogy 1, which is essentially a dispute over facts. The facts in Tetralogy 2 are not in dispute (3.1.1), but this does not mean the dispute is easily resolved, for the defendant refuses to accept the prima facie assignment of guilt that these facts would traditionally entail. In this way, Antiphon introduces the complex issues of cause and responsibility that constitute the main focus of this Tetralogy. As in Tetralogy 1, he also provides a subtext analyzing the relation of facts to arguments, though in this case he is concerned not with the value of probability arguments,[38] but rather with the relationship between the facts (*pragmata*) and the litigants' speeches (*logoi*).

The essential facts are succinctly stated by the plaintiff (3.1.1): "My boy, on the training field, struck in the side by a javelin thrown by this young man, died on the spot." We later learn a few more details—that the youth was practicing javelin-throwing with some of his contemporaries, and the boy was helping pick up the javelins that had been thrown.[39] The charge is unintentional homicide, a crime that in Athens was punished by exile, perhaps for a year. The argument we might make today, that the whole affair was an accident, would evidently carry no legal weight in the hypothetical world of Tetralogy 2, and probably not in the actual world of fifth-century Athens either. So the defendant does not attempt this defense, but instead presents a subtle, clever, and (as far as we know) new argument to the effect that the thrower did exactly what he rightly intended to do (throw his javelin), but the victim erred by running out to pick up the javelins at the wrong time; therefore, the boy is the sole cause of, and thus bears the sole responsibility for, his own death. And since he has already been punished with death, the case has been resolved and there is no need of any additional punishment for the defendant.

The plaintiff is understandably stunned by this argument; he cannot believe his son could be accused of being his own killer, and he argues that

---

[38] Likelihood (*eikos*) has no role in the litigants' arguments in Tetralogy 2. The word does occur twice at the beginning of the defendant's second speech (3.4.1), where he says that the plaintiff "probably" was not paying attention to his arguments and that it is "likely" that litigants look favorably on their own arguments.

[39] We are later told that the boy was sent out to pick up the javelins by a trainer (3.3.6), but although the defendant suggests that this might make the trainer the killer (3.4.4), this line of argument is not developed.

even if the boy is partly to blame, the thrower is also partly to blame and therefore deserves punishment for unintentional homicide. As noted above (5.2), the doctrine of pollution excludes the possibility of partial responsibility. In his final speech, the defendant reiterates that his son did nothing that all his friends did not also do; the only reason his javelin happened to hit and kill someone is that the boy, unlike the other boys who were picking up javelins, ran out on the field at the wrong time. Thus his son should be acquitted, for the victim has been convicted of killing himself.

These arguments constitute the earliest known extended analysis of cause and responsibility. General ideas about responsibility are often implicit in poetic accounts, especially in Homer and tragedy, and in *Helen* Gorgias takes up the idea that an individual might not be to blame if a god is the ultimate cause of an act[40] and extends it to other forces affecting human decisions. But whether or not *Helen* is earlier than Tetralogy 2, it is much more traditional in its handling of the general issue of responsibility, and Antiphon's discussion is significantly more sophisticated.[41] The argument employs several hypothetical antitheses that contrast the actual events with hypothetical events that would differ in specific ways and would require a different assignment of guilt (3.2.4–5). If the young man's javelin had gone astray (but in fact it did not), or if the boy had stayed where he was and been hit (but in fact he ran out), then the young man would indeed be guilty, but since neither of these is the case, he is innocent. These antitheses[42] help clarify the precise reasons why the defendant in this case should be treated differently from others who may have accidentally struck and killed someone with a javelin, and they point the way to the defendant's generalization that even if both (or several) parties contributed to an unintentional act, only the one who made a mistake (*hamartia*) is responsible. Since the boy made a mistake (in running out at the wrong time) but the young man did not (he threw at the same time as all the other throwers), the boy is responsible for his own death (3.2.6–8).

In his second speech, the plaintiff first complains that having wasted his first speech, he now has only one speech in which to make his accusation,

---

[40] The idea is already present in the *Odyssey* (e.g., 3.269–70, 23.222).

[41] Antiphon marks the novelty of his approach by having the defendant admit that he himself hardly understands the subtlety (*akribeia*) of the issue and apologize to the jurors if he speaks more subtly than usual (3.2.1–2).

[42] Antithesis is "an effective means of isolating and therefore clarifying concepts, and its vogue in fifth-century style . . . at bottom springs from the desire for forceful clarity" (Finley 1967: 70).

and therefore the defendant's speech will go unanswered (3.3.2).[43] He argues first, in essence, that the young man threw the javelin and is therefore the killer, even if he did not intend to kill (3.3.5–6). Second, the law prohibiting just and unjust killing (see above, 2.2) requires that every killing, even if unintentional, be punished—and rightly, since the harm to the victim is just as great no matter what the intent (3.3.7). If fortune or the gods played a role, moreover, the killer still deserves to be punished for it (3.3.8). The defendant's argument about *hamartia* is wrong, for his son made no mistake, but the thrower did (3.3.9). And finally, in a hypothetical antithesis of his own, the plaintiff concludes that the young man would be absolved of the blame only if he had not thrown his javelin at all; since he did throw it, then if it is right to blame the boy because he ran into the path of the javelin, then it is also right to blame the young man for throwing the javelin (3.3.10). In other words, when more than one agent contributes to an action, both should be held responsible for the action and punished for it.

In his response, the defendant returns to his earlier antitheses. The boy acted differently from the other spectators, who all stayed still while he ran out on the field; the young man, on the other hand, acted exactly the same as the other throwers, who all threw their javelins. The boy happened to run in front of his javelin, whereas no one ran in front of the other throwers' javelins (3.4.5–6). The boy's mistake was preventable, since he could have seen that the young men were throwing their javelins and not run out, whereas the young man could not have foreseen that the boy would run out (3.4.7). The defendant is clearly worried about the possibility of joint responsibility (which would require full punishment for each), and thus continues to insist that his son made no mistake at all and thus does not share the fault (3.4.8).

Although some of these arguments about cause and blame seem unsophisticated, Antiphon raises many of the same issues concerning negligence that common-law courts and legislators have long been debating, such as contributory negligence and comparative negligence.[44] At the very least, this is a serious exploration of the issue of cause and responsibility, which advances the discussion further than any thinker before Aristotle, a century later.[45] Tetralogy 2 does not, however, give a final answer to these questions

---

[43] In fact, 3.3.9–10 is a response to the defendant's first speech. The defendant similarly notes that the plaintiff's speech was an accusation, not a response (3.4.1).

[44] See, e.g., the standard textbook on torts (Prosser 1971), which devotes almost a quarter of its more than 1,000 pages to negligence and related issues, such as proximate cause.

[45] The fourth-century *Rhetoric to Alexander* is no more sophisticated than Antiphon: "You [a defendant] must regard as a crime (*adikia*) a wicked deed done deliberately; . . . a

but tries to do justice to both sides. The arguments on one side may seem stronger, but both have valid points, and, of course, no verdict is rendered at the end. From one perspective, the work is a protest against the traditional rule that unintentional homicide must be punished, but it also suggests that a homicide victim's need for requital cannot be ignored. Thus it should lead the reader to understand better the complexity of factors that can affect one's judgment about cause and responsibility.

In addition to their arguments about cause and responsibility, both sides also contribute to the Tetralogy's metadiscourse on the relationship of actions (*pragmata*) to discourse (*logoi*) about those actions. This analysis begins with the plaintiff's opening words, which divide cases into those where the *pragmata* are agreed on and those where they are disputed. Since in a legal case any dispute about *pragmata* will manifest itself in the two litigants' *logoi* that present the dispute to the jurors for their verdict, he implies a direct, unequivocal relationship between *pragmata* and *logoi*: a specific set of *pragmata* entail one and only one *logos* ("speech," "account," "argument"); if the litigants' *logoi* disagree, this can only reflect disagreement about the *pragmata*. This direct equivalence of *pragmata* and *logos* appears obvious to the plaintiff, and he is stunned that the defendant replies that even though he agrees with the plaintiff about the *pragmata* in this case, his *logos* will disagree with the plaintiff's *logos*.

The defendant prefaces his first speech with some extended remarks about the *logos* he is about to present. As he explains, he is forced to deliver his defense speech with regard to *pragmata* differently than he is accustomed to doing; indeed, he himself can hardly understand the *akribeia* ("precision" or "subtlety") of the *pragmata* in this case, and he is uncertain how he should convey their meaning to the jurors (3.2.1).[46] He asks them not to hold this precision or subtlety against him: they should not judge his speech "by appearance (*doxa*) rather than truth (*alētheia*). For the appearance of things (*pragmata*) favors those who speak well but the truth favors those who act (*tōn prassontōn*) in a just and righteous manner" (3.2.2). The implication of these remarks is that appearance requires speaking well, whereas truth requires a direct relationship between *pragmata* and the *logos* that is

---

harmful act done because of ignorance must be called an error (*hamartia*); while the failure to accomplish some good intention, not through one's own fault but owing to someone else or to chance (*tychē*), is to be accounted a misfortune (*atychia*)" (1427a31–37).

[46] ὡς χρὴ ὑμῖν ἑρμηνεῦσαι ταῦτα. The verb ἑρμηνεύω means to "translate" or "interpret" another language (e.g., Xenophon *Anabasis* 5.4.4), an apt term for conveying the precise meaning of *pragmata* by means of *logoi* that others can understand.

spoken about them. Since the defendant's speech will convey precision, presumably in the cause of truth, his commonplace claim of uncertainty how to proceed and the implication that he is not a good speaker cannot be taken at face value. On the contrary, anyone reading what he knows is a work of Antiphon will expect the "inexperienced" speaker to develop a skillful argument, with an abundant display of sophistic cleverness.

More important, this methodological apology introduces a crucial point about the relationship of facts and words: since the *pragmata* have both an appearance and a truth, and these can evidently differ, then there can be (at least) two different *logoi* corresponding to these *pragmata*, *logoi* that may convey their appearance or their truth. To confirm this conclusion, the defendant begins his argument with a restatement of the *pragmata*: "The young man, not through any insolence (*hybris*) or lack of self-control (*akolasia*) but simply practicing with his friends on the playing field, threw his javelin but did not kill anyone, according to the truth (*alētheia*) of what he did" [47] (3.2.3). With this account, the defendant replaces the plaintiff's *logos* of appearance ("my son was hit by a javelin and killed unintentionally") with a *logos* of truth ("my son threw a javelin but did not kill anyone").[48] And he insists that this truth resides in or belongs to the *pragmata* ("according to the truth of what he did"), even though the *logos* that conveys his truth is just the opposite of the plaintiff's *logos*, which presumably conveyed the truth as the plaintiff understood it. Thus, we have two competing *logoi*, both claiming to represent truthfully the same, agreed-on *pragmata*, and thus far Antiphon has provided no guidance for deciding between them. Traditional readers would probably find the defendant's claim preposterous (as the plaintiff does) and would consider it the weaker *logos* (above, 1.5), but others might view it more favorably and admire the skill with which it was crafted. In any case, the defendant's *logos* requires a skillful explanation, which Antiphon provides (as we have seen) by a series of hypothetical antitheses.

The first of these continues the metadiscourse about the relationship between *pragmata* and *logos*: "If the javelin had hit and wounded the boy because it carried outside the boundaries of its proper course, then no argument (*logos*) would be left for us against the charge of homicide" (3.2.4). In other words, a different set of facts would have precluded this *logos*, or any

---

[47] κατά γε τὴν ἀλήθειαν ὧν ἔπραξεν.

[48] The defendant's argument makes use of the ambiguity of the Greek verb βάλλω, which can mean either "throw" or "hit with a throw."

other *logos* that claimed the youth was innocent. This means that although more than one *logos* (and even two opposed *logoi*) may legitimately correspond to a given set of *pragmata,* the *pragmata* also restrict or set limits on the *logoi*. This particular *logos* arguing for the defendant's innocence is thus valid because it corresponds to the actual *pragmata* in this case, but a slightly different set of *pragmata* would rule out this *logos*.

In his second speech the plaintiff introduces his *logos* with remarks that continue this metadiscourse: "I think this man has shown by actions (*erga*), not words (*logoi*), that need can compel anyone to speak (*legein*) and act (*dran*) against his nature" (3.3.1, cf. 3.2.1). He complains that the defendant has two speeches to his one and adds, "with such an advantage over us in his speeches (*logoi*) and a much greater advantage in his actions[49] . . ." (3.3.3). Now, the only action the defendant has taken that could inspire these remarks is to speak, so that in one sense, in all three instances of the word/deed antithesis, the inclusion of action, though strictly speaking irrelevant, suggests that the defendant's words are in some sense also an action.[50] This is the first hint that *logoi* and *erga* not only correspond but are in some sense identical, a notion that is also hinted at by Thucydides.[51]

These repeated antitheses also foreshadow the plea that follows (3.3.3–4): "I ask you [jurors], where the facts (*erga*) are clear, do not let yourselves be persuaded by a wicked precision (*akribeia*) of words (*logoi*) to think that the truth (*alētheia*) of what was done (*ta prachthenta*) is really false (*pseudos*);[52] for the former [i.e., precision] is persuasive rather than true, while the latter [i.e., truth] is less deceitful, but also less powerful." These words reverse the defendant's earlier claim that although he will not dispute the facts, he will use precision to present their truth (3.2.1–2); the plaintiff argues instead that precision is merely a tool for false persuasion. Despite this difference about the role of precision, both litigants present truth as somehow disadvantaged: the defendant was forced to use extraordinary means to convey the truth, and now the plaintiff explicitly calls the truth less powerful.[53]

---

[49] ἐν οἷς ἔπρασσε.

[50] The plaintiff tells the jurors a few lines later, "I seek refuge in your pity in fact, not in word (ἔργῳ καὶ οὐ λόγῳ, 3.3.3)." Here, too, he is seeking words—a verdict of guilty—but these words are also an action—the punishment of the defendant.

[51] Thucydides is aware that *logos*, "as what men think and say, is itself a vital force in the action of the war" (Parry 1957: 85). The whole discussion in Parry (ibid.: 76–89) is relevant.

[52] μὴ ἔργα φανερὰ ὑπὸ πονηρᾶς λόγων ἀκριβείας πεισθέντας ψευδῆ τὴν ἀλήθειαν τῶν πραχθέντων ἡγήσασθαι.

[53] Presenting oneself as disadvantaged is, of course, a standard rhetorical move.

These observations about *logoi* and *erga/pragmata* in the first three speeches culminate in the defendant's preface to his second speech (3.4.1–2): "You [jurors] must recognize that since we litigants judge the action (*to pragma*) from our own point of view, we both naturally (*eikotōs*) think we speak with justice (*dikaia legein*). You, however, must examine the facts (*ta prachthenta*) impartially (*isōs*), for their truth (*alētheia*) is only discernible from what has been said (*ek tōn legomenōn*)."[54] This extraordinary admission of a litigant's natural bias would almost certainly not be expressed in court by a real litigant, but Antiphon's metadiscourse is not aimed at persuading the (hypothetical) jurors, and so he expresses frankly his views about language, truth, and reality. Each litigant will understand an agreed-on set of *pragmata* from his own perspective and will then produce a *logos* that he considers just. Each also considers his *logos* true in the sense of corresponding to the *pragmata* in question.[55] But the overall truth (in some larger sense) of these *pragmata* can only be determined by the impartial jurors, who must judge not directly from the facts themselves (which are not in dispute) but from the opposed *logoi* of the litigants, each of which presents a different account or interpretation of these facts. Thus, one can only understand *pragmata* by means of *logoi;* any given *pragmata* can give rise to different *logoi*, each of which may truly correspond to these *pragmata;* and there exists an overall, impartial truth that can be discerned from the individual, self-interested *logoi* of the litigants. In essence, this is the principle underlying the discourse of *Antilogiae:* the opposed *logoi* each present one perspective on an issue, and from these the reader reaches an overall understanding (*logos*) that comprehends and supersedes the two individual *logoi*.

The defendant then continues (3.4.2): "For my part, if I have lied about anything, I agree that whatever I have said correctly (*orthōs*) can also be discredited as unfair (*adikos*); but if I have spoken the truth (*alētheia*) but with subtlety (*lepta*) and precision (*akribeia*), then it is only fair (*dikaios*) that any hostility that results should be directed not at me the speaker (*legōn*), but at him [the boy] who acted (*praxas*)." The defendant continues to insist, in other words, that his *logos* is true (presumably because it corresponds to the actions) and that it differs from the prosecution's *logos* primarily in being more subtle and precise. Antiphon does not explicitly draw the conclusion,

---

[54] ὑμᾶς δὲ χρή, γιγνώσκοντας ὅτι ἡμεῖς μὲν οἱ ἀντίδικοι κατ᾽ εὔνοιαν κρίνοντες τὸ πρᾶγμα εἰκότως δίκαια ἑκάτεροι αὐτοὺς οἰόμεθα λέγειν, ὑμᾶς δὲ ἴσως ὁρᾶν προσήκει τὰ πραχθέντα· ἐκ τῶν λεγομένων γὰρ ἡ ἀλήθεια σκεπτέα αὐτῶν ἐστίν.

[55] As the defendant noted earlier (3.2.4), if the facts were different, his *logos* would have to change in order to conform to the facts.

though he may wish to imply it, that the more precise account is the better (or stronger) one. Indeed, he provides no clear guidance to the jurors (or the reader) how to evaluate the opposed *logoi,* and the defendant's final contribution to this metadiscourse does not help (3.4.3): "The plaintiff agrees that the deed (*ergon*) occurred as we say (*legomen*), but he disagrees on the question of the killer, although it is impossible to show who the killer is in any other way than from what has been done (*ek tōn prachthentōn*)." This statement further reinforces the sense of identity between words and deeds but still leaves the question of deciding between the two accounts unanswered.

In sum, if the truth can only be discerned from what is said, and the killer can only be shown from what is done, an identity of words and deeds must be the basis for judicial decisions, even though that identity is neither simple nor straightforward. Tetralogy 2 thus moves the discourse about the relationship of language and reality to another level compared to the discussion in Tetralogy 1, where the issue was one important type of *logos,* the argument from likelihood, and its relation to factual evidence. There *logos* and *pragma* are opposed, but Tetralogy 2 presents a complex symbiosis of the two in which facts control words, but words also control facts, since the truth of these facts depends on the words that represent them. Language corresponds to reality, but since reality is complex, that correspondence does not necessarily involve a single *logos* and a single reality.[56]

This metadiscourse of Tetralogy 2 resonates with the views of several other fifth-century thinkers. The conclusion that words represent reality is in sharp contrast to Gorgias's argument in *On Not-Being* that language cannot convey reality.[57] On this issue Antiphon may be closer in some ways to Parmenides, for whom the truth about reality is not in what people observe but in what they think, and thinking and being are closely associated. But a stronger parallel is to Protagoras, whose example of the warm and cold wind could be similarly expressed: one *logos* (the wind is warm) is opposed by another (the wind is cold), and an overall truth encompassing both these *logoi*—perhaps that the wind is both warm and cold—may be determined by a third party. We can also discern parallels with Thucydides, who uses some of the same ideas to create a more complex analysis of language and reality. In his famous statement of method (1.22), he notes the difficulty of

---

[56] Cf. fragment 1 DK of *Truth* and the discussion above (section 3.5).

[57] Cf. Gorgias *Palamedes* 35: "If it were possible to make the truth of actions (*erga*) clear and evident to listeners through words (*logoi*), a decision based on what has been said would now be easy. But since this is not so, etc."

acquiring precise information (*akribeia*) about events (*ta erga tōn prachthen-tōn*), for many of which he depended on the *logoi* of others. "The implication is that whatever is known about an event is largely a creation of language."[58] *Logoi* may be inadequate to represent outstanding achievement, as Pericles worries at the beginning of his funeral oration (Thucydides 2.35), but *logos* is also the only way to represent the true greatness of Athens, which goes far beyond physical accomplishments to include qualities of the mind. "The *History* is an interpretation of reality which also interprets the possibilities of interpretation."[59] Antiphon's treatment of these issues may lack the vividness or complexity of Thucydides' account, but Tetralogy 2 presents a view of language and reality far in advance of anything achieved by his predecessors.

5. TETRALOGY 3

The last Tetralogy is the shortest of the three. While alluding to points made in the first two, it focuses primarily on causation, though the arguments on the issue are different from those in Tetralogy 2. It also presents a more complex set of events, which makes the analysis of responsibility less clear. Unlike its two predecessors, it concerns a situation that was probably familiar to most Greeks (a drunken fight) and thus may be intended to bear more resemblance to an actual court case, where it is often impossible to isolate and analyze a single issue in the dispute. As in Tetralogy 2, the plaintiff's first speech gives a relatively brief summary of his case: as he sees it, this is a case of intentional murder by someone who, in drunken arrogance (*hybris*) and without self-control (*akolasia*), beat an elderly man to death (4.1.6). The claim that the defendant acted with *hybris* and *akolasia* is a specific echo of Tetralogy 2, where these two states of mind are explicitly denied by the defendant (3.2.3).

 The plaintiff begins with a longer-than-usual prologue (4.1.1–5). In addition to the familiar arguments about pollution, he introduces a new point about humans as divine creations that supports these familiar arguments: because the god created us, killing is a sin against the gods, as well as a violation of human laws (4.1.2), and all killing must be punished (4.1.3). This conclusion also suggests the harmony of *nomos* ("law") and *physis* ("nature"), since the *nomoi* of humans and their *physis* as divine creations share the com-

---

[58] Parry 1957: 103; cf. 7–10, 159–71.
[59] Ibid.: 10.

mon goal of punishing any killing.[60] The plaintiff concludes his first speech with a short epilogue that calls, as usual, for the killer to be punished, and introduces in passing two further points: that witnesses have testified to these events,[61] and that the murder was planned (4.1.7).

Like his counterpart in Tetralogy 2, the defendant in this case tries to shift responsibility for the death to the victim. The facts of this case, however, do not allow him to argue that he himself should escape all blame. Thus he begins his first speech by asserting only that the victim was more responsible than he for the death, since "he began the fight" (4.2.1).[62] He also responds to the earlier charge that he was drunk (4.1.6) by claiming that the victim was drunk (4.2.1). Neither litigant denies he had been drinking, and we may conclude that both were in fact drunk—undoubtedly a familiar situation.

Someone who begins a fight could be held responsible for the consequences, although disagreement about who started the fight was probably common (as it is today), so that this factor would rarely be decisive in itself.[63] But the defendant makes much of the argument, presenting the events as a causal chain where his own blow was the immediate cause of the death, but the victim's initial blow was the prior cause.[64] This is a significantly different analysis from that of Tetralogy 2. There, two concurrent but independent events (the youth's throwing and the boy's running out) combined to produce a result (death); here (the defendant alleges) one event (the initial blow) causes a subsequent event (the defendant's blow in response), which in turn produces a result (death). The defendant's argument in the first case is that whichever party erred is guilty; in this case, it is that whoever initiated the chain of events is guilty.

---

[60] See above, section 3.2. The word *physis* does not appear in 4.1.2, but two cognate words are used to describe the creation of the human race, suggesting that this divine creation is part of our nature: ὅ τε γὰρ θεὸς βουλόμενος ποιῆσαι τὸ ἀνθρώπινον φῦλον τοὺς πρῶτον γενομένους ἔφυσεν ἡμῶν.

[61] The witnesses' testimony does not appear in the text, but it is never disputed. In the artificial world of these Tetralogies, Antiphon can take their testimony for granted.

[62] The Greek expression for "began the fight" (ἄρχων χειρῶν ἀδίκων) is a technical legal expression that is as old as Draco; see Gagarin 1997: ad loc.

[63] See Gagarin 1978a.

[64] Although one may imagine a simple example, like a billiard ball striking another ball, which in turn strikes a third, in real cases disputes about proximate cause (or "legal cause") rapidly become very complex; as Prosser observes (1971: 236), "There is perhaps nothing in the entire field of law which has called forth more disagreement, or upon which the opinions are in such a welter of confusion."

The defendant elaborates this line of defense in the next paragraph (4.2.2– 6). He argues that the response to an assault can legitimately be more severe than the initial blow, though he is aware that the law prohibiting just and unjust homicide requires punishment (see above, section 2.2). He must argue, therefore, not that he was justified, but that he did not kill at all (4.2.3). This requires an extension of the causal chain to include a new factor, the allegedly incompetent doctor who treated the victim. Since the death occurred many days after the fight, he argues, the doctor is actually the killer, and even those who advised him to see the doctor can be considered the cause of his death (4.2.4). In this way the defendant adds another link to the causal chain: his blow only caused the victim to see a doctor, and the doctor's care then killed him. The plaintiff will later note (4.3.5) that the law protects a doctor from prosecution if his patient dies, but this consideration does not weaken the defendant's argument, since he need only remove responsibility from himself and place it on someone else, without regard to the legal liability of this other person. Thus, the defendant seeks to avoid taking responsibility for the death himself, by moving responsibility either backward along the causal chain to a prior cause, the victim himself, or forward to a subsequent cause, the doctor who attended him. Other considerations he introduces—planning the death (4.2.5), bad fortune, or thoughtlessness (4.2.6)—also point to the responsibility of the victim but are of less interest and are discussed only briefly.

The plaintiff's response also echoes parts of Tetralogy 2. He begins by noting (4.3.1) that the defendant's words match his unholy deeds (cf. 3.3.1– 4), but the jurors tolerate it because they want to learn precisely what happened (tēn akribeian tōn prachthentōn, cf. 3.2.1). He also expresses incredulity that the defendant could agree that he struck the blow but claim not to be the murderer (cf. 3.3.5), and could even accuse the plaintiff of being a murderer. He repeats these points in the epilogue (4.3.6 –7). In his main argument, the plaintiff seeks to rebut the defendant's main points (4.3.2–5). He begins with a probability argument, that the victim did not start the fight because the young are more likely than the old to drink and start a fight. Since witnesses have already testified that the victim did start the fight, and since the weakness of this probability argument is accurately noted in the defendant's rebuttal (4.4.2), Antiphon's aim in raising the argument may be to echo the point made in Tetralogy 1, that probability arguments only have force in the absence of more direct evidence. And indeed, the plaintiff apparently assumes that his probability argument has failed, for he next tries to distinguish the victim's (admitted) initial blow from the defendant's retaliation on the basis of their results: only the second blow caused death, so it must have been different from and unequal to the first blow. Similarly, since the victim hit without killing, he only planned the blow, but defendant's blow killed, so he planned the death. These arguments do not make a strong case for differentiating the acts of the two parties, but the plaintiff does not need to prove the victim's complete innocence, only that the defendant shares responsibility for the death, in order to make the defendant liable for punishment according to the rule that anyone who is even the partial cause of a death must be punished.

After disputing the legitimacy of transferring blame to a prior cause, the plaintiff now rejects the transferal of blame to a subsequent cause, the doctor. Those who advised the man to see a doctor are blameless, since if they had not so advised him, they would now be faulted for this omission, and in any case the law protects a doctor (4.3.5). Finally, in an echo of the defendant's argument about prior cause, he argues that since the blow forced the victim to visit a doctor, then he who struck the blow must be the killer. In sum (4.3.6–7), the plaintiff returns to a more direct approach, confidently reasserting the traditional view that the blow caused the victim's death and that according to the law, he who strikes the blow is the murderer.

The plaintiff's confidence seems justified, since the defendant leaves before his second speech, which is delivered by a friend (4.4.1). Athenian law allowed a homicide defendant to go into exile voluntarily any time before his last speech, and despite his friend's pleas, it is hard to imagine that such a course did not influence the jurors to vote for conviction.[65] Antiphon may have his defendant choose this course in order to explore various arguments relevant to this situation, but this move also indicates the weakness of the defendant's case. The contrast with Tetralogy 1, where the defendant cites his continued presence at the trial as evidence of his confidence in his innocence (2.4.1), is clear.

The defendant's friend first challenges one of the plaintiff's probability arguments. If it were a law of nature (*physis*) that young men act with violence (*hybris*) and old men with restraint (*sōphrosynē*), as it is a law of nature that we see with our eyes, then the argument that the victim, an old man, did not start the fight would be valid; but since there are many examples of the opposite behavior, this argument is inconclusive, and since witnesses testify that the victim started the fight, the defendant is innocent (4.4.2–3). As noted above, this rebuttal confirms the relatively low value of probability arguments. The friend then returns to the issue of the defendant's position in the causal chain of events: "For if the striker, by striking a blow and

---

[65] MacDowell 1963: 115.

forcing you to seek the care of a doctor, is the murderer rather than the one who killed him [i.e., the doctor], then the initiator of the fight is in fact the murderer; for he compelled the other to strike back in self-defense and the one who was then struck to go to the doctor" (4.4.3). In other words, if the plaintiff wants to shift responsibility from the immediate cause, the doctor, back to a prior cause, the defendant, then by the same token responsibility should also be shifted one step further back to the victim. The defense thus argues, as before, for shifting responsibility either forward or backward: in either case it will be removed from the defendant.

The defense then repeats several other arguments that were made earlier: that the defendant did not plan to kill but only to strike the victim (4.4.4), that the victim erred in starting the fight (4.4.5), that he was drunk and arrogant and the aggressor (4.4.6), that even if the defendant's blows were stronger, those who start a fight are everywhere punished (4.4.7), and that the law prohibiting just and unjust homicide has been satisfied because the defendant did not kill, the doctor did (4.4.8). He then adds a new argument concerning the standard of proof: even though the defendant's innocence has been demonstrated, if both parties are jointly responsible and the defendant is equally deserving of acquittal and conviction, then the jurors should acquit rather than convict: "For it is unjust for someone to gain a conviction without showing clearly that he has been wronged, and it is wrong to convict a defendant unless the charge has been clearly proven" (4.4.9). Athenian law contained no authoritative statement of the standard of proof needed for conviction. Speakers sometimes imply that jurors should vote for the stronger case, and defendants naturally insist on a high standard of proof for conviction. In Tetralogy 1 the defendant argues that he should only be convicted if he is shown to have killed in fact not in likelihood (2.2.10), and the defense may be making a similar point here in Tetralogy 3. If the arguments fall equally on both sides, then the defendant has not been clearly proven guilty and should be acquitted.

Tetralogy 3 draws on arguments found in its two predecessors and adds new arguments of its own to produce a more complex case than either of the others. As in the two preceding Tetralogies, a situation is posited that allows for argument on both sides: a fight erupts between two men who have been drinking; the older man, who apparently started the fight, is struck by the younger man and is entrusted to the care of a doctor, but he eventually dies. As in Tetralogy 2, these facts are generally agreed on, and the one brief attempt to deny that the victim started the fight is easily rebutted. The defendant attempts to blame the victim himself for the fight, and therefore for his death, but this argument does not seem as effective as the similar argument in Tetralogy 2, and the defendant must, therefore, pursue other arguments as well, including the claim that he has no responsibility for the death since the doctor, who is the more immediate cause, is the killer. The Tetralogy does not, of course, explicitly judge the strength of the opposing arguments, but the defendant's absence at the end suggests less confidence in his case than in either of the other defendants'.

Tetralogy 3 also continues the metadiscourses of its two predecessors, in the process introducing a new issue, the relationship of *physis* and *nomos*. The discourse of Tetralogy 1 on the relative value of probability arguments reappears in Tetralogy 3 when the plaintiff attempts a probability argument (4.3.2) that would deny the validity of a witness's testimony, but this is immediately refuted by the defendant (4.4.2) with an argument, not found in Tetralogy 1, that a rule that is likely (*eikos*) is not the same as a rule of nature: a young man may be more likely to start a fight than an old man, but this claim has a different status than the rule that we see with our eyes. There can be cases, like this one, where an old man starts a fight (but not where someone sees with his ears). Thus the probability argument is contrasted not only with the direct evidence of witnesses but also with natural behavior. This suggests that probability arguments belong on the side of *nomos* or custom (young men customarily start fights).

Tetralogy 3 also refers briefly to the discourse on *logos* and *ergon* that occupies Tetralogy 2, when the plaintiff notes that the defendant's words match his unholy deeds (4.3.1). He also observes that the jurors put up with hearing the defendant's *logoi* because they want to learn "precisely what happened" (*tēn akribeian tōn prachthentōn*) (4.3.1); this recalls the defendant's argument in Tetralogy 2 (3.4.1–2), that words are necessary if we wish to understand the truth of what happened.

Finally, Tetralogy 3 also raises the question of the relationship of *nomos* and *physis*. Two passages suggest that these may not be opposed, but rather may work together. First, I have already noted that the plaintiff's story of the creation of humans by the god (4.1.2) concludes that killing is a violation of both our divine nature and human law. Second, the defendant may hint at the agreement of *nomos* and *physis* when he argues that "large penalties are everywhere prescribed for the initiator of a fight, but nowhere is any penalty written for someone who defends himself" (4.4.7). If the same laws hold everywhere, then law may be thought to reflect something in our nature.[66] These hints about *nomos* and *physis* play only a small role in Tetra-

---

[66] The defendant in Antiphon 5 similarly claims that the rule allowing the accused to leave before his second speech "is common to all" (5.13; cf. 5.17). Thinkers of this period

logy 3, but they suggest possible connections with the treatment of this issue in *Truth,* which I shall consider later (7.4).

6. CONCLUSION

The Tetralogies are a form of *Antilogiae* in which litigants present their
opposed *logoi* in an artificial forensic world. This world is shaped by Athenian homicide law and legal procedure, which litigants adhere to generally,
though not in every detail, and also by the intellectual discourse of the second half of the fifth century. For each Tetralogy, Antiphon creates a specific
situation that allows him to develop arguments and explore issues of interest
to educated Greeks at the time. His audience may have included young men
who were seeking an education, and the Tetralogies would have given them
general but not practical help in preparing discourses of their own on these
issues. But the Tetralogies were not primarily aimed at students, but rather
at the intellectual community as a whole, both in Athens and elsewhere.
Moreover, whether the Tetralogies were early works or were written when
Antiphon was a practicing logographer, they reveal some of the features
for which he was especially well known, in particular his skill in argumentation and his skill in supporting the weaker case, as we see especially in Tetralogy 2.[67] Both features would have appealed to his intellectual audience,
though they might have made him suspect in the eyes of the general public.

In addition to arguments relevant to each legal case, the Tetralogies also
engage in a metadiscourse in which Antiphon explores views on the nature
and validity of the litigants' arguments. Three issues are of particular interest to him: the value of probability arguments relative to the evidence of witnesses and other factual evidence, the interaction of words and deeds, and
the relationship of laws and nature. This discourse occupies primarily the
opening and closing parts of speeches; when it occurs in the main body of
the arguments, it is generally unobtrusive, but it keeps us aware that the author of the *Antilogiae* (as opposed to the individual speakers) has broader interests than determining the verdict in these particular legal disputes. These
interests give a purpose to the Tetralogies that goes beyond the effectiveness
or persuasiveness of any individual speech.

---

more commonly point to differences among the laws or customs of different peoples; see,
e.g., Herodotus 3.38 on different ways of treating dead ancestors.

[67] See Philostratus's report (*Vitae Sophistarum* 499) that Antiphon was accused of "selling for a high price speeches that run counter to justice, especially to those who are in
the greatest danger of conviction."

Several points suggest, moreover, that the three works were composed as a group: the second differentiates itself from the first with regard to the basic issue it raises (what would later be called its *stasis*), and the third alludes to arguments in the first two. There are also hints that the issues raised in the three metadiscourses are related. As noted above (5.5), Tetralogy 3 hints at the possible relationship of each of these issues to one another. The probability argument in Tetralogy 3 (4.3.2, 4.4.2) suggests that probability is in the realm not of nature (where behavior is determined by necessity) but of law or custom. And the difference between probability arguments and the testimony of witnesses or slaves can be seen as one instance of the difference between *logos* and *ergon*.[68] These hints suggest an alignment of probability, discourse, and law on the one hand against direct evidence, facts, and nature on the other. This is perhaps an oversimplification, but the possibility of such connections indicates that the author of the Tetralogies could think in broad terms over a range of issues. And it is no coincidence that some of the issues in the Tetralogies overlap with the similarly broad range of issues in Antiphon's *Truth*.

---

[68] Cf. "not by *eikos* but by *ergon*" (2.4.8); cf. 2.1.9–10.

VI. THE COURT SPEECHES

I. ATHENIAN HOMICIDE LAW

As a background to discussion of the individual works, I begin with a brief summary of Athenian homicide law and legal procedure in Antiphon's day.[1] The Attic orators and others refer to the Athenian homicide laws as the oldest in the land. Scholars generally accept the tradition that the first laws written for Athens by Draco around 620 were all replaced a generation later (around 590) by Solon, except for Draco's laws on homicide; thus, the homicide laws were the earliest of "the laws of Draco and Solon," which remained the basis of Athenian law until Antiphon's day. By the end of the fifth century, so many additions and revisions had accumulated that the Athenians appointed a commission to sort out and reinscribe those that should still be treated as valid. One of the first texts to be reinscribed in 409/8 was "the law of Draco concerning homicide," and this inscription on stone survives to the present day, albeit in a mutilated state.[2] From this and other evidence, primarily the orators and Aristotle's *Athenian Constitution,* we can reconstruct the main features of homicide law, though some details remain controversial.

When someone was killed, relatives of the victim normally brought a private homicide suit, a *dikē phonou,* against the alleged killer. They made a proclamation in the agora naming the killer and filed the suit with the Basileus, the official who oversaw religious matters in Athens.[3] The Basileus

---

[1] MacDowell 1963 remains the most useful study. Although scholars have disputed some of the details, his account is still largely accepted.

[2] *Inscriptiones Graecae* I³ 104; see Stroud 1968; Gagarin 1981.

[3] The Basileus, or "king," was one of the nine Archons or chief magistrates at Athens. Since "king" is a misleading equivalent, and the modern expression *archon basileus* does not occur in our classical sources, I refer to him as the Basileus.

held three preliminary hearings, each a month apart, then supervised the trial, which was usually heard by one of three special courts, depending on the charge, the defendant's response, and other circumstances: the Areopagus tried cases of intentional homicide; the Palladium, unintentional homicide[4] and cases involving noncitizens; and the Delphinium, homicide that was exempt from punishment by law.[5] The Athenians treated someone who had "planned" or instigated a homicide as liable for prosecution under the homicide laws just like a person who killed "with his own hand." The history of and rationale for these courts is much disputed, but we happen to have actual examples of a case from each of them: Antiphon 1 tried before the Areopagus,[6] Antiphon 6 before the Palladium, and Lysias 1 before the Delphinium. A different procedure, *apagōgē* or "summary arrest," is used in Antiphon 5, but this appears to have been unusual, perhaps even unprecedented.[7] The *dikē phonou* had religious associations, and thus its procedures differed in some respects from those in other cases; for example, the litigants had to swear more solemn and serious oaths.

In a *dikē phonou,* the plaintiff and defendant each speak in turn, then each gives a second speech in rebuttal;[8] in an *apagōgē* (Antiphon 5), each litigant gives only one speech. The jurors vote immediately. The penalty for intentional homicide is death, though exile seems to have been a common alternative; if he wished, the accused could leave and go into exile at any point before his second speech, which would then be delivered by a relative or friend, as in Tetralogy 3 (above, 5.5). The penalty for unintentional homicide is exile, probably for a limited period. If the accused claims that his act belongs to one of the specific categories of just or lawful homicide, such as killing a fellow soldier by mistake,[9] and the jurors then agree, he suffers no penalty. Since a homicide suit is a private action, it could be settled by the lit-

---

[4] Homicide was the only crime for which unintentional acts were explicitly punishable in Athenian law. This probably reflects prelegal conditions portrayed in Homer, where unintentional killings require exile (e.g., *Iliad* 23.85–90), and is another indication of the antiquity of the homicide laws.

[5] See *Ath. Pol.* 57.3. Two other homicide courts were used under special circumstances: the Prytaneium when the killer was unknown (or was an animal or something inanimate), and a court "in Phreatto" for cases where the killer was already in exile.

[6] See Gagarin 1997: 104. We have other speeches for trials before the Areopagus (such as Lysias 7), but not from a homicide case.

[7] See below, section 6.4. Lysias 13 is also a homicide case brought by an *apagōgē.*

[8] Antiphon 1 and 6 represent the litigant's first speech; cf. 6.14: "And if I am lying . . . the prosecution can refute me in their second speech on any point they wish."

[9] Demosthenes 23.53; *Ath. Pol.* 57.3.

igants themselves (i.e., the killer and the victim's relatives) at any time, and a convicted killer who is in exile can return to Athens if the victim's relatives agree. Presumably such agreements often involved a financial settlement.

In a *dikē phonou*, Antiphon wrote the first speech,[10] but he may have left the rebuttal speech for the litigant himself to compose after he had heard the plaintiff's speech. In delivering the speech, the litigant presumably followed Antiphon's version closely, since he had paid a large fee for it, though he may, of course, have altered the wording in small ways, just as any lecturer may sometimes diverge from the prepared text. It is unlikely that Antiphon revised the speech later.[11] A litigant probably presented his entire case in one speech, though he may have left some points for his second speech, and no issue was decided separately, as in common law today a point of law might be decided separately from questions of fact. All factual evidence and every argument on substance or procedure, fact or law, had to be presented together. Thus, speeches combine narrative, argument, and emotional appeal, often with repetitions and digressions, all with the goal of obtaining a favorable verdict. There was a rule in homicide cases that one should stick to the subject (5.11, 6.9), but there was no way to enforce the rule (unless the jurors objected enough to alter their verdict), and speakers seem to have had considerable latitude in choosing their arguments. Thus litigants introduce such matters as previous service to the city, which strike a modern reader as out of place in a legal case; but Athenian law was shaped in part by its democratic political ideals, and the worth of an individual to the polis was a legitimate (though not the only) concern.[12]

A litigant's primary task in presenting his case was to take control of the issue—to direct the jurors' attention to those issues that favored his own case, while at the same time drawing their attention away from points that

---

[10] I am assuming the logographer wrote the entire speech. Dover (1968a: 148–74) suggests that logographer and litigant may have collaborated, each contributing to the final text, but this theory has found little acceptance; see Usher 1976.

[11] Some scholars argue that the texts we have of these speeches were significantly rewritten to improve the argument. But a logographer's reputation would have depended more on his success in court than on any assessment of the written version of his speech. Revision is more likely in speeches that were primarily political and thus might later function as political pamphlets. See Todd 1990: 164–67; Worthington 1991 (who relies on a doubtful analysis of "ring-composition" in the speeches); Trevett 1996.

[12] We should not exaggerate the difference on this score between Athenian and modern U.S. practice. The Athenians did not ignore objective factors of guilt or innocence (see Dover 1974: 288–301, esp. 292–95), and verdicts today may in practice be influenced by some of the same extralegal considerations as in Athens.

might favor his opponent. For Antiphon, we never have the opponent's speech and can only speculate about its contents. Nor do we know the verdict in any of these cases; even if we did, we would not know which arguments contributed most to the success or failure of the case. However, a logographer with Antiphon's reputation must have learned which points had been successful in past cases, and would be likely to use similar approaches and arguments in other cases.

A hallmark of Antiphon's argumentation is its flexibility. He follows the traditional four-part division of a speech into prologue, narrative, proof or argument, and epilogue only loosely, fitting his presentation to the needs of the case. Thus the narrative in 1 is more detailed and relatively much longer than in 5 or 6, in part because 1 is a speech for the prosecution, and the speaker must thus present the first account of the facts to the jurors, but also because without much other evidence, the narrative needs to bear the main weight of the case. Antiphon sometimes blurs the line between the different parts of a speech, moreover, so that even where he signals an explicit move from narrative of the facts (*ta pragmata*) to arguments about likelihood (*ta eikota*) in 5.25, he in fact continues to present a mixture of both with only a shift in emphasis.

In the course of his narrative (or elsewhere), the litigant could call for various kinds of evidence to be presented to the court, such as the testimony of witnesses, the text of a law or other written document, or the text of a proposed oath or challenge to interrogate a slave. This evidence comprises what Aristotle later called *atechnoi pisteis,* or "nonartistic proofs" (because, he says, they are simply "found," not created by the skill of the speaker).[13] Later in the fourth century, such evidence was written down at a preliminary hearing and deposited in a sealed container for use at the trial, where it could be introduced during the course of the litigant's speech. In Antiphon's time, witnesses may have given their own testimony, though they were never cross-examined. In our manuscripts, the introduction of these supplementary items is usually designated by a single word, such as "law" or "witnesses." In some cases, though never in Antiphon, the full text of such a document is sometimes included in the manuscript text of the speech, and at least a few of these texts appear to be genuine.

Previous scholars have tried to find common structural principles in Antiphon's three court speeches. The most important of these attempts was

---

[13] *Rhetoric* 1.15, cf. 1.2.2. Aristotle mentions laws, witnesses, contracts, interrogation by torture (of slaves), and oaths.

Solmsen's, who noted the frequent reference to oaths and the interrogation of slaves under torture, and argued that the selection and development of arguments in the court speeches was conditioned by the lingering importance of these nonartistic proofs.[14] In early Greek law, Solmsen argued, nonartistic proofs operated automatically, so that, for example, the swearing of a specified oath in itself decided the case. Even though this system of "proofs" had largely disappeared by Antiphon's time, its earlier importance accounts for the prominent role of such proofs in Antiphon. Solmsen's thesis was widely acclaimed, but is now generally rejected.[15] Not only is there virtually no evidence that nonartistic proofs played this kind of role in early procedure,[16] but it is now recognized that the logographers manipulate these elements just like artistic proofs, according to the needs of the case.[17] Moreover, Antiphon actually puts little emphasis on oaths, and his arguments about the interrogation of slaves are very different in 1 and 5 and are in each case determined by the circumstances.[18]

The three surviving court speeches were probably all written during the last decade of Antiphon's life. Antiphon 6 can be securely dated to 419/8, and the other two are likely to be later, or at most just a few years earlier. I shall examine them in what may be their chronological order, but is in any case a convenient sequence: 6, 1, 5.[19]

2. ANTIPHON 6: ON THE CHORUS BOY

The speaker of Antiphon 6 is generally designated "the choregus," since it was in his role as the "producer" (*chorēgos*) of a choral performance, responsible for training the chorus, that he was accused of homicide after one of the boys in the chorus, named Diodotus, died from drinking some drug (perhaps intended to improve his voice) while training in the choregus's house. The choregus tells us that in their accusation, "the plaintiffs swore

---

[14] Solmsen 1931, drawing on the work of Latte 1920.

[15] E.g., Vollmer 1958; Due 1980; Goebel 1983; Gagarin 1990d.

[16] But cf. Thür 1996 (followed by Duran 1999), who continues to argue that automatic oaths decided all cases in early Greece.

[17] Carey 1994.

[18] Carawan (1998) revives Solmsen's theory, modifying it to apply to Antiphon 1 and 6, but not 5 (which was not a *dikē phonou*). I find Carawan's version no more plausible than Solmsen's and will discuss some of his specific arguments below.

[19] Dover (1950) argues for this order on stylistic grounds, but it is doubtful that stylistic criteria could allow us to specify the order of speeches written so close in time.

that I killed Diodotus by having planned his death, but I [swore] that I did not kill him either with my own hand or by planning" (16).[20] He adds that the plaintiffs agree that the death occurred "unintentionally and without preparation" (19).[21] Much about this accusation is puzzling: on the surface, "planning" an unintentional death seems a contradiction in terms, but the charge was evidently allowed, and "planning" in this case must therefore refer to the sort of involvement or responsibility that for us would make someone potentially liable to a charge of negligence.[22] Athenian law did not have an explicit concept of negligence, but the rule that unintentional homicide was punishable could lead (as in Tetralogy 2) to a charge similar to our negligent homicide. This rule, when combined with the rule that a "planner" or instigator of a homicide was equally guilty—a rule normally used only for intentional homicides—gave the plaintiffs the opportunity to accuse the choregus, despite the fact that he apparently had no direct connection with the actual death.

After a prologue emphasizing the importance of the homicide laws and the need for a correct verdict (1–6), the choregus begins his defense by asserting that the plaintiffs have ignored the rule about sticking to the issue and have instead accused him of various public crimes in addition to the actual accusation of homicide (7–10). He then briefly describes the careful domestic arrangements he made for the boys' training, just as he had done for past choruses he had trained (11–13): he furnished a special room in his house and selected the best boys he could without unduly pressuring anyone. Then, since he could not be present in person, as he was involved in a public prosecution for impeachment,[23] he selected several experienced colleagues to supervise the boys' training. He thus presents himself as an important public figure who aggressively guards the public interest, but who made the most responsible arrangements possible for the chorus, so that despite his own

---

[20] διωμόσαντο δὲ οὗτοι μὲν ἀποκτεῖναί με Διόδοτον βουλεύσαντα τὸν θάνατον, ἐγὼ δὲ μὴ ἀποκτεῖναι, μήτε χειρὶ ἀράμενος μήτε βουλεύσας.

[21] μὴ ἐκ προνοίας μηδ' ἐκ παρασκευῆς.

[22] See Gagarin 1990b. In the U.S., we are increasingly familiar with the idea that anyone in a position of responsibility, such as the director of an organization, can be sued for damages incurred accidentally in any area of the organization, no matter how remote the director's own connection with the events.

[23] There was no public prosecutor in Athens; public crimes had to be prosecuted by individuals who voluntarily undertook to bring the case themselves. Citizens generally watched for and prosecuted offenses committed by their political enemies.

absence, caused by his undertaking a public service, the boys still received the best possible training.

At this point we might expect the choregus's own account of Diodotus's death (of which the plaintiff presumably had already given a version), but instead he simply states his claim that he was not directly involved in the boy's death: "I did not order the boy to drink the drug, I did not force him to drink, I did not give him the drink, and I was not even present when he drank" (15). He then calls witnesses to support these assertions. He takes this line of defense, he explains, because the plaintiffs "base their accusation on the argument that whoever ordered the boy to drink the drug or forced him to drink or gave it to him is responsible" (17). He does not claim that they accused him explicitly of these acts, and they presumably did not, for if they had, the choregus's witnesses would deny them, and the plaintiffs apparently did not have any witnesses of their own who had direct knowledge of the administration of the drug. Thus the choregus's claim that the facts are well known (18–19) is probably true, and the case hinges, therefore, like Tetralogy 2, on an interpretation of these facts. The plaintiffs probably argued that even though they did not know the exact arrangements for administering the drug, since these would have been made in private, the choregus was responsible because he had overall supervision of the chorus. They may have mentioned specific acts conditionally ("if anyone ordered the boy to drink, etc., he would be guilty") to support the argument that the choregus would be responsible no matter what his specific involvement in administering the drug.

It is puzzling that the choregus's denial of involvement in the death is so narrowly circumscribed (15–19). The jurors must have wondered what actually happened: Who did administer the drug, and for what reason? Perhaps these details were provided by witnesses (15), but in that case one would still expect the speaker to mention them. More likely this limited denial is intentional. The choregus does not want to describe in detail what happened, since these facts might not provide good support for his case; or they might implicate his associates, who were more directly involved. But he does not want the blame shifted to anyone else: "I am not emphasizing these points in order to absolve myself and put the blame on someone else. No, I blame no one, except fortune" (15). Underlying this case is an ongoing struggle between the choregus and his political opponents, and it would not strengthen his case if he argued for his own innocence by shifting the blame to one of his political allies. So Antiphon decided to direct the jurors' attention to the plaintiff's conduct, where he must have felt he had the strongest case.

The choregus's denial in 16–19 is his only direct discussion of what in U.S. law would be the central issue of the case—responsibility for the boy's death.[24] He spends much more time (20–51) discussing the plaintiffs' actions during the days and months after Diodotus's death, taking these as evidence that they had ulterior motives for prosecuting him. He has already suggested that his opponents' behavior will be a significant issue (7–10); he now recounts how, on the day of Diodotus's funeral, Diodotus's brother, Philocrates, came to the court where the choregus's impeachment case against Philinus and others was to be tried the next day and accused him of killing Diodotus by forcing him to drink a drug (21). Philocrates' motive can only have been to prevent the choregus from prosecuting his impeachment case, since anyone formally accused of homicide was immediately banned from most public places, including the courts.

To demonstrate the evident falseness of the accusation, the choregus reports that he challenged Philocrates to question all those present at the death, free men and slaves, and he dwells at some length on this challenge and its implications (23–32). Challenges were a common pretrial maneuver among litigants in Athens.[25] One litigant would challenge the other to undertake or allow some course of action, such as swearing an oath or allowing slaves to be interrogated (under torture). Some challenges may have been honest attempts to find points of agreement with an opponent, but many were little more than rhetorical provocation: one side issues a challenge knowing that the other side will refuse, and then this refusal becomes a point in one's argument in court.

The choregus's challenge clearly belongs in the latter category. Philocrates must have already had an account of events from someone present, and the choregus does not need to issue a challenge in order to introduce the

---

[24] Carawan takes a different approach. He notes the choregus's request that the jurors should decide which party swore "more truthfully and better. They swore that I killed Diodotus by planning his death, but I swore I did not kill him either by my own hand or by planning" (16); Carawan concludes (1998: 280), "The judges are not asked to determine a question of fact. . . . The objective questions of what was done and what the law requires are fundamentally matters for the litigants to investigate and decide for themselves. . . . The judges are asked only to decide between the sworn claims of the two litigants, which of the two has conducted his case with moral certainty." But since the two sworn statements present each side's case in a nutshell, judging these oaths is equivalent to judging the litigants' cases. If the oaths per se and the litigants' moral certainty were the central issue, we would hear much more about them.

[25] The standard work is Thür 1977; see also Gagarin 1996; Johnstone 1999.

testimony of free witnesses; but Philocrates' refusal of the challenge does allow the choregus to argue that the refusal is a sign of the weakness of Philocrates' case. The choregus's challenge is aimed at reinforcing his one factual argument, that he was not present at the time of Diodotus's death. On this point (and only on this point), he has the strong evidence of witnesses, and so he makes much of Philocrates' refusing the challenge and contrasts his own willingness to seek the truth (23–26). In a common rhetorical move termed "hypothetical role-reversal" (27–29), he argues that if their roles were reversed, Philocrates would be asserting that the witnesses were the most reliable evidence. In summary (30–32), the choregus claims he has facts (*erga*) to support his plausible arguments (*eikotes logoi*).[26] "What else can I do to show that I am acquitted of the charge?"

The choregus answers his own rhetorical question with a further examination of the plaintiffs' behavior after Diodotus's death (33–51), arguing that Philocrates charged him with homicide only because he was "persuaded" (i.e., bribed) by the choregus's political enemies, whom he was in the process of prosecuting. Philocrates was friendly with him at first and did not accuse him until three days after Diodotus's death, just as the choregus's impeachment case was about to go to trial. Then Philocrates filed the request for an indictment even before Diodotus's funeral rites were finished. The choregus managed to have the case rejected on a technicality, however,[27] thus freeing him to continue with his impeachment. He and Philocrates were then reconciled. Later, when the new Basileus took office, Philocrates did not refile the indictment for fifty days, and in the meanwhile associated publicly with the choregus. Only when the choregus brought another impeachment case against various public officials did Philocrates refile his accusation, which led to this trial. This account, which occupies more than a third of the speech, shows clearly that Philocrates did not really hold the choregus to blame for the boy's death but only prosecuted him for these ulterior motives.

One of the difficulties in assessing Antiphon's strategy in this case is that we do not know the plaintiffs' case. It seems likely, however, that they, too, introduced matters that may at first glance appear extraneous to the homi-

---

[26] Or perhaps "arguments from likelihood." The choregus actually claims that the *erga* support the witnesses, that he has witnesses and facts in addition to *logoi,* and that the facts support the witnesses. But the facts (*erga*) are nothing more than the witnesses' own testimony.

[27] There was not enough time left in the Basileus's annual term of office for the required preliminary hearings (see Gagarin 2000).

cide case, namely the choregus's public prosecutions. As he says, "They are conspiring against me by inventing falsehoods and slandering me for my public activities" (9). Quite possibly they accused the choregus of neglecting the chorus boys' training in order to pursue his own selfish political goals, and they may well have portrayed his political activity as inimical to the interests of Athens. He was more concerned (they might have argued) to bring baseless charges against honest public servants and advance his own political career than to discharge his duties as choregus; as a result, many young boys doing their civic duty were put at risk, and one even died. They may also have justified refiling the homicide case only after some delay by pointing out that they only acted after the choregus violated a reconciliation agreement by undertaking a new public prosecution. Even if they could not know precisely the choregus's role in Diodotus's death, it is clear that he could have done more to prevent it. Now (they might conclude), no boy in Athens will be safe, if this death is allowed to go unpunished!

Arguments such as these may have been presented to support the plaintiffs' unorthodox charge of homicide by means of "planning."[28] If there is any truth to the choregus's narrative of events after Diodotus's death, then it appears that the boy's relatives were willing to consider the death an accident (the result of *tychē*), or at most bring a charge against one of the subordinates who was more directly responsible. At the urging of the choregus's opponents, however, a charge of unintentional homicide by planning was brought against the choregus in order to force him to drop his impeachment case. As we saw in Tetralogy 2 (above, 5.4), the issue of responsibility for an accidental death could give rise to some complex and subtle arguments,[29] though we do not know how much of their speech, if any, the plaintiffs devoted to such arguments. For his part, although Antiphon was obviously capable of developing a full analysis of this issue (and might have done so if he were writing a Tetralogy about this event), such subtle arguments would be out of place in a court speech.[30]

---

[28] The Basileus who rejected the charge on a technicality may have been troubled by the questionable nature of this charge; see Gagarin 2000.

[29] The different circumstances in this speech would, of course, necessitate different arguments.

[30] The jurors in this case were a special group called *ephetai*, who heard certain homicide cases. They were probably better educated on average than the jurors in the popular courts, but they would still be very different from the intellectual audience of the Tetralogies.

Thus Antiphon simplifies his direct response to the accusation, maintaining simply that the choregus had nothing to do with the death. Specifically, he denies the most obvious ways in which one might be indirectly responsible (such as by telling someone else to administer the drug) and provides witnesses to support this denial. Beyond this, he avoids the complex and tricky issue concerning the precise nature of the choregus's supervision of arrangements for the chorus, on which score he might be held responsible for the death, whatever he did. Instead, he directs his main argument to the issue of the plaintiffs' motives. Devoting only a brief time to answering the specific accusation of involvement in the death not only allows him to devote more time to the issue of the plaintiffs' motive, but also conveys the impression that the specific charge of homicide is trivial and baseless in comparison with the real issue, namely, will these public criminals be allowed to divert attention from their crimes and use this specious accusation to attack a man for doing his civic duty?

Antiphon's strategy is thus to contrast the choregus's responsible and socially useful behavior with the crimes and manipulations of his opponents. To this end, he establishes a pattern of responsible behavior on the part of the choregus, as seen both in his arrangements for the boys' training and in his prosecutions of public criminals, and a pattern of dishonest behavior on the part of the plaintiffs, as seen in their refusal of his challenge and their casual treatment of the accusation. In strict legal terms,[31] the public conduct of the litigants may not be relevant to the question, whether the choregus is guilty of unintended homicide by planning; and this case might thus be taken to support the view that Athenian law was less concerned to secure "justice" in a narrowly legal sense than to negotiate the balance of social and political power between the two litigants. But in fact, the broader consideration of the choregus's public behavior is relevant to the question of "planning" or negligence, both because the choregus's public activity was probably presented (by the plaintiffs) as the cause of his absence during the boys' training and because his responsible career of public service would lend support to his claim that his provisions for the boys' training were responsible, not negligent. Similarly, the plaintiffs' ulterior motives are a legitimate consideration, for if these motives are entirely political, this implies that even they do not believe the accusation of homicide, and this in turn suggests that

---

[31] I am aware of using "legal" in the narrow sense it has today of "directly relevant to the law"; it is ultimately misleading to use the term in this sense of Athenian forensic discourse, which did not share our modern understanding of legal relevance.

their case has no basis in fact. Indeed, I suspect that if similar circumstances in the U.S. today prompted a civil suit, where the standard of proof is less than certainty,[32] Antiphon's line of argument would be just as effective.

3. ANTIPHON 1: AGAINST THE STEPMOTHER

Antiphon 1 was delivered by a young man who is accusing his stepmother of poisoning his father. The woman is defended by her son, the speaker's half-brother.[33] In his opening remarks, the speaker says he will show that she "murdered our father intentionally and with premeditation, and indeed that she was caught in the act of contriving his death not just once but many times before" (3). Most scholars agree that since the plaintiff presents no witnesses or other direct evidence of the stepmother's intentions, his case is very weak and probably failed to win a conviction. I shall suggest a different assessment.

In a short prologue, the speaker emphasizes his inexperience and introduces the issue of family loyalty. His half-brother, who speaks for the defense, has forsaken their father, the innocent victim, out of loyalty to his mother, a foul murderer (2–4). This introduces the basic polarity of the speech—an innocent male victim set against his evil, murdering wife—which evokes, among other things, the myth of Agamemnon and Clytemnestra, with whom the speaker later explicitly associates his stepmother (17).

The argument proper (5–13) begins by asking how the defendant can say he is "quite certain"[34] of his mother's innocence (6), when his refusal of a challenge to interrogate his own slaves indicates that he did not want certainty (6–8). The speaker himself "wanted to interrogate the defendant's slaves, for they knew that once before this woman had contrived to poison our father, that he had caught her in the act, and that she had not denied it, except to claim she was giving the drug as a love potion, not to kill him" (9). By a hypothetical role-reversal quite similar to the one we noted earlier, in Antiphon 6 (27–29), the speaker argues that the defendant's refusal to let the slaves be questioned amounts to strong evidence in the plaintiff's favor (11–13).

---

[32] In the U.S., the requirement for a verdict in a civil case is usually "a preponderance of the evidence," rather than proof "beyond a reasonable doubt."

[33] The stepmother is almost certainly not in court (Gagarin 1998), and the speaker sometimes speaks as if his half-brother were the defendant.

[34] The expression εὖ οἶδεν occurs repeatedly (6, 8, etc.), suggesting that this is a direct quotation from the defendant's oath (8, 28).

The speaker then presents an account of his father's death and the events leading up to it (14–20), the longest uninterrupted narrative in Antiphon.[35] His father had a close friend, a merchant named Philoneus. One day his stepmother summoned Philoneus's *pallakē* ("mistress") and told her that Philoneus would soon cast her aside, and that she herself was losing her husband's love. She asked the *pallakē* to help her so that they could both regain the men's love. The *pallakē* agreed, and some days later during a dinner she slipped a drug the stepmother had provided into the men's drink, giving Philoneus a larger than recommended dose in the hope that he would love her even more.[36] Philoneus died on the spot; the speaker's father became sick and died twenty days later. Philoneus's relatives immediately had the *pallakē* executed for her role in the death, but the stepmother, who was really responsible, remains unpunished.

The speaker gives no explanation how he learned of the events he recounts, and he presents no witnesses or any other evidence to support this account. But his vivid story of the women seeking desperate remedies when they fear they are losing their men's love would fit comfortably into most of the (all-male) jurors' preconceptions about the kinds of steps desperate women take for the sake of love. At least some of the jurors had undoubtedly heard Euripides' Medea observe perhaps fifteen years earlier that "no mind is more murderous than that of a woman wronged in love" (*Medea* 265–66) and then watched in horror as her actions validated this stereotype. Antiphon's tale of two women conspiring to administer a drug to men who were on the verge of abandoning them would have found a sympathetic audience, and few would have paused to reflect that the speaker could not possibly have known what the two women said to each other, let alone what they were thinking.

The speaker next returns to the dichotomy with which he began: he is seeking revenge on behalf of his most cruelly murdered father, whereas his brother has no concern for their father and seeks only to defend his criminal mother (21–27). He repeats the rhetorical question, how can the defendant have "certain knowledge" when he was not there (28)—an argument that would apply equally, of course, to his own account, though he may not have claimed the same degree of certainty. The speaker then recalls how just before his death, his father, realizing what had been done, enjoined the speaker—then just a boy—to see that the crime would be duly punished

---

[35] In Antiphon 5 and 6, the narrative bits are dispersed throughout the speeches.

[36] Faraone 1999: 128–29 discusses the possible composition of the drug in this case.

(29–30). The speech ends with a brief plea to the jurors to vote in accordance with justice (31).

Scholars treating this case have almost all assumed that the central issue is whether the stepmother intended to give her husband a love potion or intended to poison him.[37] They then observe that the speaker presents no evidence on this point, and they conclude, naturally, that his case is weak. It has even been suggested this is a rhetorical exercise. Carawan argues that the case is stronger than generally thought, but he gives a similar assessment of the issue: "The argument in this case centres on the defendant's state of mind. . . . The trial would turn upon the question of malice aforethought."[38]

To support this analysis, scholars often adduce a passage from the *Magna Moralia* (1188b29–39), an ethical treatise included among Aristotle's works but widely judged to be a later work of his school (i.e., at least a century after Antiphon's speech). Here, in a discussion of intentional and unintentional acts, the example of giving a love potion is used; the decisive factor is the absence of deliberate intent—*dianoia:*

> When someone strikes or kills or does something like that to another without prior deliberation (μηδὲν προδιανοηθείς), we say he acted unintentionally (ἄκων), since intentional action (τὸ ἑκούσιον) is a matter of deliberation. For instance, they say that a woman once gave someone a love potion (*philtron*) to drink, and the man then died from drinking it. The woman was tried by the court of the Areopagus, which acquitted her for no other reason than that she did not act intentionally (οὐκ ἐκ προνοίας), since she gave the love potion for love but failed to achieve this goal. Therefore her act was not considered intentional (ἑκούσιον) because she did not give the love potion with the deliberate intention of killing him (μετὰ διανοίας τοῦ ἀπολέσθαι). In this case, the intentional is included in the [category of acting] with deliberation.

This case is presented as a historical example, and some scholars have suggested it may refer to the very case for which Antiphon 1 was written. This

---

[37] Gernet (1923: 35–36), for example, notes specifically the absence of "proofs or indications which would establish premeditation" and suggests that arguments on this point may have dropped out of our text. One discussion that seems to take a different approach, connecting the case to its literary background, is Faraone 1994. But Faraone 1999: 114–16 takes a more traditional approach, arguing that the women's only mistake was to give too large an amount of the drug and taking it as a "fact" that "the wives [*sic*] were acquitted on the grounds that they were trying to mix love potions" (128).

[38] Carawan 1998: 217.

is not impossible, but even if the story is based on a real case, the Athenian legal system would not allow Aristotle or anyone else to know the jurors' reasons for acquittal.[39] But scholars are comfortable with the philosopher's reasoning, which reduces the case to a clear legal issue: Did the woman kill with deliberate intent? The same line of argument would probably be expected in a similar case today, where a charge of intentional homicide would require that the woman know the drug was a poison. Of course, even today an actual case might be considerably messier. Consider a woman who suspects she is losing her husband to a younger woman and in desperation procures some Viagra and slips it into her husband's drink. She has mistaken the dosage, however, and the Viagra proves fatal. How would our law treat her? Not as a murderer, perhaps, but probably not as completely innocent either. If the charge were criminal negligence, many factors might be raised in addition to knowledge or intent. At the very least, the simple distinction between intentional and unintentional homicide would not exhaust the possibilities.

Nonetheless, modern scholars are generally comfortable with the Aristotelian analysis of Antiphon 1. But Athenian court speeches were not composed for an audience of philosophers or scholars, and the speech itself clearly reveals different concerns. The speaker seems to have no interest in the question of whether his stepmother deliberately intended to kill or not. He gives no argument that she thought the drug was a poison rather than a love potion, and only mentions this issue casually in alluding to her claim of innocence when she was earlier accused of attempting to kill her husband: she did not deny the allegation "except to claim she was giving the drug as a love potion, not to kill him" (9). This qualification, which most scholars see as central to the case, is presented as trivial and as having little or no relevance to the question of the stepmother's guilt.[40] It may be possible to read the narrative as implying that the stepmother knew the drug was a poison and deceived the *pallakē* into thinking it was a love potion, but in fact, everything she does in the plaintiff's account is consistent with her thinking the drug was a love potion.[41] Even if the stepmother had previ-

---

[39] Litigants presented many different arguments, jurors gave no reasons for their votes, and the jurors who voted for acquittal probably did so for different reasons.

[40] Just as it had no relevance for the guilt of the *pallakē*, who certainly believed (according to the speaker's account) that the drug was a love potion, and who acted out of love with no intent to kill, and yet, in his view, fully deserved her punishment (20).

[41] The only hint to the contrary is the statement that the *pallakē* did not realize she had been deceived by the stepmother until afterwards (19).

ously admitted that she had provided the drug,[42] this would not mean that she knew it was a poison and intended it to be fatal. The speaker is clearly not interested in her intent or state of mind when she provided the drug.

His concern is rather to show that the stepmother planned the whole matter. He represents her as saying that "her own job was to contrive the plan, the *pallakē*'s was to carry it out" (15), and he implies that she gave advice on the best time to administer the drug (17). He later reiterates this point: now that the *pallakē* has been duly punished, "the woman who was really responsible and who thought up the plan and carried it out"[43] deserves the same fate (20). And he repeatedly calls her the killer and insists that she pay for her crime: "She killed him intentionally, planning the death . . . by sending the drug and ordering [the *pallakē*] to give it to him to drink, she killed our father" (26).[44] In other words, the speaker is concerned to show that the defendant contrived the plan to give the drug, provided the drug, and persuaded the *pallakē* to help administer it, but he is not concerned to show that she knew the drug was a poison, rather than a love potion.

Antiphon's strategy, in other words, is to portray the stepmother as the primary agent in a plot to give her husband a drug. She is represented scheming against her husband and victimizing the innocent *pallakē*. Whatever the motive, dealing in drugs was a dangerous business,[45] which in literature is commonly associated with evil, men-destroying women, such as Circe and Medea. Even the ill-fated Deianira of Sophocles' *Trachiniae*, who is represented as killing her husband Heracles by mistake, only reinforces the view that no woman should give a drug to her husband, even out of love, and that any woman who takes aggressive action to win back her husband's love is a dangerous threat. Surely no male Athenian would want his own wife slipping a drug into his drink, even if her motive was love. If the step-

---

[42] Carawan (1998: 221–23) speculates that the defense agreed beforehand that the stepmother provided the drug, but in that case, surely the speaker would mention this fact; cf. Antiphon 5.28, 6.19, 6.29, where admissions by opponents are mentioned. Carawan suggests that the half-brother would mention this stipulation in his own defense speech, but he could hardly be expected to have helped the plaintiff with his arguments.

[43] ἡ δ᾽ αἰτία τε ἤδη καὶ ἐνθυμηθεῖσα καὶ χειρουργήσασα. Many editors move καὶ χειρουργήσασα ("and carried it out") so that their subject is the *pallakē*, but the speaker may be intentionally exaggerating the stepmother's role; see Heitsch 1984: 31 n. 80.

[44] ἑκουσίως καὶ βουλεύσασα τὸν θάνατον ⟨ἀπέκτεινεν⟩ . . . πέμψασα τὸ φάρμακον καὶ κελεύσασα ἐκείνωι δοῦναι πιεῖν ἀπέκτεινεν ἡμῶν τὸν πατέρα.

[45] The difference between a poison and a love potion must have been difficult to determine. Even today, a small change in dosage may make a beneficial drug lethal.

mother's plotting caused her husband's death, her motive probably did not matter to most of the jurors.

On the other hand, it could be significant to establish that this was not an isolated incident, an innocent mistake, but part of a pattern of dangerous scheming by the stepmother against her husband. This is why the speaker dwells on the allegation that once before she was caught red-handed, although on that occasion, too, her intent seems unimportant. It is her conduct that is significant, not her motive. The speaker also introduces the conduct of her son, who sides with his mother against his father, in contrast to the speaker, who is loyal to his father. If the stepmother is a Clytemnestra (17), it is particularly important that the son should assume his proper role and emulate Orestes by avenging his father and punishing his mother, as the speaker himself is doing.[46] Antiphon's overall strategy is thus to tell the story of a woman who thinks she is losing her husband's love and contrives a fatal plot to regain it. For this she deserves to be punished, no matter what precise knowledge she had about the drug.

We can only speculate about the defense strategy, but it might have been to try to remove the stepmother entirely from this story by denying the plaintiff's account and telling a different story[47]—perhaps that of a wife who remained loyal to her husband and who now, as a grieving widow, is viciously attacked by a hostile stepson. Such a story would surely give more importance to the *pallakē*'s role and would probably deny that the stepmother planned to have the drug given to her husband, though it may have allowed that the stepmother provided the drug for the *pallakē*'s use, perhaps at her request. Other arguments are possible,[48] but the important point is that the defense almost certainly did not accept the story that the stepmother planned the whole affair, and did not base their argument on the claim that she acted out of love and not with malicious intent.

---

[46] There may be other allusions to the story of Orestes in 21, 25, and 29; see Gagarin 1997: ad loc.

[47] The speaker hints at this when he notes that his half-brother swore he was "quite certain" that his mother did not do these things.

[48] The defense might have argued, for instance, that the death, which did not occur until twenty days after the drug was given, was caused by something else, such as disease or the doctor's incompetence. They might also have proposed a challenge to interrogate slaves on certain points, and then attacked the speaker for his refusal to accept these sure means of learning the truth. Finally, they may have noted the long time that has passed since their father's death and questioned the motive for bringing the case at this time.

In sum, the decision to bring this charge of homicide was probably not so straightforward as the plaintiff makes it appear. At the time of the death, Philoneus's relatives had contented themselves with punishing the *pallakē*, who administered the drug; this suggests that they had no good evidence linking the stepmother to the death. Now, quite a few years later,[49] the son of the other victim brings charges against her, even though after so much time has passed he probably has even less direct evidence. Antiphon devises a strategy that does not require direct evidence but depends instead on portraying the accused as a disloyal and dangerous plotter whose scheming was the ultimate cause of her husband's death. One suspects that underlying the case is a dispute (perhaps over inheritance) between the son who brings the charge and his half-brother, who defends the stepmother. The centerpiece of Antiphon's strategy is a narrative account of a woman plotting to give a drug to her husband, just as she had tried to do before. To this are added several arguments directed at the behavior of the son who is defending his mother: that by siding with her against his father he violates proper family relations, that by refusing to let his slaves be interrogated he shows a lack of concern for the truth, and that he cannot justify his sworn claim that he has "certain knowledge" of his mother's behavior that he did not himself witness.

The later philosophical version of this story, on which most scholars rely, provides a neat rule for deciding the case—guilt requires the woman's knowledge that the drug was a poison—but is of no relevance to Antiphon's case. Consideration of what the speaker actually says, particularly in the context of (male) Athenian views of women as shaped by the literary and mythological tradition, reveals a different set of concerns—concerns much more likely to resonate with the jurors. This suggests that the plaintiff's case may have been considerably stronger than modern scholars have assumed; perhaps it was not strong enough to guarantee a victory, but it ought to have stood a reasonable chance of success.

4. ANTIPHON 5: THE MURDER OF HERODES

As in Antiphon's other two cases, the charge of homicide in Antiphon 5 has been brought for questionable reasons. The speaker, Euxitheus, is a citizen of Mytilene (on the island of Lesbos) who is charged by an unorthodox procedure with murdering an Athenian named Herodes. It is the longest

---

[49] The speaker was a boy at the time of his father's death (30) and must now be at least eighteen.

and most complex of Antiphon's surviving speeches and is often considered his best.[50]

After a prologue with some commonplaces about the difficulty of matching words to deeds (1–7),[51] Euxitheus turns immediately to one of the main points in his defense, that the wrong procedure is being used: he is accused of homicide, but he was denounced and then arrested by a procedure (*endeixis* followed by *apagōgē*) intended for common criminals, not for homicide (8–19). The normal procedure, the *dikē phonou*, requires open-air trials and solemn oaths, and sets a fixed penalty for conviction; *apagōgē* does none of these (9–12). Moreover, the prosecutors imprisoned him as soon as he reached Attica and kept him in jail until the trial, despite his willingness to provide the customary sureties (13, 17–18), and they leave open the possibility of a second trial by the regular homicide procedure if they do not succeed in convicting him in this case (16).

Next, in a brief and selective narrative (20–24), supported several times by the testimony of witnesses (20, 22, 24), Euxitheus relates how he and Herodes left Mytilene on the same boat, bound for Thrace. A storm forced them to take shelter in a small harbor, where they moved to a larger boat with a roofed deck to wait out the storm and began drinking (20–23). The next morning Herodes was missing. Euxitheus helped search for him, but when no sign of Herodes was found, he resumed his journey to Thrace (23–24).

Euxitheus then turns to his arguments, or, as he says, to "the likelihoods" (*ta eikota*) of the case (25–63). His main point is that the prosecutors have fabricated the case against him. They did not accuse him at all until after he had left for Thrace; then, even though he never left the boat on the night in question and they could not find Herodes' corpse or explain how he disappeared, they concocted the story that he killed Herodes and threw his body into the sea (25–28). In his absence they interrogated witnesses, one of whom, a slave, was persuaded by torture to confirm this story (29–32). When this slave later recanted, they killed him, despite the pleas of Euxitheus's friends, so that no one else could question him and determine the truth (33–35, 38). This shows that the recantation was probably true (36–37, 40–41). Another witness who was interrogated, a free man, said Euxitheus never left the boat (42). The prosecution's story is implausible, since he would

---

[50] It was highly regarded in antiquity ([Plutarch] *Moralia* 833d). In addition to the commentary in Gagarin 1997, Edwards and Usher 1985 has a translation and commentary; for the details of the case, see also Gagarin 1989.

[51] See below, section 7.4.

not have enlisted help in killing Herodes, someone would have noticed a murder taking place, and disposing of the body would have left evidence at the scene (43–45). Putting the slave to death illegally can only have been intended to prevent Euxitheus from learning the truth (46–48). The free man sided with Euxitheus consistently and is more likely to have told the truth; the slave's testimony in favor of Euxitheus is more likely to be true than his accusation (49–51). If Euxitheus were guilty, he would have eliminated the witnesses (52). The prosecutors introduced a letter he allegedly wrote to a certain Lycinus admitting the deed, but they probably forged this and planted it on the boat (53–56). Neither he nor his alleged accomplice Lycinus had any motive for murder, and he would not have killed Herodes for Lycinus's sake (57–63).

Euxitheus then adds several peripheral arguments: he does not know and should not be expected to know what happened to Herodes (64–66); three examples from the past show that in some cases the murderer is never found and in others the wrong person is convicted, so the jurors should not decide hastily (67–73); his father is a good and loyal citizen, even though he may have participated in the Mytilenean revolt a few years earlier (74–80); and the gods have signaled their belief in his innocence by allowing him to participate in sacrifices and to travel by boat without bringing harm to anyone (81–84). The speech ends with a long epilogue reiterating some previous points (85–96): he should be acquitted now, since conviction for homicide is irreversible; he can always be tried later by the proper homicide procedure, which because of its special features would be more likely to reach a true verdict; he has a clean conscience, and the jurors should not be persuaded by the prosecution's false slanders.

It should be evident even from this brief summary that the speech is far from straightforward, and we may suspect that Antiphon has intentionally made it difficult to disentangle the different arguments. But before considering his strategy, we must examine these arguments in more detail. For convenience I divide them into substantive issues (the facts of the alleged murder), procedural issues (the procedure used in this case and the treatment of witnesses and other evidence), and supplementary arguments (Euxitheus's father and signs from the gods).[52]

---

[52] I do not mean to imply that the Athenians themselves would have recognized this categorization of substantive and procedural issues, but the division of arguments in Euxitheus's speech to some extent falls along these lines.

The prosecutors' case is apparently based largely on the testimony of the slave who provided details about Herodes' murder and admitted his own participation in it. In their speech they must have provided a detailed account of the crime, probably supported by witnesses. They apparently did not know Euxitheus's exact motive for the crime but argued that Lycinus and he planned the murder together. Antiphon's response to the charge is first to provide a clear, straightforward narrative account of events before and just after Herodes' disappearance, showing that Euxitheus could not have planned Herodes' death since the events before Herodes' disappearance were determined by chance (*tychē*) and compulsion (*anankē*), which are unpredictable and uncontrollable. It was mere chance that the two men were on the same boat together; the storm came by chance and forced them to move to another boat with a roof. Moreover, Euxitheus did not behave afterwards as if he had killed Herodes: the next day he participated fully in the search, as he would not have done if he had been guilty. This clear, detailed account of events before and after Herodes' disappearance helps conceal the fact that Euxitheus provides little information about the central episode: "We began drinking, and it is clear that Herodes left the boat and did not return again, but I did not leave the boat at all that night. The next day . . ." (23). He later claims the support of a witness for this account but provides no further details. Either he is concealing these details or, perhaps more likely, he was drinking and does not know exactly what happened. In any case, Antiphon concentrates on a clear account of those events which point to Euxitheus's innocence.

Antiphon then turns to arguments, explicitly distinguishing them from the facts just presented—"these are the facts; now consider the likely conclusions that follow from them" (25) [53]—though in fact, more facts emerge in the course of these arguments. The simple, direct, diachronic narrative seems to confirm Euxitheus's innocence; by contrast, the complex, repetitious, and chronologically disordered sequence of arguments that follows suggests that these matters are debatable and uncertain. Antiphon may not be able to make a strong direct argument for Euxitheus's innocence, so his strategy seems rather to be to cast doubt on the prosecution's arguments by demonstrating the complexity and uncertainty of all arguments in this case. To this end, he breaks up his arguments and scatters them around. For example, the free man who supported Euxitheus's claim of innocence is first

---

[53] τὰ μὲν γενόμενα ταῦτ' ἐστίν· ἐκ δὲ τούτων ἤδη σκοπεῖτε τὰ εἰκότα.

mentioned in 30 but is not mentioned again until 42. Only later (49) do we learn that he was not a slave. In this way information is introduced piecemeal, generally in connection with other arguments. Thus, we learn that this man is a free man only when Antiphon wishes to emphasize that a free man is a more reliable witness than a slave (49).

The purpose of these arguments seems to be more to discredit the prosecution's case than to construct a positive case for the defense. Just as the narrative provided no information about Euxitheus's actions on the night in question, so, too, in the section of argument, we learn only that the free man said that Euxitheus "did not leave the boat at all" (42), and that the free man "said nothing bad about me" (49). It has puzzled scholars that Antiphon does not make more of this alibi, supported as it apparently is by the direct testimony of a witness,[54] but he is clearly more concerned to rebut the slave's incriminating testimony, which occupies the bulk of this section. This testimony was probably presented in considerable detail by the prosecution, and without a similarly detailed account of his own, which Euxitheus apparently cannot provide, he was forced to attack the testimony in other ways. So Antiphon challenges the slave's reliability, raising one objection here and another there in a confusing but forceful attack, and introducing facts from the slave's account only as needed for his attack on the slave's truthfulness.

Antiphon begins by summarizing the prosecutors' story without mentioning the slave, who (we later learn) was the source of their information: "They say the man died on land when I hit him on the head with a stone" (26). However, they cannot explain Herodes' disappearance, and he himself did not leave the boat (27). He then reveals that the prosecutors say that Herodes was thrown into the sea, but they have no evidence for this either (28). By emphasizing the absence of evidence and saying nothing about the slave,[55] Euxitheus gives the impression that the prosecution's account has no source and thus has no more support than a mere story.

Only in 30 does Euxitheus mention the slave, and everything he then says about him is directed at casting doubt on his testimony and on the prosecution's conduct. The slave, he claims, was probably lying in the hope of gaining freedom in exchange for his testimony. When only one side is asking questions, a slave will say what the interrogator wants to hear; and the prosecutors apparently agree, for they executed the slave so that no one

---

[54] Of course, Euxitheus may not have such a strong alibi; see Gagarin 1989.

[55] Of course, the prosecution would have given information about the slave.

else could question him further (30–38).[56] In all this we are not told the slave's words, only that he incriminated Euxitheus. Later Euxitheus claims that the prosecution misrepresented the slave as saying that he helped kill Herodes, whereas in fact he said only that he led Herodes off the boat and helped dispose of the body (39).[57] Euxitheus repeats the arguments why the slave probably lied (40–41), and then introduces the free man's testimony (42), explaining that it conflicts with the slave's story: according to the slave, Euxitheus left the boat and killed the man, and the slave helped dispose of the body. The details just trickle in, but Euxitheus's strategy is clearly to attack the slave's credibility without revealing much of what he actually said.

Euxitheus's next argument, that the slave's story is in itself implausible (43–45), reveals a little more of the prosecution's story: Herodes was killed near the sea, and his corpse was put in a small boat. Euxitheus repeats that the slave should not have been put to death (46–48) and adds another reminder of the conflicts in testimony with no further details (49–51). Finally, in connection with the letter to Lycinus, he presents a version of the slave's testimony (54) that contradicts his earlier version (39) on the question of whether the slave said he killed or helped to kill Herodes.[58] Although the slave's testimony may have allowed either interpretation, Antiphon's argument requires a different version in each place. He may have hoped that the jurors would not notice the contradiction (they did not have the luxury of going back and checking the earlier passage); but in any case it is more important to support the particular argument he is making in each place than to be consistent from one argument to another. His overall goal is to negate the effect of the slave's account, and to this end he marshals any arguments he can.

Another example of the method of introducing only those facts needed is the figure of Lycinus. Although the prosecution must have discussed him,[59] Euxitheus mentions his name only when he takes up the question of the let-

---

[56] In reality, Herodes' relatives probably began to question witnesses without knowing who might be incriminated. Once the slave implicated Euxitheus, they could have summoned him to question the slave himself, but they probably were not required to, and in any case, he was probably still in Thrace. Euxitheus confuses things in part by alluding to the more common situation of a challenge between two litigants, where both sides had to be present at any interrogation, but this rule would not apply in this situation.

[57] It is not clear that there is in fact any contradiction between these two versions.

[58] In 39 Euxitheus says the slave admitted only to helping Euxitheus, whereas in 54 he relies on the opposite claim, that the slave testified that he himself killed Herodes.

[59] Euxitheus must show "that their charge against [Lycinus] is also unreasonable" (60).

ter (53–56) and gives no information about him until he considers the issue of motive (57–59) and the allegation that he was acting for Lycinus. Then, in arguing that Lycinus also had no motive for murder (60–63), Euxitheus gives us glimpses of Lycinus's financial situation, but no more. He remains a shadowy figure to the end.

In sum, Antiphon's strategy throughout this section of argument (25–63) has been directed primarily at casting doubt on the slave's veracity and the prosecution's conduct and motives rather than at presenting facts that would contradict their story or would support an alternative version. This strategy may have damaged the prosecution's case, but it leaves Euxitheus's case fragmented and confusing, and it provides no effective alternative account of his actions. He gives a reasonable defense of his refusal to speculate about what really happened to Herodes (64–66), and the historical examples he gives (67–73) reinforce his point that if the jurors do not know what happened, they should not convict; but Antiphon knows that a plausible alternative story would strengthen his case (as the defendant in Tetralogy 1 realizes, 2.4.3).[60] His hope seems to be that the jurors will be so skeptical of the prosecutors' case and so troubled by their misconduct that they will not notice, or will not be bothered by, the absence of an alternative account.

Antiphon treats the prosecution's use of an abnormal procedure in much the same way, moving back and forth among arguments and providing only the information necessary at each point. His basic objection is that the prosecutors' behavior is illegal, violent, and motivated by financial self-interest. First, the use of an *apagōgē kakourgōn* ("arrest of common criminals") to prosecute a homicide case is unprecedented and wrong. This may be correct, but Antiphon cannot cite any law specifically prohibiting the use, for Athenian laws were normally worded to allow a procedure for a crime but not to require it or prohibit other procedures. Thus Euxitheus relies more on moral and religious considerations, especially the solemn religious nature of the *dikē phonou* that should properly be used in this case (10–12).

At first we are not told why the prosecutors chose the procedure of *apagōgē*, only that they defended their choice, evidently aware of the unusual nature of this move (9). Euxitheus suggests vaguely that they did so for their own financial benefit and promises to give more information about this

---

[60] It may be that Euxitheus does not offer a detailed account of his own actions or an alternative explanation of Herodes' disappearance because he is in fact guilty and has no plausible alternative to offer; see Gagarin 1989.

later (10). Presumably part of the punishment could be a fine paid to the prosecutors. Euxitheus then abruptly mentions another feature of *apagōgē*, that he was arrested when he reached Attica and so could not leave voluntarily, as in a *dikē phonou*. Apparently the prosecution argued that if he had not been arrested, he would not have awaited trial (13). This maneuver is understandable, since a Mytilenean citizen might have less reason than an Athenian to remain for a homicide trial. Euxitheus also complains that he was not able to post sureties and remain free before his trial, as the law allows (17). The posting of sureties, though perhaps not a legal requirement, was a common practice, and the prosecutors' refusal to allow it bolsters the impression that they are not playing by the rules.

Euxitheus brings two more complaints against the prosecutors' use of *apagōgē* (15–16). First, their witnesses can testify without swearing solemn oaths, as they would in a *dikē phonou*. Although this is probably not an important factor in their strategy, the charge raises the suspicion of false testimony, to which Antiphon will return later. Second, by using an *apagōgē*, they are keeping the *dikē phonou* procedure in reserve in case they lose. If they win a conviction, they will demand the death penalty,[61] but if they lose, they can retry the case by a *dikē phonou*. It is unlikely that such "double jeopardy" would be allowed,[62] but by raising the possibility Euxitheus creates more doubt about the prosecution's motives.[63]

Even if some of Euxitheus's objections to the use of *apagōgē* are minor, they all contribute to the picture of the prosecutors as violating the normal rules of law and interested primarily in their own enrichment. These arguments on procedure set the tone for the rest of the speech, where the same charges are repeated: the prosecutors have fabricated their story; their treatment of the slave violated basic rules; and they have even forged a letter and planted it on the boat. As we noted, this strategy leaves Antiphon's argument fragmented, as he moves from one point to another and back again, but taken together the arguments make a strong case that the prosecution's conduct is corrupt, unlawful, and self-interested. In this sense, the speech has

---

[61] This assertion conflicts with Euxitheus's earlier assumption that the prosecutors will request a monetary fine, not the death penalty (10), though they could probably request both.

[62] Athens had a rule against trying the same case twice, but this may not have applied to trials of the same issue by different procedures. U.S. law also has a rule against double jeopardy, but in some cases the same issue is tried more than once by different procedures.

[63] Euxitheus reverses this argument in the epilogue (90, 96), urging the jurors to acquit him now because they will still have a chance to convict him in a second trial.

an overall cohesion that may not be apparent if one looks only at the logical structure of individual arguments.

Even Euxitheus's two supplementary arguments—about his father and about divine signs—are shaped to reinforce this message. Anyone who prosecuted a Mytilenean in Athens during this period of lingering resentment over the Mytilenean revolt (in 427) would undoubtedly seek to tie the accused to the rebellion. Euxitheus is careful not to raise this issue until after his main argument is complete. He distances himself from the revolt, since he was very young at the time (74–75), and defends his father's conduct during the revolt and afterwards, claiming he has remained loyal to Athens and has acted in Athens's interests (76–79). His father's only reason for moving to Thrace was to escape from "sykophants"—those who prosecute others purely for the sake of money (78)—and he appeals to the jurors to help him resist these present sykophants (i.e., the prosecutors) and show others that they cannot profit in this way (80). Euxitheus then introduces the signs from heaven that were in his favor (81–83), turning this argument, too, against the prosecutors by noting that even though all the facts are against them, they are hoping their words will make the jurors disbelieve the facts (84).

Antiphon 5 is considerably longer than either 1 or 6, in part because the procedure of *apagōgē* allows each speaker only one speech, whereas the speeches from the two *dikai phonou* would have been followed by rebuttals. This may also explain why 5 contains such a diverse collection of arguments, including the two self-contained arguments at the end (74–83), some of which might have been omitted if Antiphon were writing only a first speech.[64] The complexity of Antiphon 5 is also caused in part by the unorthodox legal maneuver of the prosecution, which created considerable difficulty for the defense. Antiphon's response is indirect and deceptive, and in places seems designed to produce confusion rather than clarity. But in response to the prosecutors' tricky strategy, he needed every bit of forensic skill he could muster. The fact that they used an unorthodox procedure to bring the case provided an opening that Antiphon seizes on to argue that in this and other ways, their handling of the case has violated the normal rules of procedure, and that this has allowed them knowingly to create a false case against Euxitheus solely for their own financial gain. The high reputation of the speech in antiquity suggests that this strategy succeeded.

---

[64] It is generally accepted that a logographer normally wrote only the first speech for a case; otherwise we ought to hear of many duplicate titles of speeches. But he may have advised his client about issues that should be included in the second speech.

5. ANTIPHON'S SPEECH IN HIS OWN DEFENSE

In addition to the three surviving court speeches, the titles of about twenty other speeches are preserved in ancient sources.[65] Little or nothing remains of these speeches, and in most cases the scattered words or phrases cited by ancient lexicographers give little sense of the content of a speech and no hint of Antiphon's overall strategy in the case. Among the wide range of subjects, however, political concerns can reasonably be surmised in about half the speeches and may have played a role in others. Antiphon wrote two speeches concerning the tribute paid to Athens by allied cities, Lindos (9) and Samothrace (15); these probably protested the amount or manner of the levy. He also wrote speeches for cases involving prominent public figures, such as the general Demosthenes (3).[66] In addition, political issues were probably involved in several other speeches,[67] and it is possible that even cases that appear completely free of political concerns were in fact politically motivated.[68] It is clear, then, that during the last fifteen years of his life,[69] Antiphon devoted a substantial portion of his logography to cases involving public figures and political issues. As we would expect, several titles suggest that he represented more conservative political figures and causes, but his prosecution of Laispodias, who led an embassy under the 400, suggests that we should be cautious about too rigidly categorizing the political forces during this period.

Antiphon's most famous political speech was his unsuccessful plea in his

---

[65] I include two works that were not true speeches. The "Invective against Alcibiades" (20) appears to have the form of a speech, even though it was probably circulated as a pamphlet, not delivered in court. And *Proems and Epilogues* (21) was a collection of standard sentiments, such as a father lamenting the loss of his son, that were perhaps meant to be rehearsed by students. I follow Thalheim 1914 for the numbering of the fragments.

[66] Others include *Against Laispodias* (8), a general associated with the 400, and *Against Hippocrates* (6), if this is the general, not the doctor.

[67] In *Against Nicocles* (11), Hyperbolus, a leading political figure, is mentioned; *Against Philinus* (18) is probably the impeachment case referred to in Antiphon 6.12; and the titles of 12, *Accusation of an Illegal Proposal*, and 14, *Against the Prytany* (if genuine), in themselves indicate political disputes.

[68] Even if we do not accept Cartledge's admittedly speculative conclusions about 16, *Against Erisistratus Concerning the Peafowl* (Cartledge 1990), we may legitimately suspect that political issues underlie the speech.

[69] None of the fragments can be dated earlier than about 425 (Dover 1950: 53–56); in some cases, however, there is no indication of a date, and so some speeches may be earlier than this.

own defense at his trial in 411, the one speech whose outcome we know. In antiquity this speech was one of his most celebrated, but only a few words survived into the modern era until early in the twentieth century, when a papyrus revealed a few more sentences.[70] These indicate that Antiphon, like Socrates in 399 (at least as Plato presents him in the *Apology*), used the occasion of a trial to defend his career as a whole, not just to refute the specific charge against him. Although both speeches failed to convince the majority of jurors at the time, the uncompromising endeavor to make a forensic speech into an *apologia pro vita sua* won both speakers the admiration of other intellectuals both at the time and in the years to come.[71]

Almost all of Antiphon's colleagues in the group of 400 who formed the short-lived new government in 411 left Athens after the democracy was restored rather than face trial.[72] Only Antiphon, Archeptolemus, and Onomacles are named in the official indictment that is preserved, and the last of these apparently escaped before the trial, since the verdict, which is also preserved, names only Antiphon and Archeptolemus.[73] The flight of all the other leaders suggests that it was predictable that any member of the 400 who stood trial immediately after the restoration of democracy would be convicted, and Antiphon must have known that his chances of acquittal were slight. He almost certainly had connections outside Athens,[74] who would have given him refuge if he had wanted to flee, and so he must have had strong reasons for staying to face trial. Again, it is tempting to compare his conduct to Socrates'.

We cannot discern the overall strategy of this speech, but the arguments that survive suggest that Antiphon was more concerned to defend his career than to win an acquittal. The fragments do not indicate how he addressed the specific charge against him, which was misconduct on an embassy to Sparta, but speak instead to the general charge of treason and harming the city. The longest fragment presents two arguments about motive:

⟨What was supposed to be my motive for conspiring against the democracy? Was it⟩ that I had been selected for a public office where I had

---

[70] Nicole 1907.

[71] For similarities between the defenses of Socrates and Antiphon, see Gagarin 1997: 249; and more fully Gagarin forthcoming.

[72] One member, Andron, saved his own life by proposing the decree indicting Antiphon.

[73] See [Plutarch] *Moralia* 833e–834b.

[74] Antiphon 5 (for a citizen of Mytilene) and the speeches for Lindos and Samothrace suggest friends in at least these three places.

handled large sums of money and faced an accounting that I feared? Had I been disenfranchised? Had I done you some wrong? Did I fear an impending trial? Surely I had no such motive, since I faced none of these situations. Well, were you depriving me of property? Or ⟨was it because of⟩ wrongs done by my ancestors? . . . ⟨Others⟩ desire a different form of government from the one they have because they want to escape punishment for crimes they have committed or take revenge for what they have suffered and not suffer in return. But I had no such motive.

My accusers say I used to compose speeches for others to deliver in court and that I profited from this. But under an oligarchy I would not be able to do this, whereas under a democracy I have long been the one with power because of my skill with words. I would be worthless in an oligarchy but very valuable in a democracy. Surely then it's not likely that I desire an oligarchy. Do you think I'm the only man in Athens who cannot figure this out or cannot understand what is to my own advantage? [75]

The first argument is similar in form to others in Antiphon that list possible motives for a crime and then deny them (e.g., 5.57–58): he had none of the standard reasons for desiring a new government. The second argument is positive: in fact, he had every reason to favor retaining the democracy, since his skill with words would be more valuable under that form of government. This argument is framed as a response to the charge that he profited from his logography, though it may have cut both ways. The response suggests that his opponents were trying to strengthen their case by appealing to the jurors' prejudices against logography and sophistic cleverness with words, for which he had become suspect in the eyes of many (Thucydides 8.68). By connecting logography to democracy, Antiphon turns the charge in his favor, but the cleverness he exhibits in doing so may also have reinforced prejudices against this sort of ingenuity.

Two other sentences survive: one [76] suggests that his accusers sought to link Antiphon to his ancestors, who may have sided with antidemocratic forces a few generations earlier; again, Antiphon's logical response may have

---

[75] The translation is from Gagarin and MacDowell 1998: 91–92.

[76] "On the charges brought by Apolexis, that like my grandfather I was a political partisan . . . the ancestors would not have been able to punish the tyrants but have been unable to punish their bodyguards." The argument apparently is that although Antiphon, like his grandfather, may have been on the side of those no longer in power, his grandfather was not punished for this (though he could have been), and so Antiphon should not be punished either.

struck the jurors as more clever than respectful of tradition. The other sentence[77] suggests that the prosecution anticipated an emotional appeal from Antiphon, to which he apparently will not resort.

These fragments indicate that Antiphon was more concerned to defend his career and display his powers of argument than to win his case.[78] This may help explain why the speech was written down and preserved. The speeches he wrote for clients needed to be written down, of course, but he would not need to write down a speech he was going to deliver himself unless he wanted others to read it. Most Athenians with political or intellectual interests probably attended the trial and heard the speech delivered,[79] but some, like Thucydides, would not have been present to hear it. For him and others like him, and for posterity, Antiphon left a written version. In doing this, he introduced a practice that was soon widely adopted, first by Andocides and then by Lysias and others.

6. ANTIPHON'S LOGOGRAPHIC STRATEGIES

The court speeches of Antiphon stand as pioneering works of logography. The three that survive in full show that he carefully constructed each speech to fit the needs of his clients. Although certain kinds of argument occur in all three, the overall structure of each is quite different, and Antiphon is clearly able to employ a wide range of different approaches and forms of argument as needed. It is in the construction of these logographic strategies that his talent is most evident.

The fundamental factor affecting the strategy of a forensic speech is whether it is composed for the plaintiff or the defendant.[80] Both of Antiphon's surviving defense speeches (5, 6) must respond to unorthodox legal maneuvers on the part of the prosecution. In both speeches he focuses primarily on the prosecution's handling of the case, though his strategy is a bit different in each case. In 5, he not only repeatedly attacks the prosecution's

---

[77] "[The prosecutor] asked that you not pity me, since he feared that I would try to persuade you with tears and supplication."

[78] The sophistic nature of Antiphon's speech is particularly evident in contrast to the more straightforward pleas Andocides composed in his own behalf not long afterwards (Andocides 2, composed in 410–405; Andocides 1 in 400 or 399). Andocides directs all of his arguments to persuading the jurors.

[79] These included Agathon, who praised the speech afterwards (Aristotle *Eudemian Ethics* 1232b7–9).

[80] See Johnstone 1999.

procedural innovation, but he constructs most of the rest of the speech around this procedural attack: from the presentation of the facts to the question of motive, every argument is directed, at least in part, at portraying the prosecution as devious and dishonest "sykophants" interested only in financial profit. In 6, on the other hand, Antiphon does not directly comment on the unorthodox nature of the charge ("planning unintentional homicide"), directing his arguments instead to the larger political issues concerning the choregus's own public activities and the ulterior, ultimately political, motives of the plaintiff; the case becomes one of civic responsibility versus public criminal conduct.

The sole prosecution speech (1) gives Antiphon wider leeway in developing his strategy, though he is of course constrained by his client's situation: years after his father's death, the young man wants to bring a homicide charge against his stepmother, who was apparently not implicated at the time; he has little or no good evidence and must thus rely entirely on the power of Antiphon's logography. Here Antiphon must essentially create the evidence, from the challenge to interrogate slaves about a different incident that is only distantly related, to the vivid narrative of events in which the defendant explicitly reveals her intentions, to the recollection of the victim's deathbed plea. These elements, none of which is supported by other evidence, are integrated into the overall controlling model of a love-scorned wife scheming against her respectable husband, which is largely drawn from literary and mythological stereotypes.

In all three cases Antiphon devises strategies that are rational approaches to the particular circumstances. Certain features of his argument in each (especially in 5) might appear ineffective, like repetition, confusion, and even self-contradiction, and some of Antiphon's points undoubtedly failed to impress the jurors. But each speech has a clear basic structure in which the parts are well demarcated. The traditional division into preface, narrative, argument, and epilogue is loosely followed, though these categories oversimplify the reality in which different elements, especially narrative and argument, are often mixed together. More specifically, in both 1 and 5 we have prologue, argument, narrative, arguments,[81] and epilogue; and in 6, prologue, narrative, argument, narrative, and epilogue. There is some repetition and fragmentation of points, and some sections are more fully developed

---

[81] This long section of arguments in 5 (25–84) is subdivided into several clearly demarcated points: circumstantial evidence, the accounts of the slave and the free man, the note to Lycinus, motive, precedents against hasty judgment, his father, and divine signs.

than others, but it is clear that after devising an overall strategy, Antiphon organized his speeches into distinct parts.

Nonartistic proofs occur in all three speeches (as they do in many speeches by the other logographers), but they do not play an unusually large role in Antiphon's strategy in any of them. Arguments concerning oaths or challenges to torture are structured to fit the speaker's needs, and there is no trace of a world of automatic proofs, as Solmsen and others once suggested (see above, 6.1). Though there are obvious differences in detail, the intellectual world and legal context of Antiphon's day is not so different from our own, and the main task for a logographer, as for a trial attorney today, was to present the case in such a way that the jurors would not just arrive at the desired answers but would be asking the desired questions. In each case, Antiphon clearly takes control of his material and presents a coherent set of arguments tailored to the specific circumstances. Without knowing the facts or having any external evidence for his opponents' strategies, it is impossible fully to evaluate his success, but as I have indicated in the analysis of each case, I think each would have stood a fair chance of winning. Thus, we have no reason to doubt the tradition that Antiphon was successful in his career as a logographer.

Finally, we should note that in all three cases, the speaker devotes considerable attention to the conduct and motivation of his opponents before and during the trial. In 1, the stepson emphasizes the misplaced loyalties of his half-brother, who is conducting the defense; in 5, Euxitheus repeatedly returns to the charge that the prosecutors have fabricated the case against him and have violated normal procedures in order to gain a conviction; and in 6, the choregus engages in a sustained attack on the plaintiff's conduct, particularly his motive in bringing the case. These ad hominem arguments may be presented in an extended account (6.20–51) or spread throughout the speech, as in 1 and 5. In 6, especially, the personal attack appears to dominate the speech at the expense of the legal[82] issue of responsibility for the boy's death; and even in 1, the factual and legal questions concerning the accused's precise intentions seem to be of less interest to the speaker than her character and conduct in general. Such factors may lead a modern reader to conclude that Antiphon stressed the personal and political aspects of these contests at the expense of legal considerations. This conclusion would reinforce the currently popular view that Athenian trials were intended to pro-

---

[82] For the sense of "legal," see above, note 31.

vide competitions between individuals rather than decisions about factual and legal issues.[83]

But such a view is based on a false dichotomy. The attention paid to personal considerations in Antiphon's court speeches does not prevent speakers from treating the factual and legal issues of the case, though their treatment of these issues differed from what a modern reader might expect in two respects. First, the Athenians had a broader view of the "justice" they expected their judicial process to deliver, and would have considered communal norms of conduct to be valid legal considerations even if they were not written into statutory legislation. This is clear from the nature of Athenian statutes, which specified offenses in the most general terms ("impiety"), thereby forcing litigants and jurors to use communal norms to clarify the relevance of the statute to the case at hand. In 1, for example, modern law might take the question, Did the stepmother plan her husband's death? to mean, Did she knowingly intend to kill her husband? A fifth-century Athenian, however, would take the same question to mean, Did the stepmother plot against her husband using drugs that had the potential to kill him? This, not our modern question, is the issue Antiphon addresses. Similarly, in 6 the issue is, Was the choregus, by neglecting his duties, indirectly responsible for Diodotus's death? And in 5 Antiphon asks, Since the prosecutors' evidence is either lacking or contradictory and their arguments are muddled, is there any reason to accept their case, or is it not more plausible that they are simply looking for financial gain?

Second, we must bear in mind differences in material conditions between antiquity and today. Physical evidence was difficult to obtain and, when obtained, difficult to assess accurately. Is the drug (*pharmakon*) a poison or a beneficial potion? Is the note genuine or forged? The Athenians understood the importance of such evidence, but without an eyewitness to the crime or similarly conclusive evidence, one could almost never meet the standards of proof we require today. When the relatives of Herodes discovered blood in the boat where he was last seen, they thought they had conclusive evidence of his death, but it turned out to have come from an animal sacrifice. Their remaining evidence—the confession of the slave who allegedly assisted the murderer and an apparently incriminating letter—would have given them

---

[83] "At the core of the Athenian judicial *agōn* is the comparative judgment of the parties as citizens and social beings, not according to the statutory norms (which are often hardly discussed), but according to the normative expectations of the community" (Cohen 1995: 186).

as strong a case as one could reasonably expect. In such circumstances, Antiphon's concentration on the deficiencies (real or supposed) in the prosecution's handling of the case would be an effective and necessary strategy.

There are real differences between Athenian law and our own, but they are not so large as scholars often assume, especially if one considers modern law in practice (as some highly publicized cases have recently made clear).[84] And Antiphon's forensic strategies, directed as they are at the specific situations in each case, do not differ widely from strategies employed in court today.

7. CONCLUSION

In the last fifteen years of his life, Antiphon undertook, among other things, to compose speeches for litigants to deliver in court. By 420, use of the legal system had grown to the point that Aristophanes could make jurors the central subject of one of his plays (*Wasps*) and could have one of his characters joke that if no juries are sitting, the place cannot be Athens (*Clouds* 207–8). The forensic experience Athenians were thereby acquiring, together with the increased awareness of more sophisticated forensic strategies and methods of argumentation brought about by the Sophists, increasingly made the courts important battlegrounds for competing public figures as well as arenas where these figures could display skill and innovation in forensic discourse. Two of Antiphon's speeches (5, 6) show that others had also learned how to make the most of the legal system to advance their own interests, so that the forensic skill for which Antiphon became famous was not an isolated phenomenon.

In both of these cases, Antiphon was forced to devise a strategy to respond to a novel, or at least unorthodox, use of the legal system. In 5, he attacks this use of the law directly; in 6, he ignores it and directs his arguments to other matters. In his other speech (1), he sets the direction with his speech for the plaintiff, constructing a fairly strong case out of little or no evidence. These three speeches reveal a diverse range of strategies that can be fitted to the needs of the many different cases on which Antiphon was consulted. One overall feature of these strategies stands out, namely the ability to merge personal and political arguments with more narrowly legal and factual ar-

---

[84] Most notably, of course, the homicide trial of O. J. Simpson, where the issue of racism in the U.S., thought by many to be extraneous to the legal issues in the case, played a significant role, whereas the forensic evidence, strong as it was, failed to win a conviction.

guments. Without any other examples of forensic oratory from this period, we cannot say whether this was common to many litigants or an innovation of Antiphon, but in any case he was clearly expert at bringing these different considerations together into a single case. From these three speeches alone, it is not hard to see why his reputation was so high.

VII. FROM THE SOPHISTS
TO FORENSIC ORATORY

I. THE COMPLETE ANTIPHON

As we have seen (above, 2.1), most ancient authorities did not distinguish another Antiphon ("the Sophist") from Antiphon of Rhamnus. As far as we can tell, those who did make this distinction did so for stylistic reasons and had no biographical information about this supposed other Antiphon; and the Antiphon described by Thucydides so resembles a typical Sophist that he would probably have been considered a Sophist by many of his contemporaries and would thus be the most likely source for Xenophon's character "Antiphon the Sophist." In subsequent chapters, examination of the various works attributed to Antiphon shows that these share many common features, most notably an interest in law, justice, and the nature of *logos*. Perhaps even more important is a common approach or attitude that challenges traditional views and explores novel ideas and methods of argument. This attitude is naturally more evident in the Tetralogies and sophistic treatises than in the court speeches, but even these show clear traces of it, especially in his last speech in his own defense.

There are also, of course, some important differences among these three groups of works, but these can in large part be attributed to their different forms and purposes: the Tetralogies and *Truth* were intended to be read by students and other intellectuals. The former were an experiment in using the new form of *Antilogiae* to explore legal and philosophical issues; the latter has the form of a standard treatise, though the method is questioning, not dogmatic. *Concord* may have been intended for oral presentation to a larger, less intellectual audience; it challenges common views, but in a more constructive and moralistic fashion. The court speeches were composed for oral delivery to a group of jurors, though Antiphon's last speech, which was written down and later circulated, was also aimed at a wider audience. These differences affected the contents of the works, their methods of argument, and their styles, leading some ancient scholars who found them all grouped under the name Antiphon to question whether the same man could have written so differently. In part, this question reflects the spirit of the Hellenistic age, when generic categories were more clearly established and prose styles were being studied, categorized, and differentiated. Such divisions were relatively unknown in the late fifth century, when prose texts, especially Attic prose, were still a relative novelty, and experimentation with forms and styles of discourse was common. In such an intellectual climate, it is readily understandable that one man could produce this diversity of works.

2. STYLE

Since antiquity, the criterion of style has been used to divide Antiphon, for the sophistic treatises differ stylistically from the court speeches, as do the Tetralogies. Whatever the differences, it is clear that Antiphon paid considerable attention to style. His earlier works were aimed at other intellectuals,[1] and he therefore wrote them in a complex, analytical style generally unsuited for oral delivery, a style that was to influence the historian Thucydides (said by some to have been Antiphon's pupil). Later, since he was the first to write speeches for delivery in court, he had no models to follow other than the extemporaneous oral discourses he would have heard there. He was thus forced to create a new style, different from the intellectual argumentation of his other works, that would be more suitable for oral delivery.[2] The resulting speeches may not achieve the vividness and smoothness we find in Lysias's work, but they provide clear narratives and forceful arguments, and compare favorably with the speeches of his closest successor, Andocides, who can give a good narrative account but has no skill for argument.

Thus Antiphon's style changed over time. When he began writing, perhaps as early as 450, Attic prose was still in its infancy, and Ionic was the common dialect of intellectual communication. Even if the report that his father was a Sophist and had a school is not true,[3] as a young, wealthy aristocrat with intellectual interests and abilities, Antiphon would certainly have been exposed both to visiting Sophists and other intellectuals (such as medical teachers) and to a range of intellectual discourses written primarily

---

[1] Although we cannot date the Tetralogies or the treatises with any certainty, they are very likely earlier than the surviving court speeches, which may all date from the last eight years of Antiphon's life.

[2] For more on the differences between writing for oral delivery and writing for circulation to readers, see Gagarin 1999.

[3] [Plutarch] *Moralia* 832c; see Edwards (1998: 83–85), and below, 7.5.

in the Ionic dialect. It is thus not surprising that Ionicisms creep into the Tetralogies,[4] which may have been his earliest compositions, and perhaps also occasionally into his sophistic works.[5] When Antiphon came to write speeches that would be delivered in court, however, not only was he careful not to admit any Ionic forms, but he also reduced considerably the intensely intellectual quality of his style (above, 3.7). In the court speeches, sentences are generally less complex than in the Tetralogies, the clusters of adjectival participles characteristic of the Tetralogies are reduced, and oral markers like *touto men . . . touto de* become more common.[6] This sort of development is only to be expected, and is perfectly consistent with the view that the same person wrote all these works.

3. ARGUMENT

In the Tetralogies, Antiphon experiments with the new, sophistic form of discourse called *Antilogiae,* or "opposed arguments," which was invented by Protagoras and was popular among the Sophists. The Tetralogies are the only examples we know where each side is represented by two *logoi,* a form that copies, and probably was inspired by, the procedure in Athenian homicide cases and certain other private suits. Although the Tetralogies imitate a trial, however, they differ significantly from actual forensic discourses. They set narrow parameters for the argument, allowing both sides to focus on a limited range of issues and forms of argument; individual arguments in the opposed *logoi* can respond directly to one another, as they often did not in court speeches; and no verdict on the merits of the opposed *logoi* is explicitly indicated. The overall purpose of a Tetralogy cannot be to persuade jurors; rather, its purpose is to explore interesting and important new ideas about or perspectives on the issues raised by a certain type of case. This antilogistic structure suggests, moreover, that readers should not expect to judge one side right and the other wrong, but rather that they should treat the *logoi* on both sides as having at least some validity, and should look to both for help in furthering their understanding of the issues they raise.

---

[4]Dover 1950: 57–58. Note that both the "Old Oligarch," written in Attic perhaps around 430, and the *Dissoi Logoi,* written in Doric around 400, contain occasional Ionic forms (Treu 1967: 1976; Robinson 1979: 89 n. 63).

[5]Possible Ionic usages are ἥδοντα in *Truth* (44B4.17–18, see above, chapter 3, note 58) and δειμαίνει in *Concord* (58 DK).

[6]Dover (1950: 56–59) supplies the evidence, though his own focus is on the dating of the Tetralogies and court speeches.

The structure of opposing *logoi* representing different perspectives on an act or event is also incorporated, though in a rather different form, into *Truth*. Here Antiphon introduces the two perspectives with a single voice, proposing, for instance, both that justice is conformity to the law and that justice is not wronging anyone who has not wronged you. These views are not resolved in *Truth* (at least not in the text that survives) any more than in the Tetralogies, and thus here, too, the reader is left with the sense that the opposed views both have some validity. On the other hand, Antiphon also seems to be urging the reader, as the defendant in Tetralogy 2 urges the jurors, to recognize that each perspective has its limitations, and that an impartial consideration may be able to determine a more comprehensive truth based on everything that has been said (3.4.1–2).[7] Thus an intelligent reader can reach an understanding beyond the opposed *logoi* of the Tetralogies and beyond the two perspectives juxtaposed in *Truth*. The possibility of greater understanding is also urged in several fragments of *Concord,* which suggest that the limitations of traditional human perceptions and judgments can be overcome by the application of intellect, a view perhaps grounded in a theory of perception set forth at the beginning of *Truth*. *Concord* may be directed at a more popular audience, for it tends to state, or at least imply, the truer or better view, whereas *Truth* and the Tetralogies force readers to think through the consequences for themselves; but there is an essential consistency in the views all these works convey.

Naturally, the court speeches must employ different methods. They must convey one side of an issue and claim that it is true or just and that the other side is not. They must also include the full range of issues and arguments that might support the case. But the court speeches nonetheless show the influence of the methods of argument of the other works. This is most evident in the similarities between the arguments in Tetralogy 1 and those in Antiphon 5, both cases where some evidence points to the defendant as the killer but the case is far from conclusive. Tetralogy 1 is primarily devoted to probability arguments, but the speakers also explore the role of probability arguments and acknowledge the greater importance of facts where these are available. They also seek to support their cases with facts as well as probabilities, the plaintiff by citing the evidence of the witness just before he died,

---

[7] "You [jurors] must recognize that since we litigants judge the action (*to pragma*) from our own point of view, we both naturally (*eikotōs*) think we speak with justice (*dikaia legein*). You, however, must examine the facts (*ta prachthenta*) impartially (*isōs*), for their truth (*alētheia*) is only discernible from what has been said (*ek tōn legomenōn*)."

the defendant by invoking a strong alibi. The defendant in 5 also invokes facts, namely his alibi, supported by witnesses, and probability arguments both in support of his own innocence and in his attack on his opponents' procedures and motives. Neither the facts nor the probability arguments are as straightforward or conclusive in 5, for the nature of real cases is such that straightforward and conclusive arguments are rarely available. But Tetralogy 1's exercise of combining and assessing facts and probability displays the same skills as the more complex interweaving of the two in Antiphon 5.[8]

Antiphon 6, on the other hand, consciously avoids the subtle arguments of the defendant in Tetralogy 2; it gives no analysis of the complexities of cause and responsibility, and directs its attention instead to the plaintiff's conduct. The reasons for this are clearly foreshadowed in Tetralogy 2, when the defendant asks the jurors not to hold it against him if he speaks with more subtlety than usual (3.2.2). Speakers in court in the late fifth century had the difficult task of finding the right level of complexity, somewhere between a subtlety that might satisfy intellectuals and a simplemindedness that would appeal to the least educated of the jurors.

4. THOUGHT

Two general subjects stand out as of special concern to Antiphon: first, nature, law, and justice; and second, words, deeds, and truth. The first occupies most of the text of the papyrus fragments of *Truth*, though these probably give an unbalanced impression of the work as a whole; the second issue is explored implicitly in *Truth* and explicitly in the Tetralogies. To understand the connections between these and the rest of Antiphon's works with regard to these two interrelated subjects, it is best to start from the conclusions we reached in chapter 3.

As we saw, in *Truth* Antiphon first locates justice in the matrix of *nomos* ("law") and *physis* ("nature"); on one account, at least, justice requires adherence to the former, even though this imposes restrictions on behavior where the latter does not. There are good reasons for obeying justice under some circumstances, but at other times justice may be harmful, both in unnecessarily requiring a person to act in ways not required by *physis* (B3) and

---

[8] On one issue, the desirability of producing an alternative explanation, 5 seems to reject the implication of Tetralogy 1, that the likelihood of another person being the criminal adds support to the defendant's claim of innocence. In 5, the defendant explicitly refuses to suggest a different murderer and justifies this position with very different arguments from those in Tetralogy 1 (5.64–66).

in putting innocent persons at a relative disadvantage (C1–2). Antiphon seems to suggest that these harmful effects are a consequence of the existing system of justice (which, as far as it is described, is Athenian)[9] and are not necessarily inherent in all systems of justice per se. He seems to imply that society would benefit from improving the existing system of justice, in part by making punishment more certain and by giving victims a greater advantage in bringing those who wronged them to justice.[10]

Although *Truth* appears to pose a strong opposition between *nomos* and *physis,* the work also suggests a breakdown in this polarity and a closer union of the two (see above, 3.6). *Concord* also implies that justice may often be to one's own advantage. And Tetralogy 3 suggests further connections between justice and *physis,* notably when the plaintiff maintains that justice is grounded in the divine nature of humans: the law rightly prohibits anyone from destroying the life that the god has created (4.1.2–3).[11] And the defendants in both Antiphon 5 and 6 maintain that the homicide laws have the support of the gods, so that to violate them is to disobey the gods (6.3–5, cf. 5.81–84). The law (*nomos*) prohibiting just and unjust homicide, which is introduced into Tetralogies 2 and 3, suggests a similar view, that justice prohibits any destruction of life. And the speakers for the defense in Tetralogy 3 also indicate a difference between *physis* and likelihood (*eikos*): they respond to the argument that the young are more likely to get drunk and start a fight by observing, in an echo of the view of *physis* presented in *Truth,* that there is a difference between behavior that is natural (*kata physin*), such as seeing with the eyes and hearing with the ears, and behavior that is likely, such as that the young are more likely to get drunk (4.4.2). This suggests that natural behavior is certain and thus is a more legitimate concern of justice than likely behavior.

Litigants in court must praise justice, of course, and claim its support, but their view of justice is broad, encompassing the social and political context of behavior, and emphasizing the overall conduct of the two parties as citizens in the community. This emphasis encourages the inclusion of ad

---

[9] Although he criticizes aspects of Athenian legal procedure, in what survives, at least, Antiphon does not reflect the criticism of Athenian jurors found in Aristophanes' *Wasps* (produced in 422).

[10] In the last two decades of the fifth century, Athenians became more concerned about people bringing false claims of wrongdoing against innocent people (the so-called sykophants); the views expressed in 44C suggest that *Truth* predates these concerns.

[11] The word *physis* is not used here, but repetition of the root *phy-* suggests the connection of god and nature (see above, chapter 5, note 60).

hominem arguments, in which litigants try to enhance their own standing and discredit their opponents. Attacks on one's opponents' general conduct are evidently not considered diversions from the central issue of justice, as they might be today, but rather are presented as central to the justice of the case and may occur in close proximity to expressions of strong support for law and justice. This practice, which continues in fourth-century forensic discourse, may have been introduced by Antiphon, but it may also have been a feature of Athenian law before he began writing speeches. Furthermore, when speakers note deficiencies in the legal system, which is rare, they do so only obliquely, as when Euxitheus notes that innocent men have in the past been convicted (5.67, 69–70). They are more likely to blame their opponents' misuse of the system (as in Antiphon 5 and 6) for problems that in an objective assessment such as we find in *Truth* would be ascribed to the legal system. But although court speeches must mute their criticisms of the legal system, Antiphon's ability to devise different forensic strategies to meet different challenges reveals a thorough understanding of the legal system, including its weaknesses.

Antiphon's other major interest is truth and its relation to words and deeds. The surviving fragments of *Truth* do not give us a clear picture of his views on this, but as we saw (3.6), they suggest that on one level, all three are ambivalent. Multiple senses of a word may correspond to multiple aspects of reality, so that although truth lies in the correspondence of word and deed, correspondence does not yield a single, unequivocal truth. On the other hand, beyond this level there may be a larger "truth of things" that encompasses these multiple truths.

Antiphon may have made his views on this matter clearer in parts of *Truth* that no longer survive, perhaps even in the columns that immediately followed 44B. At the end of B6 he raises the issue of persuasion in his criticism of the legal process:

> For [the victim] must persuade the punishers [i.e., the jurors] that he suffered, or else be able to obtain justice by deception. But these means are also available to the agent, ⟨if he wishes⟩ to deny . . . (B7) the defendant has as long for his defense as the plaintiff for his accusation, and there is an equivalent opportunity for persuasion for the victim and for the agent.

At this point the papyrus becomes very fragmentary, and the remaining letters have been supplemented in various ways, but all the suggested restorations provide a text that continues to talk about words (*rhēmata*). It may have continued by observing, "For victory lies in words."[12] In B6 persuasion is apparently opposed to deception, and by implication, therefore, is linked to truth. In B7 Antiphon may have continued with further discussion of *logos*, persuasion, and truth, though we can only guess what he might have said.

There is much more discussion of words and truth in the Tetralogies, especially Tetralogy 2 (above, 5.4), where the defendant is particularly concerned to present "the truth of things,"[13] as he sees it, and urges the jurors also to determine this truth from their own, disinterested perspective, which encompasses the two different truths presented by the litigants. The court speeches also treat this issue, though, not surprisingly, they show more skepticism about *logoi* than do the other works. Litigants are particularly likely to call their opponents' *logoi* deceptive and unreliable in comparison with the facts. As the choregus puts it, they can say whatever they want, but facts are facts; "I do not think that what happened depends on my opponents' words but on justice and truth" (6.18). Euxitheus, too, attacks his opponents on this score: "Others test *logoi* against the facts (*erga*), but these men are trying to use their arguments to make you disbelieve the facts" (5.84). And in a similar vein, both of Antiphon's defendants urge the jurors not to judge the quality of the laws on the basis of their opponents' words, but to judge their words by the laws (5.14 = 6.2).[14]

On the other hand, words can provide important support as long as they correspond to the facts. The choregus analyzes his own case as follows (6.30–31):

If someone should present the facts (*ta prachthenta*) with speech (*logos*) without furnishing any witnesses, one would say his words are in need

---

[12] B7.13–15: ἐγίγ]νετο· ἡ / γὰρ ν[ίκη ῥή/μασι κ[εῖται.

[13] Robinson 1979: 236, commenting on *Dissoi Logoi* 8.12, where the same expression occurs, suggests that τῶν πραγμάτων ἡ ἀλήθεια ("the truth of things") may have been a "sophistic catch-phrase (and perhaps even a specifically Protagorean one)." Similar expressions are common in the Tetralogies (2.4.1; 3.2.2, 3.2.3, 3.2.10, 3.3.3).

[14] See also the prologue to Euxitheus's speech (5.1–7), especially 5.3: "Before now many who lacked speaking ability were unconvincing in telling the truth and were destroyed for this very reason, that they were unable to make the truth clear; but many others who had speaking ability were convincing with their lies and were saved in this way, because they lied. Therefore, when someone is inexperienced in legal contests, he is forced to address himself to the prosecution's arguments (*logoi*) rather than to the actual events (*erga*) and the truth of what happened (ἡ ἀλήθεια τῶν πραγμάτων)."

of witnesses; and if someone should furnish witnesses without making clear the inferences (*tekmēria*) that follow from these witnesses, one could make the same objection, if one wanted. But I am now making clear to you plausible words (*logoi eikotes*), and witnesses who agree with these words, and facts (*erga*) that agree with the witnesses, and inferences (*tekmēria*) derived from these very facts.

The choregus here presents a chain of factors that have joined together to support his case, though in fact they are all reducible to the basic categories of words and deeds: the testimony of witnesses falls into the category of facts, and the inferences that follow from the facts take the form of arguments or words. Thus the choregus is essentially claiming that his *logoi* should be accepted because they agree with and support the *erga*, which in turn agree with and support his *logoi*.

Finally, to the extent that probability (*eikos*) arguments are used in the court speeches,[15] these, too, belong to the realm of *logos*. Tetralogy 1 assumes an opposition between likelihood and fact throughout; Euxitheus moves explicitly from facts to probabilities at the end of his initial narrative (5.25); and the choregus in the passage just cited (6.31) calls his *logoi* plausible (*eikotes*). Tetralogy 3 adds that probable behavior is not the same as natural conduct, like seeing with the eyes (4.4.2). The overall structure of all these remarks, then, suggests that Antiphon would have accepted on some level the linking of *nomos, logos,* and *eikos* as opposed to *physis* and *ergon,* though from a larger perspective this polarity would break down, revealing an overall unity in them that is ultimately Truth.

5. THE CAREER OF ANTIPHON

Antiphon was born around 480 to an old and wealthy family from the deme Rhamnus, where the family probably still lived. Rhamnus was on the northeast coast of Attica facing the island of Euboea. It had a good harbor, from which a considerable amount of trade was carried out, so that it was probably more cosmopolitan than most rural demes. It is reported[16] that

---

[15] Probability arguments have no significant role in Antiphon 1.

[16] As Edwards (1998) shows, although scholars have tended to dismiss out of hand much of the information in the account of Antiphon's life preserved in [Plutarch] *Moralia* 832b–834b, most of it is not contradicted by other known facts. This is not to say the account is entirely true; but scholars should be more willing to allow the possibility that much of it may be accurate.

Antiphon's father Sophilus had a school and was (later) a Sophist.[17] Thus the young Antiphon, though raised with traditional, aristocratic values, was probably well educated and would have been exposed from a young age to people from around the Greek world (and beyond) as well as to the current ideas and activities of the new intellectuals, later to be called Sophists, who were beginning to make their presence felt around this time. He must have known the works of such figures as Protagoras, and he probably had personal contact with many other intellectuals when they visited Athens and on other occasions, such as at the Olympic festival.

By around 450 or shortly afterwards, the institutions of Athenian democracy, including the lawcourts, had reached the forms in which they remained more or less unchanged for the next half century.[18] In particular, the reforms of Ephialtes in 462 had resulted in an expansion of the number and importance of the popular courts. Pericles' introduction of pay for jurors around 450 was undoubtedly connected with this expansion,[19] since more and more jurors were needed, and the practice of requiring that certain kinds of case involving litigants from cities allied to Athens be tried in Athens further added to the prominence of the courts.[20] The young Antiphon must have followed these developments closely, and even if he himself attempted to stay in the background (as Thucydides later reports), he undoubtedly had friends who became involved in public affairs and who also regularly found themselves in court. Under these political conditions, the combination of the advantages of Antiphon's family background, his interest in the political and legal affairs of the city (even if only expressed in private), and his intellectual acumen made him a leading native Athenian thinker. Issues of law and justice were of special interest to him, but he also expressed views, often provocatively, on many of the other issues of the day, including geometry, cosmology, and the pseudo-science of dream-interpretation.

Antiphon's first written works were probably the Tetralogies, most likely composed between 450 and 430. These took the exercise of composing opposing speeches (*Antilogiae*)—the new form of intellectual expression pioneered by Protagoras—expanded it from two to four *logoi* on the model of certain Athenian trials, and used this tetralogical structure to explore issues relating to law, justice, and forensic argument. These experimental and pro-

---

[17] To say that Sophilus was a Sophist means only that he was an intellectual with a public presence, for "Sophist" was not a fixed title at the time.

[18] Ostwald 1986: esp. 47–83.

[19] The pay was raised again by Cleon, probably in 425.

[20] [Xenophon] *Constitution of the Athenians* ("The Old Oligarch") 1.16–18.

vocative *logoi* must have impressed other intellectuals for their boldness and skill in argument. They were presumably read by Antiphon's students (if reports that he was a teacher are correct), but they would have appealed to their readers' general intellectual interests and would not have provided training in the specific skills and techniques of litigation. Perhaps a bit later Antiphon composed his intellectual treatises, *Truth* and *Concord*, which explore a wider range of issues than the Tetralogies in a less dramatic format but maintain the same experimental and provocative attitude and continue to employ the technique of juxtaposing opposing viewpoints. The largest surviving fragment shows Antiphon putting his own stamp on the discussion of *nomos* and *physis*, which was one of the major topics of interest to the Sophists at this time; for Antiphon, the relation between nature and law is particularly relevant to the issue with which he is most concerned, namely justice.

Antiphon may have continued to teach during this period; certainly he remained intellectually active, and his intelligence, his ability to express himself well, his interest in both the theory of justice and the practical workings of the Athenian legal system, and his continuing desire to remain behind the scenes made him a sought-after adviser by others who were involved in litigation, especially those whose cases were particularly difficult. It was presumably this work of advising friends and associates (some of whom were prominent public figures) about forthcoming litigation that gave him the idea, some time after 430, of writing an entire speech for a litigant to memorize and deliver in court. He soon built a reputation for expertise in this new art of logography, which occupied him for the last fifteen years of his life.

Although the idea of writing a speech for someone else to deliver may seem unremarkable in retrospect, the possibilities of this practice were far from obvious at the time. Alphabetic writing had been known in Greece for more than three centuries, but only recently had the Sophists begun to use writing to communicate their ideas, and literacy, however one defines it, was still not common. For most fifth-century Athenians, communication was largely oral. Speaking in public was widespread, of course, not least in the litigation process, where the oral pleas of the litigants comprised nearly the entire trial. But no speaker had thought to write out a speech before delivering it, let alone to write one for someone else. To take a form of communication hitherto used for special tasks and a limited area of intellectual discourse and use it for assistance in communicating with a large popular audience was a bold innovation that, like other sophistic activity, was controversial not just in Antiphon's own day but well into the fourth century. A decade after his death, however, the practice of logography had grown rapidly and soon became the leading form of public discourse in Athens.

During the last two decades of his life, Antiphon probably continued to be active in other ways as well, teaching, engaging in sophistic discussions and debates, and discussing with friends the political affairs of Athens. The ongoing war with Sparta was in everyone's mind and would have focused attention on the strengths and weaknesses of Athenian leaders and institutions. Many of the cases for which Antiphon composed speeches were of a political nature or involved prominent public figures, and his legal consulting would thus have overlapped considerably with political consulting. Finally, after the Athenian defeat in Sicily in 413, Antiphon took the step from political consulting to political action, as he and some friends planned a course of action that they claimed would make the Athenian democracy more efficient and responsible. In 411 they engineered a coup, installing a group of 400 as leaders of the city, supported by a council of 5,000. When this new structure failed to achieve any significant improvements, the government rapidly fell apart, and the previous democratic institutions were reinstated. Almost all the 400 left Athens, but Antiphon remained to face trial; he must have known his chances for acquittal were slim. His speech in his own defense apparently refused to admit any wrong, claiming that his aim was to preserve the democracy under which he had prospered, not to overthrow it. His arguments were uncompromisingly rational and must have appeared sophistic to many of the jurors, though they drew the admiration of Thucydides and others, and the speech remained one of his most highly regarded throughout antiquity. It failed to win him acquittal, however, and shortly afterwards he was executed, his property was confiscated, and his family was sent into exile.

Antiphon's career was an unusual mixture: a political leader who for most of his life avoided public prominence, and a sophistic thinker whose main influence was not on later thinkers[21] but on a new genre of public discourse, forensic oratory. We can only speculate what personal qualities caused him to remain in the background politically, but his intellectual qualities are more evident. Although he was broadly interested in almost all the major sophistic issues of the day, from the beginning his main interests were issues of law and justice. In this area his intellectual and practical interests combined to produce not only innovative intellectual studies in the dramatic form of trials, but also practical advising and consulting about litigation and forensic strategies, and finally, the composition of full forensic discourses for practical use.

---

[21] Plato only mentions him as a teacher of rhetoric, and Aristotle cites him only in connection with his views on the nature of matter and on squaring the circle.

This last accomplishment is his main legacy, for logography and other forms of oratory became a major cultural institution in the fourth century and afterwards. It is traditionally (though misleadingly) said that rhetoric was invented in Sicily several decades before Antiphon began writing speeches.[22] But the theoretical work of Corax, Tisias, Gorgias, and others had a relatively narrow impact on Greek intellectual life until Antiphon turned it to practical use and created an institution that in the fourth century played a significant role in the lives many Athenians. Later critics, interested primarily in prose style, valued Antiphon less highly than some of his successors, and most of his works were lost before the modern era. But he deserves more credit than he has received as the pivotal link between the intellectual activity of fifth-century Sophists and the public oratory of fourth-century politicians and logographers.

---

[22] For a reassessment of this tradition, see Schiappa 1999.

APPENDIX A: *TRUTH:* THE PAPYRUS FRAGMENTS

The text of Fragment 44 follows Decleva Caizzi 1989.

44 (A2) ⟨The laws [the gods?] of nearby communities⟩ we know and respect, but those of communities far away we neither know nor respect. We have thereby become barbarian toward each other, when by nature (*physis*) we are all born in all respects equally capable of being both barbarians and Greeks. We can examine those attributes of nature that are necessary in all humans and are provided to all to the same degree, and in these respects none of us is distinguished as barbarian or Greek. For we all breathe the air through our mouth and our nostrils, and we laugh when our minds are happy **(A3)** or weep when we are pained, and we receive sounds with our hearing, and we see by the light with our sight, and we work with our hands and walk with our feet.

44 (B1) Justice (*dikaiosynē*) therefore is not violating the rules (*nomima*) of the city in which one is a citizen. Thus a person would best use justice to

(A2) . . . ρων
ἐπ[ιστάμε/θά τε κ[αὶ σέβομεν· /
τοὺς δὲ [τῶν τη/λοῦ οἰκ[ούν]των /
(5) οὔτε ἐπι[στ]άμε/θα οὔτε
σέβομεν. / ἐν τούτῳ οὖν / πρὸς
ἀλλήλους / βεβαρβαρώμε(10)θα,
ἐπεὶ φύσει γε / πάντα πάντες /
ὁμοίως πεφύκα/μεν καὶ βάρβα/ροι
καὶ ἕλληνες (15) εἶναι. σκοπεῖν /
δὲ παρέχει τὰ / τῶν φύσει [ὄντων /
ἀναγκαῖ[α ἐν / πᾶσιν
ἀν[θρώ(20)ποις, π[οριζόμενά / τε
κατὰ [τὰς αὐτὰς / δυνά[μεις ἅπασι,
/ καὶ ἐν [αὐτοῖς τού/τοις οὔτε
β[άρβα(25)ρος ἀφώρι[σται /
ἡμῶν ο[ὐδείς, / οὔτε ἕλην.
ἀ/ναπνέομεν / τε γὰρ εἰς τὸν
ἀ(30)έρ[α] ἅπαντες / κατὰ τὸ
στόμ[α / κ]αὶ κατ[ὰ] τὰς ῥῖ/νας
κ[αὶ γελῶ/με]ν χ[αίροντες τῷ **(A3)**
νῷ ἢ] δακρύ/ομε[ν] λυπού/μενοι·
καὶ τῇ ἀ/κοῇ τοὺς φθόγ(5)γους
εἰσδεχόμε/θα· καὶ τῇ αὐγῇ / μετὰ
τῆς ὄψε/ως ὁρῶμεν· καὶ / ταῖς
χερσὶν ἐρ(10)γαζόμεθα· καὶ / τοῖς
ποσὶν βαδ[ίζο/μεν .υβ[
(B1) (5) . . . νόμι/μον]
δικαιοσύνη / δ' οὖ]ν τὰ τῆς
πό/λεω]ς νόμιμα, / ἐν ᾗ] ἂν

his own advantage if he considered the laws (*nomoi*) important when witnesses are present, but the requirements of nature (*physis*) important in the absence of witnesses. For the requirements of the laws are supplemental, but the requirements of nature are necessary; and the requirements of the laws are by agreement and not natural, whereas the requirements of nature are natural and not by agreement. (**B2**) Thus someone who violates the laws avoids shame and punishment if those who have joined in agreement do not notice him, but not if they do. But if someone tries to violate one of the inherent requirements of nature, which is impossible, the harm he suffers is no less if he is seen by no one, and no greater if all see him; for he is harmed not in people's opinions (*doxa*) but in truth (*alētheia*). My inquiry into these things is prompted by the fact that most things that are just according to law are hostile to nature. For rules have been made for the eyes what they should (**B3**) and should not see, and for the ears what they should and should not hear, and for the tongue what it should and should not say, and for the hands what they should and should not do, and for the feet where they should and should not go, and for the mind what it should and should not desire. Thus the things from which the laws dissuade us are in no way less [more?] congenial or akin to nature than

πολι(10)τεύ]ηταί τις μὴ / παρ]αβαίνειν. / χρῶτ᾽ ἂν οὖν / ἄνθρωπος μά/λιστα ἑαυτῷ (15) ξυμφερόντως / δικαιοσύνῃ, εἰ / μετὰ μὲν μαρ/τύρων τοὺς νό/μους μεγά[λο]υς (20) ἄγοι, μονούμε/νος δὲ μαρτύ/ρων τὰ τῆς φύ/σεως· τὰ μὲν γὰρ / τῶν νόμων (25) ἐπί[θ]ετα, τὰ δὲ / τῆς] φύσεως ἀ/ναγ]καῖα· καὶ τὰ / μὲν] τῶν νό/μω]ν ὁμολογη(30)θέντ]α οὐ φύν/τα ἐστί]ν, τὰ δὲ / τῆς φύσ]εως φύν/τα οὐχ] ὁμολογη(B2)θέντα ⟦ουχ ο/μολογηθεν/τα⟧. τὰ οὖν νόμι/μα παραβαίνων (5) εἰ ἂν λάθῃ τοὺς / ὁμολογήσαντας / καὶ αἰσχύνης / καὶ ζημίας ἀ/πήλλακται, μὴ (10) λαθὼν δ᾽ οὔ· τῶν / δὲ τῇ φύσει ξυμ/φύτων ἐάν τι / παρὰ τὸ δυνατὸν / βιάζηται, ἐάν (15) τε πάντας ἀν/θρώπους λάθῃ, / οὐδὲν ἔλαττον / τὸ κακόν, ἐάν τε / πάντες ἴδωσιν, (20) οὐδὲν μεῖζον· οὐ γὰρ διὰ δόξαν / βλάπτεται, ἀλλὰ / δι᾽ ἀλήθειαν. ἔστι / δὲ τῶνδε ἕνε(25)κα τούτων ἡ σκέ/ψις, ὅτι τὰ πολλὰ / τῶν κατὰ νό/μον δικαίων / πολεμίως τῇ (30) φύσ[ει] κεῖται· νε/νο[μο]θ[έ]τηται / γὰρ ἐπί τε τοῖς ὀ/φθαλμοῖς, ἃ δεῖ (B3) αὐτοὺς ὁρᾶν καὶ / ἃ οὐ [δε]ῖ· καὶ ἐπὶ / τοῖς ὠσίν, ἃ δεῖ αὐ/τὰ ἀκούειν καὶ (5) ἃ οὐ δεῖ· καὶ ἐπὶ τῇ / γλώττῃ, ἅ τε / δεῖ αὐτὴν λέγειν / καὶ ἃ οὐ δεῖ· καὶ ἐ/πὶ ταῖς χερσίν, (10) ἅ τε δεῖ αὐτὰς δρᾶν / καὶ ἃ οὐ δεῖ· καὶ / ἐπὶ τοῖς ποσίν, ἐ/φ᾽ ἅ τε δεῖ αὐτοὺς / ἰέναι καὶ ἐφ᾽ οὐ (15) δεῖ· καὶ ἐπὶ τῷ νῷ, / ὧν τε δεῖ αὐτὸν / ἐπιθυμεῖν καὶ / ὧν μή. [ἧττο]ν οὖν / οὐδὲν τῇ φύσει (20) φιλιώτ[ερ]α οὐδ᾽ οἰ/κειότε[ρα] ἀφ᾽

the things toward which they urge us. For living and dying belong to nature, and for humans, living is the result of advantageous things, whereas dying is the result of disadvantageous things. (B4) The advantages laid down by the laws are bonds on nature, but those laid down by nature are free. Thus things that cause pain do not, according to a correct account (*orthos logos*), benefit nature more than things that cause joy. Nor would things that cause grief be more advantageous than things that cause pleasure; for things that are in truth advantageous must not harm but benefit. Thus things that are advantageous by nature . . . and those who (B5) defend themselves when attacked and do not themselves begin the action, and those who treat their parents well even when they have been badly treated by them, and those who let their opponent swear an oath when they have not sworn one themselves. One would find many of the things I have mentioned hostile to nature; and they involve more pain when less is possible and less pleasure when more is possible, and ill treatment that could be avoided. Thus, if the laws provided some assistance for those who engaged in such behavior, and some penalty for those who did not but did the opposite, (B6) then the tow-rope of the laws would not be without benefit. But in fact it is apparent that justice (*to dikaion*) derived from law is not sufficient

ὧν / οἱ νόμο[ι ἀ]ποτρέ/πουσι τοὺς
ἀν[θ]ρώπ[ους] / ἢ ἐφ' ἃ
[ἐπιτρέ(25)πουσ[ιν.] τ[ὸ γὰρ / ζῆν
ἐστι τῆς φύ/σεως κ[αὶ τ]ὸ
ἀπο/θαν[εῖ]ν, καὶ τὸ / μὲν ζῆν
αὐτ[οῖς (30) ἐστιν ἀπὸ τῶν /
ξυμ[φερό]ντων, / τὸ δὲ ἀ[ποθανεῖν
/ ἀπὸ τῶν μὴ ξυμ(B4)φερόντω[ν.
τὰ / δὲ ξυμφέρ[οντα, / τὰ μὲν ὑπ[ὸ
τῶν / νόμων κεί(5)μενα δεσμοὶ /
τῆς φύσεώς ἐ[στι, / τὰ δ' ὑπὸ τῆς
φύ/σεως ἐλεύθερα. [οὔ/κουν τὰ
ἀλγύ(10)νοντα ὀρθῷ γε λό/γῳ
ὀνίνησιν τὴν / φύσιν μᾶλλον / ἢ τὰ
εὐφραίνον/τα· οὔκουν [ἂ]ν
οὐ(15)δὲ ξυμφέρον/τ' εἴη τὰ
λυποῦ[ντα / μᾶλλον ἢ τ[ὰ
ἥ/δοντ[α·] τὰ γὰρ τῷ / ἀληθ[ε]ῖ
ξυμφέ(20)ρ[οντ]α οὐ βλά/π[τει]ν
δεῖ, ἀλ[λ' ὠ/φελεῖν. τὰ τοίνυν / τῇ
φύσει ξυμ/φέροντα [/ (25) / / /
/ (30) / / κα[ὶ / οἵτινε]ς ἂν
πα(B5)θόν]τες ἀμύνων/ται κ]αὶ μὴ
αὐτοὶ / ἄρχ]ωσι τοῦ δρᾶν· / καὶ
ο]ἵτινες ἂν (5) τοὺς] γειναμέ/νου]ς
καὶ κακοὺς / ὄντας εἰς αὐτοὺς / εὖ
ποιῶσιν· καὶ οἱ / κατόμνυσθαι (10)
διδόντες ἑτέ/ροις, αὐτοὶ δὲ μὴ /
κατομνύμε/νοι.] καὶ τούτων / τῶν
εἰρημένων (15) πόλλ' ἄν τις
εὕ/ροι πολέμια τῇ / φύσει· ἔνι τ' ἐν
αὐ/τοῖς ἀλγύνεσθαί / τε μᾶλλον,
ἐξὸν (20) ἥττω, καὶ ἐλάτ/τω
ἥδεσθαι, ἐξὸν / πλείω, καὶ κακῶς /
πάσχειν, ἐξὸν / μὴ πάσχειν. (25) εἰ
μὲν οὖν τις / τοῖς τοιαῦτα
προσ/ι]εμένοις ἐπικού/ρησις
ἐγίγνε/το] παρὰ τῶν νό(30)μων,
τοῖς δὲ μὴ / προσιεμένοις, ἀλλ'
ἐ]ναντιουμέ/νοις ἐλάττωσις, (B6)
οὐκ ἀν[ωφελὲς ἂν / ἦν τ[ὸ ἐν τοῖς
νό/μοις πεῖ[σμα· νῦν / δὲ φαίνε[ται
τοῖς (5) προσιεμ[ένοις / τὰ

to assist those who engage in such behavior. First, it permits the victim to suffer and the agent to act, and at the time it did not try to prevent either the victim from suffering or the agent from acting; and when it is applied to the punishment, it does not favor the victim over the agent; for he must persuade the punishers that he suffered, or else be able to obtain justice by deception. But these means are also available to the agent, ⟨if he wishes⟩ to deny . . . (B7) . . . the defendant has as long for his defense as the plaintiff for his accusation, and there is an equivalent opportunity for persuasion for the victim and for the agent.

44 (C1) To testify truthfully for one another is customarily thought (*nomizetai*) to be just (*dikaios*) and not less useful in human affairs. And yet one who does this will not be just if indeed it is just not to wrong (*adikein*) anyone, if one is not wronged oneself; for even if he tells the truth, someone who testifies must necessarily wrong another somehow, and will then be wronged himself, since he will be hated when the testimony he gives causes the person against whom he testifies to be convicted and lose his property or his life, all because of this man whom he has not wronged at all. He wrongs the person against whom he testifies for this reason, namely, that he wrongs someone who is not wronging

τοιαῦτα τὸ ἐ[κ / νόμου δίκαι[ον /
οὐχ ἱκανὸν ἐπι/κουρεῖν· ὅ γε
πρῶ(10)τον μὲν ἐπιτρέ/πει τῷ
πάσχον/τι παθεῖν καὶ τῷ / δρῶντι
δρᾶσαι· / καὶ οὔτε ἐνταῦ(15)θα
διεκώλυε τὸν / πάσχοντα μὴ /
παθεῖν, οὔτε τὸν / δρῶντα δρᾶσαι,
/ εἴς τε τὴν τιμω(20)ρίαν
ἀναφερό/μενον οὐδὲν / ἰδιώτερον
ἐπὶ / τῷ πεπονθότι / ἢ τῷ
δεδρακό(25)τι·] πεῖ[σ]αι γὰρ δ[εῖ /
αὐτὸν [το]ὺς τ[ιμω/ρ[ήσοντ]ας, ὡς
ἔ/παθεν, [ἢ] δύνα/σθαι ἀπ[άτ]ῃ
δί(30)κην [ἔχει]ν. ταύ/τὰ δὲ
καταλεί/πεται [ι] καὶ τῷ δρά/σαντ[ι
ἀ]ρνεῖσθαι (B7) / / / (5)
[ἀπο]λογ[οῦντί ἐ/στιν ἡ ἀπ[ολογία
/ ὅσηπερ τ[ῷ κα/τηγοροῦν[τι ἡ /
κατηγορ[ία, ἡ δὲ (10) πειθὼ
ἀν[τίπαλος / τῷ γε πε[πονθό/τι
καὶ τῷ [δεδρα/κότι ἐγίγ[νετο /
γὰρ. . . .

(C1) τοῦ δικαίου /
]ου δοκουν-/ . . . τὸ]
μαρτυρεῖν / ἐν ἀλ]λήλοις τἀληθῆ
(5) δίκαιο]ν νομίζεται / εἶναι] καὶ
χρήσιμον / οὐδέν] ἧττον εἰς / τὰ
τῶν] ἀνθρώπων / ἐπιτ]ηδεύματα.
(10) τοῦτο] τοίνυν οὐ δί/καιος]
ἔσται ὁ ποιῶν, / εἴπε]ρ τὸ μὴ
ἀδικεῖν / μηδ]ένα μὴ ἀδι/κού]μενον
αὐτὸν (15) δίκ]αιόν ἐστιν·
ἀνάγ/κη] γὰρ τὸν μαρτυ/ροῦ]ντα,
κἂν ἀλη/θῆ μ]αρτυρῇ, ὅμως /
ἄλλον π]ως ἀδικεῖν (20) εἶτα δὲ
α]ὐτὸν ἀ/δι]κεῖσθαι [ἐν μίσει / οὐ]ν
ἐνε[χόμενος. / ἐ]ν ᾧ διὰ τ[ὰ ὑπ'
ἐκεί/ν]ου μαρτ[υρηθέν(25)τα
ἁλίσκ[ε]ται ὁ κα/ταμαρτυρούμενος
/ καὶ ἀπόλλυσιν ἢ / χρήματα ἢ
αὐτὸν / δ]ιὰ τοῦτον ὃν οὐδὲν (30)
ἀ]δικεῖ, ἐν μὲν οὖν / τούτῳ τὸν
κατα/μ]αρτυρούμενον / ἀ]δικεῖ, ὅτι

him; and he is wronged by the
person against whom he testified,
in that he is hated by him (C2)
for having told the truth. And it
is not only that he is hated but
also that for his whole life he
must be on guard against the man
against whom he testified. As a
result, he has an enemy who will do
him whatever harm he can in word
or deed. Now, these things are
clearly no small injustices
(*adikēmata*), neither those he
suffers nor those he inflicts. For
it is impossible that these things
are just and that the rule not to
do wrong and not to be wronged
oneself is also just; on the
contrary, it is necessary that
either only one of these be just
or that they both be unjust.
Further, it is clear that,
whatever the result, trying cases,
giving verdicts, and holding
arbitration proceedings are not
just, since helping some people
hurts others. In the process, those
who are helped are not wronged,
while those who are hurt are wronged.

οὐκ ἀδι/κο]ῦντα ἑαυτὸν
ἀ(35)δι]κεῖ, αὐτὸς δ' ἀδικεῖ/ται
ὑ]πὸ τοῦ καταμαρ/τυρηθ]έντος,
ὅτι μι/σεῖται] ὑπ' αὐτοῦ
τὰ(C2)ληθῆ μαρτυ[ρή/σας· καὶ οὐ
μόν[ον / τῷ μίσει, ἀλλὰ κ[αὶ / ὅτι
δεῖ αὐτὸν τ[ὸν (5) αἰῶνα πάντα
φυ/λάττεσθαι τοῦτο[ν / οὗ
κατεμαρτύρ[η/σεν· ὡς ὑπάρχε[ι /
γ' αὐτῷ ἐχθρὸς τοιο[ῦ(10)τος, οἷος
καὶ λέγειν / καὶ δρᾶν εἴ τι δύν[αι/το
κακὸν αὐτόν. κα[ί/τοι ταῦτα
φαίνεται / οὐ σμικρὰ ὄντα
τὰ(15)δικήματα, οὔτε / ἃ αὐτὸς
ἀδικεῖται / οὔτε ἃ ἀδικεῖ· οὐ γὰρ /
οἷόν τε ταῦτά τε δί/καια εἶναι καὶ
τὸ μη(20)δ]ὲν ἀδικεῖν μη/δὲ] αὐτὸν
ἀδικεῖσθαι· / ἀλ]λ' ἀνάγκη ἐστὶν /
ἢ] τὰ ἕτερα αὐτῶν / δ]ίκαια εἶναι ἢ
ἀμ(25)φότερα ἄδικα. φαί/νεται δὲ
καὶ τὸ δικά/ζειν καὶ τὸ κρίνειν / καὶ
τὸ διαιτᾶν ὅπως / ἂν περαίνηται
οὐ (30) δίκαια ὄντα· τὸ γὰρ /
ἄ]λλους ὠφελοῦν ἄλ/λο]υς
βλάπτει· ἐν δὲ / τούτῳ οἱ μὲν
ὠφελού/μενο]ι οὐκ
ἀδικοῦ[ν(35)ται, οἳ] δὲ
βλαπτόμε[νοι / ἀδικο]ῦντα [ι.

APPENDIX B: *CONCORD:*
THE FRAGMENTS

48: Man,[1] who claims to be of all creatures the most godlike.

ἄνθρωπος, ὅς φησι μὲν πάντων θηρίων θεειδέστατον γενέσθαι.

49: Well, then, suppose his life moves on and he desires a wife. That day, that night begins a new spirit (*daimōn*), a new fate; for marriage is a great contest for a person. For if it should turn out to be unsuitable, what can he do about the situation? Divorce is difficult[2]—to make enemies out of friends who are like-minded, like-spirited, when he thought them worthy and was thought worthy by them. But it is difficult to possess such a possession—to marry pains expecting to possess pleasures. Well, then, let us not speak of the wretched aspects but suppose he speaks of the most congenial of all situations; for what is more pleasant for a man than a wife after his own heart? And what is sweeter, especially for a young man? But in fact, in this same place where pleasure resides, somewhere close by there is also pain, for one cannot traffic in pleasures by themselves, but pains and toils accompany them. Indeed, even Olympian victories and Pythian victories and similar contests, and intellectual accomplishments, and in fact all pleasures, tend to come as a result of many painful exertions; for honors, prizes—the baits that the god has set out for people—bring them to the necessity of great toil and sweat. For if I had a second body such as I the one I now have,[3] I would not be able to live, so many troubles do I cause myself for the health of my body, and for the daily necessities of life that

---

[1] I include all the substantial fragments (longer than three words) generally assigned to *Concord*. In an attempt to convey something of the style, the translations are fairly literal and, where possible, adhere to the Greek word order. I use the numbering and the Greek text of Diels-Kranz, except where noted.

[2] Legally, divorce was quite easy, but it could involve serious financial and social difficulties.

[3] I do not follow Diels-Kranz in adding ἐπιμελὲς ὄν to make the syntax more regular, since the manuscript text can be comprehended without supplement (see Gernet 1923: 182 n. 1).

must be gathered, and for my reputation and proper behavior and honor and good name. What, then, if I had another such body for which I was similarly concerned? Is it not clear that if a man has a wife after his own heart, the affection and pain she gives him will be no less than he gives himself, caring for the health of two bodies and for gathering their livelihood and for their proper behavior and their good name? Well then, suppose he also has children; everything is now full of concerns, and the youthful bounce is gone from his mind (*gnōmē*), and his face is no longer the same.

φέρε δὴ προελθέτω ὁ βίος εἰς τὸ πρόσθεν καὶ γάμων καὶ γυναικὸς ἐπιθυμησάτω. αὕτη ἡ ἡμέρα, αὕτη ἡ νὺξ καινοῦ δαίμονος ἄρχει, καινοῦ πότμου. μέγας γὰρ ἀγὼν γάμος ἀνθρώπῳ. εἰ γὰρ τύχοι μὴ ἐπιτηδεία γενομένη, τί χρὴ τῇ συμφορᾷ χρῆσθαι; χαλεπαὶ μὲν ἐκπομπαί, τοὺς φίλους ἐχθροὺς ποιῆσαι, ἴσα φρονοῦντας, ἴσα πνέοντας, ἀξιώσαντα καὶ ἀξιωθέντα· χαλεπὸν δὲ καὶ ἐκτῆσθαι κτῆμα τοιοῦτον, δοκοῦντα ἡδονὰς κτᾶσθαι λύπας ἄγεσθαι. φέρε δή, μὴ τὰ παλίγκοτα λέγωμεν, λεγέσθω τὰ πάντων ἐπιτηδειότατα. τί γὰρ ἥδιον ἀνθρώπῳ γυναικὸς καταθυμίας; τί δὲ γλυκύτερον ἄλλως τε καὶ νέῳ; ἐν τῷ αὐτῷ δέ γε τούτῳ, ἔνθα τὸ ἡδύ, ἔνεστι πλησίον που καὶ τὸ λυπηρόν. αἱ γὰρ ἡδοναὶ οὐκ ἐπὶ σφῶν αὐτῶν ἐμπορεύονται, ἀλλ' ἀκολουθοῦσιν αὐταῖς λῦπαι καὶ πόνοι. ἐπεὶ καὶ ὀλυμπιονῖκαι καὶ πυθιονῖκαι καὶ οἱ τοιοῦτοι ἀγῶνες καὶ σοφίαι καὶ πᾶσαι ἡδοναὶ ἐκ μεγάλων λυπημάτων ἐθέλουσι παραγίγνεσθαι· τιμαὶ γὰρ, ἆθλα, δελέατα, ἃ ὁ θεὸς ἔδωκεν ἀνθρώποις, μεγάλων πόνων καὶ ἱδρώτων εἰς ἀνάγκας καθιστᾶσιν. ἐγὼ γάρ, εἴ μοι γένοιτο σῶμα ἕτερον τοιοῦτον οἷον ἐγὼ ἐμαυτῷ, οὐκ ἂν δυναίμην ζῆν, οὕτως ἐμαυτῷ πολλὰ πράγματα παρέχων ὑπέρ τε τῆς ὑγιείας τοῦ σώματος ὑπέρ τε τοῦ καθ' ἡμέραν βίου ἐς τὴν ξυλλογὴν ὑπέρ τε δόξης καὶ σωφροσύνης καὶ εὐκλείας καὶ τοῦ εὖ ἀκούειν. τί οὖν, εἴ μοι γένοιτο σῶμα ἕτερον τοιοῦτον, ὅ γέ μοι οὕτως ἐπιμελὲς εἴη; οὐκ οὖν δῆλον, ὅτι γυνὴ ἀνδρί, ἐὰν ᾖ καταθυμία, οὐδὲν ἐλάττους τὰς φιλότητας παρέχεται καὶ τὰς ὀδύνας ἢ αὐτὸς αὑτῷ ὑπέρ τε τῆς ὑγιείας δισσῶν σωμάτων ὑπέρ τε τοῦ βίου τῆς συλλογῆς ὑπέρ τε τῆς σωφροσύνης καὶ τῆς εὐκλείας; φέρε δή, καὶ παῖδες γενέσθωσαν· φροντίδων ἤδη πάντα πλέα καὶ ἐξοίχεται τὸ νεοτήσιον σκίρτημα ἐκ τῆς γνώμης καὶ ⟨τὸ⟩ πρόσωπον οὐκέτι τὸ αὐτό.

50: Life is like a daytime watch-duty, and the length of life like one day, more or less, which we pass on to other successors after looking up at the light.

τὸ ζῆν ἔοικε φρουρᾷ ἐφημέρῳ τό τε μῆκος τοῦ βίου ἡμέρᾳ μιᾷ, ὡς ἔπος εἰπεῖν, ᾗ ἀναβλέψαντες πρὸς τὸ φῶς παρεγγυῶμεν τοῖς ἐπιγιγνομένοις ἑτέροις.

51: All of life is wonderfully easy to criticize, my friend; it has nothing outstanding or great and noble, but everything is small and weak and short-lived and mixed with great pains.

εὐκατηγόρητος πᾶς ὁ βίος θαυμαστῶς, ὦ μακάριε, οὐδὲν ἔχων περιττὸν οὐδὲ μέγα καὶ σεμνόν, ἀλλὰ πάντα σμικρὰ καὶ ἀσθενῆ καὶ ὀλιγοχρόνια καὶ ἀναμεμειγμένα λύπαις μεγάλαις.

52: It is not possible to take back one's life like a checker-piece.

ἀναθέσθαι δὲ ὥσπερ πεττὸν τὸν βίον οὐκ ἔστιν.

53: Those who work and are thrifty and endure hardship and accumulate things enjoy just the sorts of pleasures one would imagine they enjoy; but if they take things out and use them, they feel pain, as if they were taking out a piece of their own flesh.

οἱ δὲ ἐργαζόμενοι μὲν καὶ φειδόμενοι καὶ ταλαιπωροῦντες καὶ προστιθέντες ἥδονται οἷα δή τις ἂν εἰκάσειεν ἥδεσθαι. ἀφαιροῦντες δὲ καὶ χρώμενοι ἀλγοῦσιν ὥσπερ ἀπὸ τῶν σαρκῶν ἀφαιρούμενοι.

53a: There are those who do not live their present life but prepare themselves with great eagerness as if they were going to live some other life, not the present one; and in doing this, time passes them by and is gone.

εἰσί τινες οἳ τὸν παρόντα μὲν βίον οὐ ζῶσιν, ἀλλὰ παρασκευάζονται πολλῇ σπουδῇ ὡς ἕτερόν τινα βίον βιωσόμενοι, οὐ τὸν παρόντα· καὶ ἐν τούτῳ παραλειπόμενος ὁ χρόνος οἴχεται.

54: There is a story that when one man saw another man acquiring a lot of money, he asked him to lend it to him at interest; the man did not want to do this, but he was the sort not to trust or help anyone, and he took the money and stored it away somewhere. And someone saw him doing this and stole it; and some time later the man who hid the money went and did not find it. Greatly pained by his misfortune, therefore, especially because he had not granted the [first] man's request, in which case his money both would be safe and would be earning him more money, he met the man who had once wanted to borrow and lamented his misfortune, saying that he had made a mistake and that he was sorry he had not granted the man's request but had refused it, since his money was now all lost. But the man told him not to worry, but to put a stone in the same place and think he still had the money and had not lost it. "You were making no use at all of it when you had it, and so don't now think you have lost anything." For whatever someone has not used and is not going to use, he is not hurt any more or any less, if he has it or does not. For when god does not wish to give a man entirely good things, he gives him wealth of money but makes him poor in good sense—taking away the one, he deprives him of both.

ἔστι δέ τις λόγος, ὡς ἄρα ἰδὼν ἀνὴρ ἄνδρα ἕτερον ἀργύριον ἀναιρούμενον πολὺ ἐδεῖτό οἱ δανεῖσαι ἐπὶ τόκῳ· ὁ δ' οὐκ ἠθέλησεν, ἀλλ' ἦν οἷος ἀπιστεῖν τε καὶ μὴ ὠφελεῖν μηδένα, φέρων δ' ἀπέθετο ὅποι δή· καί τις καταμαθὼν τοῦτο ποιοῦντα ὑφείλετο· ὑστέρῳ δὲ χρόνῳ ἐλθὼν οὐχ εὕρισκε τὰ χρήματα ὁ καταθέμενος. περιαλγῶν οὖν τῇ συμφορᾷ τά τε ἄλλα καὶ ὅτι οὐκ ἔχρησε τῷ δεομένῳ, ὃ ἂν αὐτῷ καὶ σῶον ἦν καὶ ἕτερον προσέφερεν, ἀπαντήσας δὲ τῷ ἀνδρὶ τῷ τότε δανειζομένῳ ἀπωλοφύρετο τὴν συμφοράν, ὅτι ἐξήμαρτε καὶ ὅτι οἱ μεταμέλει οὐ χαρισαμένῳ, ἀλλ' ἀχαριστήσαντι, ὡς πάντως οἱ ἀπολόμενον τὸ ἀργύριον. ὁ δ' αὐτὸν ἐκέλευε μὴ φροντίζειν, ἀλλὰ νομίζειν αὐτῷ εἶναι καὶ μὴ ἀπολωλέναι, καταθέμενον λίθον εἰς τὸ αὐτὸ χωρίον. "πάντως γὰρ οὐδ' ὅτε ἦν σοι, ἐχρῶ αὐτῷ, ὅθεν μηδὲ νῦν νόμιζε στέρεσθαι μηδενός." ὅτῳ γάρ τις μὴ ἐχρήσατο μηδὲ χρήσεται, ὄντος ἢ μὴ ὄντος αὐτῷ οὐδὲν οὔτε πλέον οὔτε ἔλασσον βλάπτεται. ὅτῳ γὰρ ὁ θεὸς μὴ παντελῶς βούλεται ἀγαθὰ διδόναι ἀνδρί, χρημάτων πλοῦτον παρασχών, τοῦ καλῶς φρονεῖν ⟨δὲ⟩ πένητα ποιήσας, τὸ ἕτερον ἀφελόμενος ἀμφοτέρων ἀπεστέρησεν.

55: To delay where there is no need to delay.

ὀκνεῖν ἵνα οὐδὲν ἔργον ὀκνεῖν.

56: He would be a coward if, in the face of dangers that are far away and lie in the future, he is bold with his tongue and makes haste in his desire, but when the matter is at hand, he hangs back.

κακὸς δ' ἂν ⟨εἴη⟩, εἰ ⟨ἐπ'⟩ ἀπoῦσι μὲν καὶ μέλλουσι τοῖς κινδύνοις τῇ γλώττῃ θρασύνεται καὶ τῷ θέλειν ἐπείγει, τὸ δ' ἔργον ἂν παρῇ, ὀκνεῖ.

57: "Sickness is a holiday for cowards";[4] for they do not go to work.

"νόσος δειλοῖσιν ἑορτή." οὐ γὰρ ἐκπορεύονται ἐπὶ πρᾶξιν.

58: Whoever goes against his neighbor in order to do him harm but fears he may fail to do what he wishes but may achieve what he does not wish is very prudent (*sōphrōn*). For in his fear he delays, and in delaying often the intervening time turns his mind away from his wish; when it is accomplished it is not possible, but when one delays it is possible not actually to do it. And whoever thinks he can do his neighbors harm and not suffer harm is not prudent. Hopes are not altogether a good thing; for hopes have thrown many people into incurable disasters, and the harm they thought they would inflict on their neighbors, it turns out they have suffered it themselves. No one can judge the prudence (*sōphrosynē*) of another man better than one who himself resists the immediate pleasures of the heart and has been able to control and conquer himself. But whoever wants to gratify his heart immediately wants what is worse instead of what is better.

ὅστις δὲ ἰὼν ἐπὶ τὸν πλησίον κακῶς ποιήσων δειμαίνει, μὴ ἃ θέλει ποιῆσαι ἁμαρτὼν τούτων ἃ μὴ θέλει ἀπενέγκηται, σωφρονέστερος. ἐν ᾧ γὰρ δειμαίνει, μέλλει· ἐν ᾧ δὲ μέλλει, πολλάκις ὁ διὰ μέσου χρόνος ἀπέστρεψε τὸν νοῦν τῶν θελημάτων· καὶ ἐν μὲν τῷ γεγενῆσθαι οὐκ ἔνεστιν, ἐν δὲ τῷ μέλλειν ἐνδέχεται ⟨καὶ τὸ μὴ⟩ γενέσθαι. ὅστις δὲ δράσειν μὲν οἴεται τοὺς πέλας κακῶς, πείσεσθαι δ' οὔ, οὐ σωφρονεῖ. ἐλπίδες δ' οὐ πανταχοῦ ἀγαθόν· πολλοὺς γὰρ τοιαῦται ἐλπίδες κατέβαλον εἰς ἀνηκέστους συμφοράς, ἃ δ' ἐδόκουν τοῖς πέλας ποιή-

---

[4] These words could fit the meter of the end of a line of dactylic hexameter verse; therefore Diels-Kranz conclude that Antiphon is quoting a proverb.

σειν, παθόντες ταῦτα ἀνεφάνησαν αὐτοί. σωφροσύνην δὲ ἀνδρὸς οὐκ ἂν ἄλλου ὀρθότερόν τις κρίνειεν, ἢ ὅστις τοῦ θυμοῦ ταῖς παραχρῆμα ἡδοναῖς ἐμφράσσει αὐτὸς ἑαυτὸν κρατεῖν τε καὶ νικᾶν ἠδυνήθη αὐτὸς ἑαυτόν. ὃς δὲ θέλει χαρίσασθαι τῷ θυμῷ παραχρῆμα, θέλει τὰ κακίω ἀντὶ τῶν ἀμεινόνων.

59: Whoever has neither desired nor experienced shameful or evil things is not prudent (*sōphrōn*); for there is nothing that he himself has overcome to make himself orderly (*kosmion*).

ὅστις δὲ τῶν αἰσχρῶν ἢ τῶν κακῶν μήτε ἐπεθύμησε μήτε ἥψατο, οὐκ ἔστι σώφρων· οὐ γὰρ ἔσθ᾽ ὅτου κρατήσας αὐτὸς ἑαυτὸν κόσμιον παρέχεται.

60: First, I think, among human activities is education. For whenever someone makes a correct beginning of anything whatsoever, its end is also likely to turn out correctly. For whatever seed one plants in the earth, he should expect the harvest to be similar; and whenever one plants an excellent education in a young body, it lives and thrives during its entire life, and neither storm nor drought destroys it.

πρῶτον, οἶμαι, τῶν ἐν ἀνθρώποις ἐστὶ παίδευσις· ὅταν γάρ τις πράγματος κἂν ὁτουοῦν τὴν ἀρχὴν ὀρθῶς ποιήσηται, εἰκὸς καὶ τὴν τελευτὴν ὀρθῶς γίγνεσθαι. καὶ γὰρ τῇ γῇ οἷον ἄν τις τὸ σπέρμα ἐναρόσῃ, τοιαῦτα καὶ τὰ ἔκφορα δεῖ προσδοκᾶν· καὶ ἐν νέῳ σώματι ὅταν τις τὴν παίδευσιν γενναίαν ἐναρόσῃ, ζῇ τοῦτο καὶ θάλλει διὰ παντὸς τοῦ βίου, καὶ αὐτὸ οὔτε ὄμβρος οὔτε ἀνομβρία ἀφαιρεῖται.

61: There is nothing worse for people than unruliness (*anarchia*). People in the past knew these things and from the beginning accustomed their sons to be ruled and to do what they were told, so that when they reached manhood, they would not be shocked if they encountered a great change of circumstances.

ἀναρχίας δ᾽ οὐδὲν κάκιον ἀνθρώποις· ταῦτα γιγνώσκοντες οἱ πρόσθεν ἄνθρωποι ἀπὸ τῆς ἀρχῆς εἴθιζον τοὺς παῖδας ἄρχεσθαι καὶ τὸ κελευόμενον ποιεῖν, ἵνα μὴ ἐξανδρούμενοι εἰς μεγάλην μεταβολὴν ἰόντες ἐκπλήσσοιντο.

62: Whoever it is with whom one spends most of the day, he himself must necessarily become similar to that person in character.

οἵῳ τις ἂν τὸ πλεῖστον τῆς ἡμέρας συνῇ, τοιοῦτον ἀνάγκη γενέσθαι καὶ αὐτὸν τοὺς τρόπους.

63: But knowing the arrangement, they listen.[5]

ἀλλὰ εἰδότες τὴν διάθεσιν ἀκούουσιν.

---

[5] *Diathesis* may be the "arrangement" of a speech; *akouousin* ("they listen") may imply "they understand."

64: Recent friendships are bonds, but old friendships are stronger bonds.

αἱ νέαι φιλίαι ἀναγκαῖαι μέν, αἱ δὲ παλαιαὶ ἀναγκαιότεραι.

65: Many people have friends and do not know it, but they make acquaintances who flatter wealth and fawn on good fortune.

πολλοὶ δ' ἔχοντες φίλους οὐ γινώσκουσιν, ἀλλ' ἑταίρους ποιοῦνται θῶπας πλούτου καὶ τύχης κόλακας.

66: For taking care of the old resembles taking care of the young.[6]

γηροτροφία γὰρ προσέοικε παιδοτροφίᾳ.

---

[6] Clement attributes this fragment to "Antiphon the orator (*ho rhētōr*)." It is generally ascribed to *Concord,* even by separatists.

ABBREVIATIONS AND WORKS CITED

ABBREVIATIONS

Ath. Pol. [Aristotle], *The Athenian Constitution*
DK   Diels and Kranz 1952
GW   Gagarin and Woodruff 1995
M   Morrison 1972
Th   Thalheim and Blass 1914

WORKS CITED

Avery, Harry C. 1982. "One Antiphon or Two?" *Hermes* 110: 145–58.

Barnes, Jonathan. 1979. *The Presocratic Philosophers.* 2 vols. London.

Beck, Fredrick A. G. 1964. *Greek Education, 450–350 B.C.* London.

Bignone, Ettore. 1938. *Studi sul pensiero antico*, 1–226. Naples.

Bilik, Ronald. 1998. "Stammen P.Oxy. XI 1364 + LII 3647 und XV 1797 aus der Ἀλήθεια des Antiphon?" *TYCHE* 13: 29–49.

Blass, Friedrich. 1887. *Die attische Beredsamkeit.* 2d ed. Vol. 1. Leipzig.

Blundell, Mary Whitlock. 1989. *Helping Friends and Harming Enemies: A Study in Sophocles and Greek Ethics.* Cambridge.

Buccheim, Thomas. 1989. *Gorgias von Leontinoi: Reden, Fragmente und Testimonien.* Hamburg.

Carawan, Edwin. 1993. "The *Tetralogies* and Athenian Homicide Trials." *American Journal of Philology* 114: 235–70.

———. 1998. *Rhetoric and the Law of Draco.* Oxford.

Carey, Christopher, ed. 1992. *Apollodoros, Against Neaira [Demosthenes] 59.* Warminster.

———. 1994. "'Artless' Proofs in Aristotle and the Orators." *Bulletin of the Institute of Classical Studies* 39: 95–106.

Cartledge, Paul. 1990. "Fowl Play: A Curious Lawsuit in Classical Athens (Antiphon XVI, frr. 57–9 Thalheim)." In *Nomos: Essays in Athenian Law, Politics and Society,* edited by Paul Cartledge, Paul Millett, and Stephen Todd, 41–61. Cambridge.

Cassin, Barbara. 1992. "'Barbariser' et 'citoyenner' ou On n'échappe pas à Antiphon." *Rue Descartes* (Collège international de philosophie) (Jan. 3): 19–34.

————. 1995. *L'effet sophistique*. Paris.

————. 1996. "Sophistique." In *Le savoir grec*, edited by J. Brunschwig and G. Lloyd, 1021–39. Paris.

Cheney, Lynne V. 1992. "A Conversation with Bernard Knox." *Humanities* 13.3: 4–9, 31–36.

Cohen, David. 1995. *Law, Violence and Community in Classical Athens*. Cambridge.

Cole, Andrew Thomas. 1961. "The *Anonymus Iamblichi* and His Place in Greek Political Theory." *Harvard Studies in Classical Philology* 65: 127–63.

————. 1991a. "Who Was Corax?" *Illinois Classical Studies* 16: 65–84.

————. 1991b. *The Origins of Rhetoric in Ancient Greece*. Baltimore.

Davies, Malcolm. 1989. "Sisyphus and the Invention of Religion ('Critias' *TrGF* 1 [43] F 19 = B 25 DK)." *Bulletin of the Institute of Classical Studies* 36: 16–32.

de Romilly, Jacqueline. 1972. "Vocabulaire et propagande ou les premiers emplois du mot ὁμόνοια." In *Mélanges de linguistique et de philologie grecques offerts à Pierre Chantraine*, edited by Alfred Ernout, 199–209. Paris.

Decleva Caizzi, Fernanda, ed., trans., and comm. 1969. *Antiphontis, tetralogiae*. Milan.

————. 1989. "Antipho." In *Corpus dei papiri filosofici greci e latini*, edited by Francesco Adorno et al., 176–236. Florence.

Diels, H., and W. Kranz, eds. 1952. *Die Fragmente der Vorsokratiker*. 6th ed. Berlin.

Dittenberger, W. 1896. "Antiphons Tetralogien und das attische Criminalrecht I." *Hermes* 31: 271–77.

————. 1897. "Antiphons Tetralogien und das attische Criminalrecht II." *Hermes* 32: 1–41.

————. 1905. "Zu Antiphons Tetralogien." *Hermes* 40: 450–70.

Dodds, E. R. 1951. *The Greeks and the Irrational*. Berkeley.

Dover, Kenneth J. 1950. "The Chronology of Antiphon's Speeches." *Classical Quarterly* 44: 44–60.

————. 1968a. *Lysias and the Corpus Lysiacum*. Berkeley.

————, ed. 1968b. *Aristophanes, Clouds*. Oxford.

————. 1974. *Greek Popular Morality in the Time of Plato and Aristotle*. Oxford.

————. 1978. *Greek Homosexuality*. London.

————. 1988. "The Freedom of the Intellectual in Greek Society." In idem, *The Greeks and Their Legacy*, 135–58. Oxford. (Originally in *Talanta* 7 [1976].)

————. 1994. *Marginal Comment*. London.

————. 1997. *The Evolution of Greek Prose Style*. Oxford.

Due, Bodil. 1980. *Antiphon: A Study in Argumentation*. Copenhagen.

Dunn, Francis M. 1996. "Antiphon on Time (B9 D-K)." *American Journal of Philology* 117: 65–69.

Duran, Martí. 1999. "Oaths and the Settlement of Disputes in Hesiod *Op.* 27–41." *Zeitschrift der Savigny-Stiftung* 116: 25–48.

Edwards, Michael J. 1998. "Notes on Pseudo-Plutarch's *Life* of Antiphon." *Classical Quarterly* 48: 82–92.

Edwards, Michael, and Stephen Usher, eds. 1985. *Greek Orators*. Vol. 1, *Antiphon and Lysias*. Warminster.

Eucken, Christoph. 1996. "Das Tötungsgesetz des Antiphon und der Sinn seiner Tetralogien." *Museum Helveticum* 53: 73–82.

Faraone, Christopher. 1994. "Deianira's Mistake and the Demise of Heracles: Erotic Magic in Sophocles' *Trachiniae*." *Helios* 21: 115–35.

————. 1999. *Ancient Greek Love Magic*. Cambridge, Mass.

Finley, John H., Jr. 1967. *Three Essays on Thucydides*. Cambridge, Mass.

Fowler, Robert L. 1999. "The Authors Named Pherecydes." *Mnemosyne* 52: 1–15.

Freeman, Kathleen. 1948. *Ancilla to the Pre-Socratic Philosophers*. Cambridge, Mass.

Funghi, M. S. 1984. *The Oxyrhynchus Papyri* 52: 1–5. Oxford.

Furley, David J. 1981. "Antiphon's Case against Justice." In *The Sophists and Their Legacy*, edited by G. B. Kerferd (*Hermes* Einzelschriften 44), 81–91. Wiesbaden.

Gagarin, Michael. 1978a. "Self-Defense in Athenian Homicide Law." *Greek, Roman, and Byzantine Studies* 19: 111–20.

————. 1978b. "The Prohibition of Just and Unjust Homicide in Antiphon's *Tetralogies*." *Greek, Roman, and Byzantine Studies* 19: 291–306.

————. 1981. *Drakon and Early Athenian Homicide Law*. New Haven.

————. 1989. *The Murder of Herodes: A Study of Antiphon 5*. Studien zur klassischen Philologie 45. Frankfurt.

————. 1990a. "The Ambiguity of *Eris* in the *Works and Days*." In *Cabinet of the Muses: Essays on Classical and Comparative Literature in Honor of Thomas G. Rosenmeyer*, edited by Mark Griffith and Donald J. Mastronarde, 173–83. Atlanta.

————. 1990b. "*Bouleusis* in Athenian Homicide Law." In *Symposion 1988*, edited by Giuseppe Nenci and Gerhard Thür, 81–99. Cologne.

————. 1990c. "The Ancient Tradition on the Identity of Antiphon." *Greek, Roman, and Byzantine Studies* 31: 27–44.

————. 1990d. "The Nature of Proofs in Antiphon." *Classical Philology* 85: 22–32.

————. 1994. "Probability and Persuasion: Plato and Early Greek Rhetoric." In *Persuasion: Greek Rhetoric in Action*, edited by Ian Worthington, 46–68. London.

————. 1996. "The Torture of Slaves in Athenian Law." *Classical Philology* 91: 1–18.

————, ed. 1997. *Antiphon, The Speeches*. Cambridge.

————. 1998. "Women in Athenian Courts." *Dike* 1: 39–51.

————. 1999. "The Orality of Greek Oratory." In *Signs of Orality: The Oral Tradition and Its Influence in the Greek and Roman World*, edited by E. Anne Mackay, 163–80. Leiden.

————. 2000. "The *Basileus* in Athenian Homicide Law." In *Polis and Politics: Studies in Ancient Greek History Presented to Mogens Hansen on His Sixtieth Birthday, August 20, 2000*, edited by Pernille Flensted-Jensen, Thomas Heine Nielsen, and Lene Rubinstein, 569–79. Copenhagen.

————. 2001a. "The Truth of Antiphon's *Truth*." In *Essays in Ancient Greek Philosophy VI: Before Plato*, edited by Anthony Preuss, 171–85. Albany, N.Y.

———. 2001b. "Did the Sophists Aim to Persuade?" *Rhetorica* 19: 275–91.

———. Forthcoming. "Socrates and Antiphon: Intellectuals on Trial in Classical Athens." In *Antike Rechte und Gesellschaft: Festschrift für Panayotis Dimakis zum 75. Geburtstag,* edited by Johannes Strangas and Sophia Adam. Cologne.

Gagarin, Michael, and D. M. MacDowell, trans. 1998. *Antiphon and Andocides.* Austin.

Gagarin, Michael, and Paul Woodruff, eds. 1995. *Early Greek Political Thought from Homer to the Sophists.* Cambridge.

Gantz, Timothy. 1993. *Early Greek Myth.* Baltimore.

Gernet, Louis. 1923. *Antiphon, discours.* Paris.

Goebel, George. 1983. "Early Greek Rhetorical Theory and Practice: Proof and Arrangement in the Speeches of Antiphon and Euripides." Diss., University of Wisconsin, Madison.

Gomperz, T. [1896] 1901. *The Greek Thinkers.* 4 vols. London.

Griffith, Mark. 1990. "Contest and Contradiction in Early Greek Poetry." In *Cabinet of the Muses: Essays on Classical and Comparative Literature in Honor of Thomas G. Rosenmeyer,* edited by M. Griffith and D. J. Mastronarde, 185–207. Atlanta.

Grimaldi, William M. A. 1980. *Aristotle, Rhetoric I: A Commentary.* New York.

Gronewald, M. 1968. "Eines neues Protagoras-Fragment." *Zeitschrift für Papyrologie und Epigraphik* 2: 1–2.

Grote, George. 1869. *A History of Greece.* 2d ed. 12 vols. London.

Guthrie, W.K.C. 1971. *The Sophists.* Cambridge.

Hansen, Mogens Herman. 1978. "*Nomos* and *Psephisma* in Fourth-Century Athens." *Greek, Roman, and Byzantine Studies* 19: 315–30. (Reprinted in *The Athenian Ecclesia* [Copenhagen, 1983], 161–77.)

Harris, William V. 1989. *Ancient Literacy.* Cambridge, Mass.

Havelock, Eric. 1969. "*Dikaiosyne:* An Essay in Greek Intellectual History." *Phoenix* 23: 49–70.

Hegel, Georg Wilhelm Friedrich. 1831. *Vorlesungen über der Geschichte der Philosophie.* Berlin. Translated by E. S. Haldane and Frances H. Simson, *Lectures on the History of Philosophy,* 3 vols., 1: 352–84 (London, 1892).

Heitsch, Ernst. 1969. "Ein Buchtitel des Protagoras." *Hermes* 97: 292–96. Reprinted with additional bibliography in *Sophistik,* edited by C. J. Classen, 298–305 (Darmstadt, 1976).

———. 1984. *Antiphon aus Rhamnus.* Ak. der Wiss. und Lit. no. 3. Mainz.

Hoffmann, Klaus Friedrich. 1997. *Das Recht im Denken der Sophistik.* B. G. Teubner. Stuttgart and Leipzig.

Hornblower, Simon. 1991. *A Commentary on Thucydides.* Vol. 1, *Books 1–3.* Oxford.

Innes, D. C. 1991. "Gorgias, Antiphon and Sophistopolis." *Argumentation* 5: 221–31.

Jacoby, Felix. 1947. "The First Athenian Prose Writer." *Mnemosyne,* ser. 3, 13: 13–64.

Jebb, Richard. 1875. *The Attic Orators.* Vols. 1–2. London.

Johnson, William. 1994. "Oral Performance and the Composition of Herodotus' *Histories.*" *Greek, Roman, and Byzantine Studies* 35: 229–54.

Johnstone, Stephen. 1999. *Disputes and Democracy: The Consequences of Litigation in Ancient Athens.* Austin.

Kassel, R., and C. Austin. 1995. *Poetae Comici Graeci.* Vol. 8, *Adespota.* Berlin.

Keaney, John J., ed. 1991. *Harpokration: Lexeis of the Ten Orators.* Amsterdam.

Kennedy, George A. 1963. *The Art of Persuasion in Greece.* Princeton.

———, trans. 1991. *Aristotle, On Rhetoric.* New York.

Kerferd, George B. 1950. "The First Greek Sophists." *Classical Review* 64: 8–10.

———. 1957. "The Moral and Political Doctrines of Antiphon the Sophist: A Reconsideration." *Proceedings of the Cambridge Philological Society* 4: 26–32.

———. 1981. *The Sophistic Movement.* Cambridge.

Latte, Kurt. 1920. *Heiliges Recht: Untersuchungen zur Geschichte der sakralen Rechtsformen in Griechenland.* Tübingen.

Lipsius, J. H. 1904. "Über Antiphons Tetralogien." *Berichte über die Verhandlungen der kön.-säch. Ges. der Wiss.* Phil.-Hist. Kl. vol. 56: 191–204. Leipzig.

Lloyd, G.E.R. 1979. *Magic, Reason and Experience: Studies in the Origins and Development of Greek Science.* Cambridge.

———. 1990. *Demystifying Mentalities.* Cambridge.

Long, A. A. 1984. "Methods of Argument in Gorgias, *Palamedes.*" In *He Archaia Sophistike: The Sophistic Movement,* Greek Philosophical Society, 233–41. Athens.

Lugenbill, Robert D. 1997. "Rethinking Antiphon's Περὶ Ἀληθείας." *Apeiron* 30: 163–87.

Luria, S. 1963. "Antiphon der Sophist." *Eos* 53: 63–67. Reprinted in *Sophistik,* edited by C. J. Classen, 537–42 (Darmstadt, 1976).

MacDowell, Douglas M., ed. 1962. *On the Mysteries.* Oxford.

———. 1963. *Athenian Homicide Law in the Age of the Orators.* Manchester.

Maetzner, Eduard, ed. 1838. *Antiphontis, Orationes XV.* Berlin.

Maidment, K. J., ed. 1941. *Minor Attic Orators.* Vol. 1. Loeb Classical Library, Cambridge, Mass.

Mirhady, David C. 1991. "The Oath-Challenge in Athens." *Classical Quarterly* 41: 78–83.

Morrison, J. S. 1963. "The Truth of Antiphon." *Phronesis* 8: 35–49. Reprinted with additional bibliography in *Sophistik,* edited by C. J. Classen, 519–36 (Darmstadt, 1976).

———, trans. 1972. "Antiphon." In *The Older Sophists,* edited by Rosamond K. Sprague, 106–240. Columbia, S.C.

Moulton, Carroll. 1972. "Antiphon the Sophist, *On Truth.*" *Transactions and Proceedings of the American Philological Association* 103: 329–66.

Müller, Karl Ottfried. 1858. *A History of the Literature of Ancient Greece.* Vol. 2. London.

Nagy, Gregory. 1987. "Herodotus the *logios.*" *Arethusa* 20: 175–84.

Narcy, Michel. 1989. "Antiphon d'Athènes." In *Dictionnaire des philosophes antiques,* vol. 1, edited by Richard Goulet. Paris.

Nickau, Klaus, ed. 1966. *Ammonius: De adfinium vocabulorum differentia.* Teubner. Leipzig.

Nicole, Jules. 1907. *L'apologie d'Antiphon*. Paris.

O'Sullivan, Neil. 1992. *Alcidamas, Aristophanes and the Beginnings of Greek Stylistic Theory. Hermes* Einzelschriften 60. Stuttgart.

Ostwald, Martin. 1986. *From Popular Sovereignty to the Sovereignty of Law: Law, Society, and Politics in Fifth-Century Athens*. Berkeley.

———. 1990. "*Nomos* and *Phusis* in Antiphon's Περὶ Ἀληθείας." In *Cabinet of the Muses: Essays on Classical and Comparative Literature in Honor of Thomas G. Rosenmeyer*, edited by M. Griffith and D. J. Mastronarde, 293–306. Atlanta.

———. 1992. "Athens as a Cultural Centre." In *CAH* v²: 306–69.

Ostwald, Martin, and John P. Lynch. 1994. "The Growth of Schools and the Advance of Knowledge." In *CAH* vi²: 592–633.

Parker, Robert. 1983. *Miasma: Pollution and Purification in Early Greek Religion*. Oxford.

Parry, Adam. 1957. "*Logos* and *Ergon* in Thucydides." Diss., Harvard University; reprinted in 1981 by Arno Press.

Pendrick, Gerard. 1987a. "The Fragments of Antiphon the Sophist with a Commentary." Diss., Columbia University, New York.

———. 1987b. "Once Again Antiphon the Sophist and Antiphon of Rhamnus." *Hermes* 115: 47–60.

———. 1993. "The Ancient Tradition on Antiphon Reconsidered." *Greek, Roman, and Byzantine Studies* 34: 215–28.

Pfeiffer, Rudolf. 1968. *History of Classical Scholarship from the Beginnings to the Hellenistic Age*. Oxford.

Prosser, William L. 1971. *Handbook of the Law of Torts*. 4th ed. St. Paul.

Roberts, Jennifer Tolbert. 1994. *Athens on Trial: The Antidemocratic Tradition in Western Thought*. Princeton.

Robinson, T. M. 1979. *Contrasting Arguments: An Edition of the Dissoi Logoi*. New York.

Russell, Donald A. 1983. *Greek Declamation*. Cambridge.

Saunders, Trevor J. 1977–78. "Antiphon the Sophist on Natural Laws (B44DK)." *Proceedings of the Aristotelian Society* 78: 215–36.

Sauppe, Herman. 1867. *Commentatio de Antiphonte Sophista. Index Scholarum* 25 April to 17 August. Göttingen.

Schiappa, Edward. 1991. *Protagoras and Logos: A Study in Greek Philosophy and Rhetoric*. Columbia, S.C.

———. 1999. *The Beginnings of Rhetorical Theory in Classical Greece*. New Haven.

Schmalzriedt, Egidius. 1970. Περὶ φύσεως: *Zur Frügeschichte der Buchtitel*. Munich.

Sealey, Raphael. 1984. "The *Tetralogies* Ascribed to Antiphon." *Transactions and Proceedings of the American Philological Association* 114: 71–85.

Searle, John R. 1995. *The Construction of Social Reality*. New York.

Sinclair, T. A. 1967. *A History of Greek Political Thought*. 2d ed. Cleveland.

Smith, William. 1844. *Dictionary of Greek and Roman Biography and Mythology*. London.

Solmsen, Friedrich. 1931. *Antiphonstudien.* Berlin.

———. 1975. *Intellectual Experiments of the Greek Enlightenment.* Princeton.

Stanford, W. B., ed. 1958. *Aristophanes, The Frogs.* London.

Striker, Gisela. 1996. "Methods of Sophistry." In idem, *Essays on Hellenistic Epistemology and Ethics,* 3–21. Cambridge.

Stroud, Ronald S. 1968. *Drakon's Law on Homicide.* Berkeley and Los Angeles.

Thalheim, Th., and Fr. Blass, eds. 1914. *Antiphon, orationes et fragmenta.* Leipzig.

Thomas, Rosalind. 1989. *Oral Tradition and Written Record in Classical Athens.* Cambridge.

———. 1993. "Performance and Written Publication in Herodotus and the Sophistic Generation." In *Vermittlung und Tradierung von Wissen in der griechischen Kultur,* edited by Wolfgang Kullmann and Jochen Althoff, 225–44. Tübingen.

Thompson, Wayne N. 1972. "Stasis in Aristotle's *Rhetoric.*" *Quarterly Journal of Speech* 58: 134–41.

Thür, Gerhard. 1977. *Beweisführung vor den Schwurgerichtshöfen Athens: Die Proklesis zur Basanos.* Akad. der Wiss. Sitzungsberichte 310. Wien.

———. 1996. "Oaths and Dispute Settlement in Ancient Greek Law." In *Greek Law in Its Political Setting: Justifications Not Justice,* edited by Lin Foxhall and Andrew Lewis, 57–72. Oxford.

Todd, Stephen C. 1990. "The Use and Abuse of the Attic Orators." *Greece and Rome* 37: 159–78.

Treu, Max. 1967. "Ps.-Xenophon, *Politeia Athēnaiōn.*" In *Paulys Realencyclopädie der classischen Altertumswissenschaft.* 2 Reihe, 9.A.2: cols. 1927–82.

Trevett, Jeremy C. 1992. *Apollodorus the Son of Pasion.* Oxford.

———. 1996. "Did Demosthenes Publish His Deliberative Speeches?" *Hermes* 124: 425–41.

Untersteiner, Mario. 1961–62. *Sofisti: Testimonianze e frammenti.* 4 vols. Florence.

Usher, Stephen. 1976. "Lysias and His Clients." *Greek, Roman and Byzantine Studies* 17: 31–40.

van Lieshout, R.G.A. 1980. *Greeks on Dreams.* Utrecht.

Vollmer, G. 1958. *Studien zum Beweis antiphontischer Reden.* Hamburg.

Wallace, Robert W. 1994. "Private Lives and Public Enemies: Freedom of Thought in Classical Athens." In *Athenian Identity and Civic Ideology,* edited by Alan L. Boegehold and Adele C. Scafuro, 127–55. Baltimore.

———. 1998. "The Sophists in Athens." In *Democracy, Empire, and the Arts in Fifth-Century Athens,* edited by Deborah Boedeker and Kurt A. Raaflaub, 203–22. Cambridge, Mass.

Whitehead, David. 1988. "Athenians in Xenophon's *Hellenica.*" *Liverpool Classical Monthly* 13: 145–47.

Williams, Bernard. 1993. *Shame and Necessity.* Berkeley.

Winton, Richard. 2000. "Herodotus, Thucydides and the Sophists." In *The Cambridge History of Greek and Roman Political Thought,* edited by Christopher Rowe and Malcolm Schofield, 89–121. Cambridge.

Woodruff, Paul. 1985. "Didymus on Protagoras and the Protagoreans." *Journal of the History of Philosophy* 23: 483–97.

———. 1994. "*Eikos* and Bad Faith in the Paired Speeches of Thucydides." *Proceedings of the Boston Area Colloquium in Ancient Philosophy* 10: 115–45.

———. 1999. "Rhetoric and Relativism: Protagoras and Gorgias." In *The Cambridge Companion to Early Greek Philosophy,* edited by A. A. Long, 290–310. Cambridge.

Wooten, Cecil W., trans. 1987. *Hermogenes' On Types of Style.* Chapel Hill, N.C.

Worthington, Ian. 1991. "Greek Oratory, Revision of Speeches, and the Problem of Historical Reliability." *Classica et Medievalia* 42: 55–74.

Zimmermann, Bernhard. 1997. "Antiphon." In *Metzler Lexikon antiker Autoren,* edited by Oliver Schütz, 54–55. Stuttgart.

Zinsmaier, Thomas. 1998. "Wahrheit, Gerechtigkeit und Rhetorik in den Reden Antiphons: Zur Genese einiger Topoi der Gerichtsrede." *Hermes* 126: 398–422.

CITATIONS FROM ANCIENT AUTHORS

GENERAL INDEX